NURSES of the OUTBACK

Annabelle Brayley trained as a registered nurse. She has lived on an isolated sheep and cattle station in Queensland and worked in rural and remote health. After retiring from health to pursue her passion for storytelling, she has become a regular contributor to *R.M. Williams OUTBACK* magazine, and collected and edited the stories for the book *Bush Nurses*. She lives in the small south-west Queensland community of Morven with her husband, Ian.

NURSES of the OUTBACK

ANNABELLE BRAYLEY

15 AMAZING LIVES IN REMOTE AREA NURSING

MICHAEL JOSEPH
an imprint of
PENGUIN BOOKS

MICHAEL JOSEPH

Published by the Penguin Group
Penguin Group (Australia)
707 Collins Street, Melbourne, Victoria 3008, Australia
(a division of Penguin Australia Pty Ltd)
Penguin Group (USA) Inc.
375 Hudson Street, New York, New York 10014, USA
Penguin Group (Canada)
90 Eglinton Avenue East, Suite 700, Toronto, Canada ON M4P 2Y3
(a division of Penguin Canada Books Inc.)
Penguin Books Ltd
80 Strand, London WC2R 0RL England
Penguin Ireland
25 St Stephen's Green, Dublin 2, Ireland
(a division of Penguin Books Ltd)
Penguin Books India Pvt Ltd
11 Community Centre, Panchsheel Park, New Delhi – 110 017, India
Penguin Group (NZ)
67 Apollo Drive, Rosedale, Auckland 0632, New Zealand
(a division of Penguin New Zealand Pty Ltd)
Penguin Books (South Africa) (Pty) Ltd
Rosebank Office Park, Block D, 181 Jan Smuts Avenue, Parktown North,
Johannesburg, 2196, South Africa
Penguin (Beijing) Ltd
7F, Tower B, Jiaming Center, 27 East Third Ring Road North, Chaoyang District,
Beijing 100020, China

Penguin Books Ltd, Registered Offices: 80 Strand, London WC2R 0RL, England

First published by Penguin Group (Australia), 2014

Text copyright © Annabelle Brayley 2014

The moral right of the author has been asserted

All rights reserved. Without limiting the rights under copyright reserved above, no part of this publication may be reproduced, stored in or introduced into a retrieval system, or transmitted, in any form or by any means (electronic, mechanical, photocopying, recording or otherwise), without the prior written permission of both the copyright owner and the above publisher of this book.

Cover design by Alex Ross © Penguin Group (Australia)
Text design by Samantha Jayaweera © Penguin Group (Australia)
Cover photograph of Catherine Jurd by Louise M Cooper: louisemcooper.com
Photographs in the book were supplied by the subjects of the story unless otherwise stated
Typeset in Sabon 11pt/18pt by Samantha Jayaweera, Penguin Group (Australia)
Printed and bound in Australia by Griffin Press

National Library of Australia
Cataloguing-in-Publication data:

Brayley, Annabelle, author.
Nurses of the outback / Annabelle Brayley.
9781921901362 (paperback)
Rural nurses–Australia–Biography.
Nurses–Australia–Biography.

610.73430994

penguin.com.au

Contents

Map	*viii*
Introduction	*xi*
Foreword	*xiv*

1   **OUTBACK ANGEL**   I
Neen Hawkes, *Darwin, Northern Territory*

2   **INVESTING IN FUTURES**   19
Anna Burley, *Georgetown, Queensland*

3   **TARMACS AND TOOLBOXES**   37
Geri Malone, *Fleurieu Peninsula, South Australia*

4   **PUSHING THE BOUNDARIES**   55
Catherine Jurd, *Julia Creek, Queensland*

5   **A PATH LESS TRAVELLED**   69
Christine Foletti, *Cocos-Keeling Islands,
Indian Ocean*

6   **HEART OF THE TERRITORY**   87
Margie McLean, *Victoria River and Barkly Regions,
Northern Territory*

7   **THE MAGIC OF MOOMBA**   109
Chris Belshaw, *Moomba Oil and Gas Field, South Australia*

8 LOST AND FOUND 129
Aggie Harpham, *Kununurra, Western Australia*

9 BEYOND THE BLACK STUMP 145
Maureen Ker, OAM, *White Cliffs, New South Wales*

10 NURSE ON A MISSION 163
Karen Schnitzerling, *St Helens, Tasmania*

11 FINISHING-UP BUSINESS 181
Fred Miegel, *Alice Springs, Northern Territory*

12 WALKING HER MAGIC LINE 197
Jo Appoo, *Elliott, Northern Territory*

13 FINDING HOME 211
June Andrew, OAM, *Marree, South Australia*

14 CALLING AUSTRALIA HOME 227
Shamiso Muchando, *Derby, Western Australia*

15 WEST-COAST NIRVANA 243
Sue Stewart, Bidyadanga, *Western Australia*

Acknowledgements 261

*Dedicated to those of you who nurse those of us
who live in the Australian outback.*

Locations

1. Neen Hawkes
2. Anna Burley
3. Geri Malone
4. Catherine Jurd
5. Christine Foletti
6.a Margie McLean
6.b Margie McLean
7. Chris Belshaw
8. Aggie Harpham
9. Maureen Ker
10. Karen Schnitzerling
11. Fred Miegel
12. Jo Appoo
13. June Andrew
14. Shamiso Muchando
15. Sue Stewart

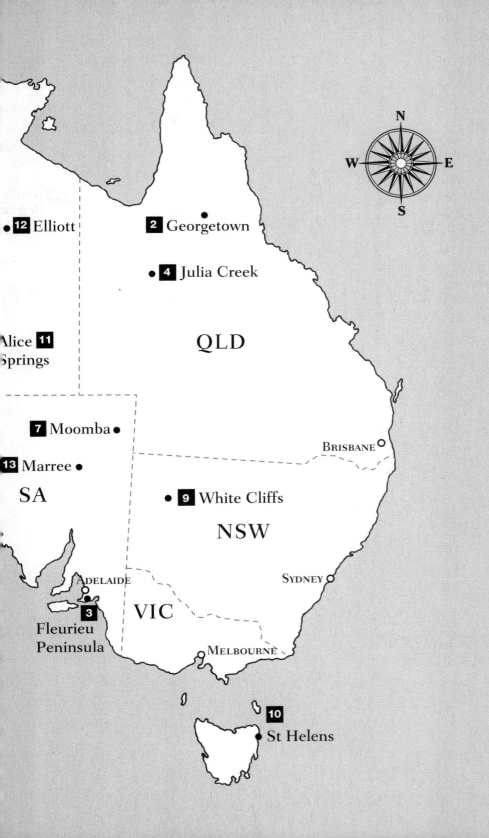

Introduction

Annabelle Brayley

Despite the fact that I trained as a nurse in the 1970s, my heart was never really in it. I was much more interested in the idea of chronicling the patients' lives than knowing their medical histories – although, back then, I hadn't yet realised a potential for storytelling.

I could, however, appreciate the talents of the nurses working around me. I believe true nurses are called to their profession, even though many of them don't necessarily recognise the initial summons. Some of the people in this book had no idea what they really wanted to do when they ventured into nursing, but they soon fell in love with their profession and quickly understood that it provided them with great personal and professional satisfaction.

Marrying my husband, Ian, and moving to live on an isolated sheep station in Queensland gave me another perspective on nursing when I joined the 'waiting room' of the Royal Flying Doctor Service (RFDS) clinic that flew into a neighbouring station once a month. Most of my antenatal and postnatal care and our two children's milestones and vaccinations were recorded at those clinic visits. The child health nurse, Sally Gorman (nee Ball), who flew with the RFDS, saved all our bacons as she guided me through the mysteries of early motherhood. Sally was and is an extraordinarily talented nurse who continues to work in a rural and remote context. Even though her story doesn't grace these pages, it was she who first made me realise that the inland actually runs on nurse power.

When I had finally established a fledgling career as a storyteller, my cousin Sally Ford said to me, 'You should write about Margie McLean.' I pricked my ears up as she reminisced about Margie, a registered nurse and midwife who, until 2009, used to run the Health Clinic at Elliott, just down the road from where Sal lived at Newcastle Waters Station in the Northern Territory. Some of Margie's stories sounded spine-tingling.

Naturally, when it came time to write this book, Margie was one of the first nurses I thought of. Having spent the better part of forty years working in the Victoria River and Barkly Tableland regions of the Territory, she'd seen a lot of changes in four decades and some of her anecdotes definitely raised the hair on the back of my neck.

Like Margie, the other nurses in these stories are without exception courageous, adventurous, strong, reliable and responsible nurturers of the people of the outback. They are also innovative, dedicated, well qualified and highly experienced. These people represent the best of the many women and some men who devote their lives to nursing in remote areas.

And yet they are often invisible angels. Most of us take them for granted and just assume they'll be there when we need them because, since the early 1900s, there have always been nurses in the outback.

When John Flynn initiated the Australian Inland Mission he sent nurses out to staff the hospitals and clinics that he established. He went on to launch the Royal Flying Doctor Service, but most people don't realise that around four out of five RFDS emergency rescues

INTRODUCTION

are actually undertaken by a flight nurse. While she (or he) will have radio or telephone access to a consulting doctor back at the base, they will usually be on their own with just the pilot for company; a doctor only goes out for extenuating medical emergencies.

There are many health clinics across the inland that are run by nurses and sometimes a lone nurse. Some of those small towns and communities only continue to exist because there is a nurse living and working there.

All of the nurses in this book were surprised and/or hesitant to be included because they thought their contribution to the world around them was pretty ordinary. And yet, the fact that they are ordinary people doing extraordinary things in geographic isolation just makes them even more heroic. They understand, on a personal level, that they make a difference, but they're used to working under the radar. Like nurses all across Australia, they provide some of the most essential services on the planet, and yet their work is often undervalued.

While this book is a celebration of the lives of the particular nurses within it, it's also a salute to all nurses who work in remote areas of the globe. May you all now be a little less invisible and a lot more appreciated.

Foreword

Kylie Rutledge, *Moble Station, Quilpie, Queensland*

The dash to town with an injured loved one is the most desperate trip of all. As a mother living 70 kilometres from the small remote town of Quilpie in western Queensland, it is the one I dread most. As my husband, Brian, and our four daughters are each blessed with an over-adventurous mind, coupled with an underdeveloped sense of self-preservation, it's a trip I know well!

The panicked tone in the garbled voice over the two-way radio always strikes fear into my heart; I know instantly someone is hurt and that it must be serious. Our children, like many others in outback Australia, have grown up with the mantra, 'Unless there is blood, bone, fire or a snake, don't whinge!'

I have no medical training and most of my first-aid experience is with four-legged patients. The anguish and helplessness I feel seeing one of my children in pain shocks me anew every time. Ridiculously, the recovery position is the only first aid I ever recall in these scenarios; I'm certain this is some sort of Freudian subconsciousness willing the situation to be over and the recovery at hand.

The various rescues, usually from the most inaccessible parts of the property, are completed in stages with whatever mode of transport is able to reach the patient. We have transferred the injured via

FOREWORD

the back of a motorbike, then onto the back of a quad bike, then onto our station plane when Brian can find somewhere close enough to land.

The rescues are fraught and tense times when all our focus is on finding the injured person and then trying to move them with the least possible pain inflicted. At times we have to track them when they are a little vague on their whereabouts, usually when they have hit their head. Head injuries terrify me and the vacant stare and the accompanying mad conversations reduce me to tears.

Extended crying was always our indication of a serious injury with the children. I remember the time one of our daughters had to be carted out of the mulga on her grandfather's quad bike. She was insisting on just going home but could not stop sobbing. When her father picked her up, she was duly flown to Quilpie Hospital, where they patched her up before sending her on to Brisbane for a total knee reconstruction.

While mustering with their father, my girls once found him knocked out and then carefully ferried him home. They all commented afterwards that goat mustering in the hills was a breeze compared to mustering Dad home that day.

No matter how or where we have retrieved the injured from, it all culminates in that final dash for the hospital that, on reflection, now seems a muddled blur of family drama. What does remain clearly etched in my mind is the nurse's voice on the end of the telephone, willing me to be calm, quietly explaining what to do next.

It will be the nurse who will meet us somewhere en route with the ambulance, a white beacon of hope emerging from the dust, or awaiting our arrival at the hospital doors, their reassuring aura of calmness like arms enveloping me. Quilpie nurses have patched us, stitched us, monitored us, put us to bed, sent us home and, on occasion, called the Royal Flying Doctor Service to fly us east to city hospitals. They have delivered my children, just as their nursing predecessors delivered previous generations. They have dealt with the endings as well as the beginnings, providing dignity in death and great comfort to families and friends.

The experiences I've described will strike a chord with many families spread throughout remote Australia. The nurses in these regions are educated and highly skilled professionals dealing with the unexpected horror in our lives. That they often manage these situations under very basic conditions and with limited resources is testament to their intelligence, ingenuity and faith.

The stories that unfold in this book are the makings of our nation's modern legends, and thank goodness Annabelle has embraced the task of writing them down for perpetuity. She is a bush woman with a nursing background and, perhaps more importantly when it comes to knowing about outback health, a mother. Remote health care has loomed large in her life and is reflected in the integrity of the stories in this book. Her innate understanding of the situations and characters portrayed allows for an honesty that belies the enormity of the nurses' achievements. These are ordinary people living truly extraordinary lives and Annabelle has swaddled their stories close to her heart.

I know Annabelle has also driven the desperate dash with an injured loved one. Through this book she has connected the people of the outback, despite the hundreds of miles of dusty roads between us.

xvi

1
OUTBACK ANGEL

Neen Hawkes, *Darwin, Northern Territory*

In late January 2000, registered nurse Neen Hawkes was at home with her two young daughters when she heard a panicked call over the two-way radio. Linda Kruger, wife of Jason, the overseer from Mt Marlow Station, was radioing Neen to say that the station manager had been badly hurt in a terrible accident. As another person took over, Neen recognised Sue Tully's voice screaming for her to come quickly: 'I think John Paul's dying!'

Neen's blood ran cold knowing that the people involved were her good friends and neighbours, John Paul and Sue Tully. Without knowing the details of the incident, Neen understood that John Paul had been seriously injured next door at Mt Marlow, the property he and Sue managed 50 kilometres west of Yaraka in central-west Queensland, and that they needed her there urgently.

Neen's husband – who is known by his surname, Hawkes – had

been flying his ultralight plane over at Mt Marlow since daylight that morning, spotting the sheep that John Paul and the Krugers had been mustering to bring into the yards for crutching. Hawkes was on his way home to refuel before going to another mustering job when he heard Linda's call for help. He flew back to view the situation so he could report it to Neen and then direct her to the accident site. He elected to stay in the air to relay any messages Neen needed to send or receive as she organised appropriate help.

Roughly dragging her wispy honey-blonde hair back into a ponytail and shoving sunglasses over her pale green eyes, Neen grabbed her nurse's bag, whooshed the girls into the car and drove the 30 kilometres next door as fast as possible. As she drove she called Andrew McCarthy at the Yaraka police station on her two-way radio, quickly told him what she knew and asked him to ring the Royal Flying Doctor Service (RFDS) and request that they be on standby for further updates. With Sue's distraught voice repeatedly cutting in, screaming for her to hurry, she and Hawkes both tried to calm her, reassuring her that Neen was on her way. Flying overhead, Hawkes guided her across country, ensuring that she took the quickest possible route to the accident. As she drew nearer, he landed his plane on a road so she could collect him and he could show her the rest of the way. Hawkes landed so quickly that a wheel came off the plane, though he still managed to pull up safely.

Before the accident, John Paul had called Sue on her radio and asked her to come out and pick up any sheep struggling in the summer heat. Jason, the overseer, was mustering in the next paddock, where his wife Linda was driving another vehicle and also collecting weak sheep. Sue had met John Paul, who was on his motorbike, and together they collected a few and put them through to the next paddock, after which Sue followed him down the fence.

2

As she drove, Sue looked out through the fence to where she could see Linda driving across the open plain. Wondering whether they'd have enough sheep in hand, Sue was hoping that she and John Paul could have an easier time the next day to celebrate their twenty-ninth wedding anniversary. She glanced over again to see if she could spot Jason behind any sheep and, as she looked back at the road, realised too late that her husband had pulled up in front of her. Despite slamming on the brakes, she could not avoid hitting him.

On impact, the back wheel of his motorbike was caught up under the bull bar, hard against the left front wheel of the Toyota utility. Jammed upright, the bike crimped in the middle, lightly pinning John Paul, who was flung back across the bull bar then forward again.

Just over the fence in the next paddock and close enough to hear Sue's screams, Linda sped across, radioing Neen and then Jason as she went. From the little coherent information Neen had, she didn't know for sure what to expect, but as soon as she saw him, she knew it was beyond bad. All of her training and experience kicked in and Neen Hawkes set about saving her good friend's life.

Neen Gall grew up on Eastwood, her family's sheep station outside Blackall in central-west Queensland. She remembers an idyllic childhood with a sister and two brothers, until she went to boarding school, which she hated. She spent the term time counting the days till she could go home.

Her paternal grandmother was a bush nurse, and, with her encouragement, Neen always wanted to pursue the same career. After her final year of school, she went home to jillaroo for her father for a year, until she started nursing training at the Royal Brisbane Hospital. She says she didn't realise the significance of her hospital training at the time, but ever since has been grateful that it was so practical. As soon as she graduated, she and an old friend, Fiona Armstrong, took off overseas. The two bush girls had become firm friends at boarding school and had done their training at the same time. Initially neither had any specific plans to return to work in the outback and, instead, simply looked forward to travelling. They both picked up a little casual nursing work in London, in between roaming around Europe and the UK.

Upon her return, Neen worked for a nursing agency in and around Brisbane. She filled in at whichever hospital required her, in whichever department needed her. 'Living and working in the city was pretty full-on and one day I woke up and thought, *When they ring me today, I'm going to ask if they have any country placements*,' she recalls. Accordingly, when the coordinator at the agency rang a short time later to tell her she would be working in intensive care that day, Neen jumped straight in and asked if they ever had any country placements.

'Oh, yes,' she said. 'We didn't realise you'd be interested.'

'Do you have any available at the moment?' Neen asked.

'Well, yes, we have one at Alpha. Do you know where that is?'

Neen laughed excitedly, as that was near where she grew up. 'Of course I do. When would you like me to start?'

'Really?'

'Yes, really.'

'You can start Monday.'

Neen packed up, drove the 800-odd kilometres home to Blackall for a day or two, then on a further 180 kilometres north-east to Alpha. True to her word, she started work on Monday morning at the little local hospital.

She loved everything about it, including the matron, Jean

Williams, who mothered her staff at the same time as she supervised them. 'She met me at the quarters on that first day and said, "Now, Neen, every Monday morning you must meet me in the office and you must tell me everything you've done over the weekend." I was a little surprised and asked her why. She said, "Because I talk to the school teachers and the publican and the police and everyone else in town and I like to be able to stick up for my nurses, so, if there's any rot being talked about around town, I like to know exactly what you've done so I can back you up." She was lovely!' remembers Neen.

The most significant difference she noticed professionally was the smallness of the nursing team and the huge amount of the responsibility for each of them. As the registered nurse on night duty, Neen would be the only nurse there overnight and was accountable for any child, aged, maternity, surgical or medical inpatients, as well as lots of unexpected things, such as outpatients, taking X-rays, setting up the theatre for when the flying surgeon came and doing all the pre-operative preparations.

Neen was excited by the work and delighted in knowing everyone she was working with. 'As a country girl it was normal for me to know everyone in the community and at Alpha I wasn't that far from home,' she says. She quickly realised that she loved emergency nursing and loved knowing that, because word gets around fast in a small community, she'd have plenty of opportunity to help out in any emergency situation that arose. It's 'all hands on deck' in the bush.

After a year at Alpha she took off overseas again, roaming around until she was very broke, then returned to the town to refill her bank account. When an opportunity arose for her to work at Blackall Hospital, she couldn't resist, despite someone telling her, 'That'll be it. You'll never leave again.' Not long after she moved to Blackall, she went out to visit one of her nursing friends, Kerry

Parkinson, whose family owned a sheep station outside Yaraka. There, Neen met John Hawkes, a stockman who was working on the station for Kerry's father. Hawkes was an entertaining young fellow with the clever wit of a natural bush poet, and the two were destined to become good mates.

While she was working in Blackall, Neen was asked if she would go to Tambo to relieve for three weeks. Tambo was a tiny, single-nurse clinic that provided primary health care (equitable access to essential health care that is socially, culturally and economically sustainable) and was located about an hour south of Blackall and, for the first time, she was completely on her own. 'It was pretty daunting,' she says. 'On the first morning, handover included everything from patient files to the cash tin to where the gardening tools were stored and then there was all the paperwork.' At 5 p.m. she locked the door, staggered to her quarters and fell on the bed exhausted. Then the doorbell rang . . .

She found a distressed father holding a little boy in his arms and a trail of blood behind them all the way up the pathway to the clinic. His sister had run over his foot with the lawnmower and cut off several toes. Neen packed a pressure bandage on the foot, called the Blackall Hospital, loaded them into the ambulance and drove them to meet an ambulance from Blackall at a halfway point. The boy was flown out by the time Neen got back to Tambo, cleaned up the mess and collapsed on the bed again, wondering whether she'd survive the next three weeks.

Needless to say, three weeks turned into three months and Neen got a crash course in primary health care, realising that running a remote clinic was so much more than just responding to emergencies. It would stand her in good stead years later when she returned to nursing in a single-nurse clinic.

In the meantime, however, she and Hawkes had fallen in love and decided to get married. She relieved at the Blackall Hospital until their wedding at the end of 1989, when they moved to Yaraka and she joined Hawkes in the contract mustering business he was steadily building. She enjoyed being back in the paddock doing stock work and they were never short of employment. They set up house in Yaraka, which has a permanent population of twenty, and a district headcount of around 150, give or take the odd shearing team, main roads camp or grey nomad. After eighteen months they bought Merrigal, a small property about 20 kilometres to the west.

Neen kept her hand in with clinical work by doing occasional relief shifts at the Isisford health clinic and, as time went on, the locals began to rely on her for their immediate medical advice. Acknowledging that she was following in the footsteps of many brilliant bush women who had pitched in and helped in their communities, Neen loved people asking her for help. The RFDS flew in to Yaraka once a month to provide a clinic and, as more and more people turned to Neen for assistance, she built up a rapport with the RFDS staff and acted as an intermediary when problems arose. As a registered nurse, she was well able to describe signs and symptoms, which expedited the medical response.

Ultimately, several people wrote letters to appropriate departments and politicians asking that a position be created in Yaraka for Neen to run a proper clinic in the room the RFDS used at the town hall. Laughing, Neen now says she thinks it must have been an election year because, in fact, money was provided for Queensland Health to build a brand new clinic, which she was selected to work at.

Operating the clinic as a primary health care centre, she encouraged and coordinated appropriate allied health teams – including a dental, mental health and women's health team – to travel out to the clinic on a regular basis, ensuring the people of the Yaraka district had access to better care.

As the local bush nurse, she did a lot of veterinary work for her neighbour John Paul Tully, but she was also available to the rest of the district. The nearest vet was at Longreach, 220 kilometres away, and Neen built a similar relationship with the vets to what she had with the RFDS. The vets and the doctors both knew her capabilities and what she carried in her clinic, so they were happy to advise her over the phone. There were limits though . . .

One day a lady rang her and said quickly, 'Mate, I'm so glad you answered the phone. You've gotta come quickly.'

'What's wrong?' Neen inquired.

'I need you to do one of them caesar things for me.'

'Excuse me?'

'You know, one of them caesar things. I've got this little dog that's in pup to a big dog. It's had one pup but I think there's more.'

'Absolutely not!' said Neen, 'You've got to go to a vet . . .'

It took her half an hour to convince the lady that she was definitely not doing 'one of them caesar things'.

Regularly called out as she was to dog injuries, Neen had only two hard and fast rules: the dogs had to be restrained, and if they were biters, she wouldn't treat them. With a rueful smile, she says, 'Some of the biggest, ugliest pig dogs were the gentlest dogs while the only one that ever bit me was a sheep dog belonging to John Paul!'

The first time Neen met John Paul was back in 1993 when he turned up at the clinic, not long after he and Sue moved to Mt Marlow as managers. He had stitches that needed to be taken out, the first of a long list of medical assistance she provided him with. He was a bit accident-prone and, between him and his dogs, kept her in regular suturing practice. So much so that one day he decided to treat himself instead of bothering Neen. She and Hawkes were away and John Paul and Sue were minding their girls. John Paul was out in the shed, working under the bonnet of a vehicle with the motor running, and somehow managed to get his hand caught down the side of the battery. His hand was burnt before he was able to extricate it. He didn't want to tell Neen so he fixed it himself, thinking she need never know. However, he only made it worse and had to own up and get her to fix it anyway. They laughed together about so many of his escapades and, in fact, Neen nicknamed him Jack (Russell) for quite a long while after he accidentally took dog worming tablets instead of Panadol for a headache. As neighbours they helped each other out and spent quite a lot of time together. They were all such good friends.

When Neen arrived to treat John Paul on the day of his accident, she noted at first glance that there were lacerations on his head, that his right arm was sitting at an awkward angle and that he was coherent but badly dazed. Having heard the radio calls, help turned up from all around the district, so she quickly organised a couple of men to take over supporting him, she checked his vital signs (pulse, breathing, blood pressure and pupil response), and established a drip line getting intravenous fluids into him to keep him hydrated. Beginning a record of her findings, she then checked him out a little more thoroughly, assessing that he had a definite fracture of one arm, a probable head injury, a very possible spinal injury and potential internal injuries.

Being the one person on the ground with appropriate medical training, Neen was in charge. As well as managing John Paul's status, she would need also to support Sue, who was in shock. In addition, she was supervising and directing everyone else, including her two girls and two other children from the station who had been helping with the muster. She quickly sent Hawkes to the homestead to get the RFDS medical box, some pillows, blankets and the Tullys' new Toyota wagon so that they could transport John Paul to the airstrip back at the homestead. She then sent one of her daughters, Holly, to her car to radio Andrew McCarthy at the police station in Yaraka, where he was waiting to hear her assessment of the accident.

Though still in primary school, her daughters, Holly and Jess, were both accustomed to going to emergencies with Neen, who was never going to leave them at home alone and rarely had anywhere else to leave them. They both knew how to do things to help their mother and Holly capably called Andrew to tell him that 'Mum's at Mt Marlow and she needs the oxygen and a stretcher from the clinic urgently'.

'Andrew and I'd worked together before and I knew he would know where to find them and what else to bring,' Neen explains. 'Via Holly, I also asked him to call the RFDS and let them know what was happening and that they needed to get here "PDQ" [pretty damn quick].'

On top of this, she asked Andrew to ask his wife, Kirsty, to standby at the police station to continue relaying information to and from Dr Bob Balmain, the doctor at the base.

Having rapidly established some order, she was then able to call Kirsty herself to relay her assessment of John Paul to Dr Balmain, including his vital signs. While he was still conscious, she felt compelled to get him off the bike, however, Dr Balmain directed her very clearly not to move him at all until he arrived and insisted that she should maintain him in the position he was in. She organised a rotation of helpers to very carefully brace John Paul, relieving them as soon as it became a strain, so that he always had firm, steady support.

Acknowledging Sue's distress, Neen tried to keep her busy. Sue and John Paul always kept frozen bottles of water at home to take out with them on the run. Finding the day's bottle still half frozen in his saddle bag, Neen got Sue to carefully chip bits of ice out of the bottle with a screwdriver and feed them to John Paul when he was able to manage them. Her offsiders, who included the locals who had come to help, pulled another vehicle around in front of the bike and rigged a tarpaulin between the vehicles to provide shade over the scene.

In the meantime, she checked his vital signs every fifteen minutes. As soon as Andrew McCarthy arrived with an oxygen cylinder, she set John Paul up with the oxygen mask to help maintain his sats (blood oxygen saturation). Then they settled down to wait, knowing full well that everyone in the district was waiting with them, glued to their radios to listen to the exchanges between Neen and Dr Balmain as they were relayed by Kirsty at the police station. In between those exchanges, she kept Sue and everyone else on track.

Bob Balmain says it was reassuring knowing Neen was at the scene. 'Whatever the situation, Neen always did everything exactly as I asked and would report back exactly what I needed to know,' he says. 'I always knew that if she said it was serious, then it was very serious. At that point, I told her not to move him and to follow the ABC of first response: airway, breathing and circulation.'

Likewise, Neen says she was very grateful that he was the flying doctor based in Charleville. 'I admire and respect him so much,' she says. 'Dr Bob taught me procedures that still stand me in good stead today. He knew my capabilities and he knew just how much I could manage on my own. My instinct was to get John Paul off the bike but I trusted Dr Bob implicitly and I couldn't have asked for better medical back-up.'

While the minutes crept away, the day became much hotter as the sun rose higher and shimmered brightly across the open plain. All the while, Neen was, outwardly, quietly confident and reassuring but, inwardly, was feeling sick because she knew that John Paul was critically compromised and they were a very, very long way from the kind of medical intervention he would need. She didn't really think he would survive.

Neen and Andrew McCarthy had worked together several times before when they were called out to accidents and she knew that, as a former surf lifesaver, he was well able to assist with basic life support. Keeping up her appearance of calm confidence despite her emotional connection to the Tully family, Neen told only Andrew that John Paul was steadily deteriorating and they were getting low on oxygen. He was suffering increased periods of apnoea – meaning that he stopped breathing momentarily – and his level of consciousness was deteriorating so much that Neen had begun to assist his breathing with a bag manually squeezed to push air into the lungs. Incidentally, and just to add an extra level of complexity to the challenges, Neen had broken her wrist in a bike accident two weeks before and had one arm in plaster. As she pumped air into John Paul, her wrist was getting sore, but she was able to rely on Andrew to relieve her periodically.

In the midst of it all, one of the helpers fainted from the heat. Neen suddenly realised that she might soon have other patients on her hands. 'It was a horrible feeling and one that I had to keep to myself, but it confirmed that I needed to keep a good eye on everyone and keep everything under control,' she says.

Finally they heard the plane. Remembering back with a glimmer of tears in her eyes, Neen says, 'I've never been so pleased to hear the sound of an aircraft in my life.' It took another fifteen minutes for the plane to land on the airstrip up at the homestead and for Hawkes to bring them down to the scene of the accident.

'Dr Bob stepped out of the car, came straight over and said in his calm, gentle voice, "It's okay now, we'll take over." It was such a huge relief to have him there,' Neen says. As she handed over to him, she was unable to get a viable blood pressure reading, his heart rate was rapid and the oxygen cylinder was pretty much empty.

'Dr Bob sedated John Paul and then, under his direction, using full spinal precautions, several men lifted him very carefully up and off the bike and laid him onto the stretcher on a tarp on the ground. Dr Bob examined him and got him stabilised, all the while explaining everything to Sue. He was just wonderful,' Neen says.

In due course, accompanied by Sue, they got him loaded and away to the plane and, as they heard it taking off shortly after, the crowd on the ground began cleaning up and leaving, starting the long process of debriefing among themselves. Everyone was stressed. They had been out there for nearly five hours by the time the plane took off. Neen and Hawkes packed up all her gear and the girls and headed home. The radio and the phone ran hot as friends and family called to talk about the accident and speculate about the outcome. Neen rang the RFDS for an update and heard that John Paul had further deteriorated in-flight and that they had to land in transit to Brisbane to restabilise him.

Hawkes could see that Neen was overwhelmed and in shock, so, later in the afternoon, he and some friends took her fishing. 'It was a helluva day and one of Neen's finest moments,' he reflects. 'It was as though all her training had led to this. What she did was huge. She kept him alive until the flying doctor got there,' he says. They camped out all night surrounded only by the silence and peace of the bush.

With intensive care, John Paul managed to hang on in the plane to Brisbane and the crucial days that followed. Worrying every day that they might not be looking after him well enough in a big, busy ward, Neen kept in regular contact with the staff at the Royal Brisbane Hospital, where he was being treated. She learnt that his injuries were even more extensive than they'd first thought. 'His lung collapsed, his spleen had ruptured with accompanying blood loss and he had a spinal injury. I don't know how he didn't die. He had so many injuries. It really was just awful,' she says.

John Paul's journey from there on was long and complicated. Initially he had his spleen removed and his arm pinned. After several days, a belated MRI showed he had, after all, broken his back and injured his spinal cord. Following surgery on his back, many months in hospital and further weeks in rehab, he recovered enough to go home on crutches, but, after a few weeks, he realised he couldn't manage Mt Marlow Station. He and Sue moved to Toowoomba where, many months later, he developed syringomyelia – a rare disorder in the spinal cord in which a growing cyst presses on the spinal cord, impacting on nerve impulses – which started spreading up his spinal column. In early 2003, surgery to install a shunt to drain the fluid resulted in him being paralysed from the waist down.

Any time John Paul tells his story, he says, 'Neen's the angel who saved my life.' In the beginning he told Neen that he wished she hadn't, a sentiment that worried her for a long time. Now, with the support of his son and daughter who live close by, an extended group of friends, visiting staff from Blue Care and a private carer, he lives alone and productively on the outskirts of Toowoomba. His and

Sue's marriage succumbed to the burden of the tragic circumstances in which the accident happened, but they remain friends. As an entertaining raconteur, John Paul practises his excellent storytelling skills on anyone and everyone who comes to call. Now when he says that Neen is the angel who saved him, he smiles and looks pleased.

In 2002 the Yaraka district was struggling in the clutches of a ceaseless, soul-destroying drought. At this point Neen began to realise she wasn't equipped to deal with the extent of heartbreak and despair in the community. 'People were more and more needy and I felt less and less able to help,' she reflects. Called to a suicide one day, she was devastated not to have been able to help the poor man who took a gun and shot himself. Although they fought to save him, he died.

Now, looking back, Neen wonders if she spread herself too thin in her determination to look after everyone else. She wonders whether she should have listened to all the people who used ask her, 'What happens if something happens to you?' To which she'd reply, 'I'll be right.' She'd be the first aid person at gymkhanas and other sporting events, but would compete in them as well. 'What happens if you fall off?' people would ask. She'd grin and say, 'I won't . . .'

Neen says she was caught unawares when Hawkes said he was leaving her, although in hindsight she acknowledges the signs were there. In the end, Hawkes moved up to Longreach to live and she moved to Toowoomba to be near the girls, who were at boarding school down there.

In the aftermath of the breakup, Neen bought Hawkes' share of their property, Merrigal, and employed a caretaker to look after it from day to day in her absence. However, she continued manage it from Toowoomba, with frequent trips home to muster cattle, wean and brand calves, check country and generally keep things going until the drought eventually broke. Holly and Jess became daygirls and Neen got a job at St Vincent's Hospital in Toowoomba. While the Yaraka community recovered from the shock of losing their nurse and another good family from the district, Neen struggled to understand the turn her life had taken. Negotiating traffic in the city every day was a nightmare and working inside four walls, trying to understand the politics and protocols of a big hospital, was challenging. 'Even living with constant noise was awful but at least I was so busy I had no time to think,' she says.

After seventeen years of running her own clinic in the outback, she found her new environment claustrophobic, both physically and professionally. After pretty much total autonomy, suddenly she had to second-guess everyone and everything. She stuck it out until after the girls had left school and then decided to get out of town. She loved St Vincent's but hated being closed inside and the repetitiveness of ward work.

Missing the wide-open spaces of western Queensland, she felt desperate to be working somewhere outside. One shift, on night duty, serendipitously, she read an online advertisement for a flight nurse position with CareFlight out of Darwin. She printed off the position description, wrote an application, had a phone interview and started work in Darwin two weeks after that. On the way up there, she drove via Merrigal, mustered and branded everything that needed to be and tidied up a few loose ends before heading north on her new adventure. Everything about it felt right. Although the first few weeks were hectic as she settled into a new town, new home and new job, Neen slotted straight into the role, loving everything about it.

Every day – and sometimes every hour – is different for her, as the flight crews respond to emergency call-outs up to three times a day and one or two times a night around the Top End, using either helicopters or fixed-wing King Air planes, depending on the circumstances.

In any given situation, people call or go to their clinic staff, who in turn call the district medical officer, who in turn calls the logistics coordinator unit (LCU) at CareFlight if they need a retrieval. High acuity cases always go to Darwin, so the crews there generally do those retrievals, though there are occasions when they will collaborate with other services. For example, one road accident involving eight children required CareFlight to attend as well as two RFDS planes from Alice Springs. The LCU's job is to work out the best and most effective options.

Like the RFDS, CareFlight retrievals are mostly undertaken by one flight nurse and one pilot, although, pre-flight, the nurse can specifically request a second nurse or a doctor to be on board if they believe it is necessary. The crews are interdependent and everyone values everyone else on the team because their safety and viability depends on each person doing their specific job perfectly.

Explaining some of the intricacies, Neen says, 'Flight nurses need to understand aviation physiology because chest drains, catheter bags and intravenous drip bags function differently under pressure. Sometimes we have to fly to sea-level cabin pressure if there's air trapped in a cavity in the patient, like a pneumothorax or a gut obstruction, or if it's an eye injury or suspected head injury.'

In the three years Neen has worked for CareFlight, she has undergone winch training, which means she is the nurse who can be lowered down from a helicopter to a patient in an awkward retrieval, such as down a gorge, on top of a ridge or onto a ship. 'It's exciting, adrenaline-pumping work,' she attests.

It was a particularly busy year for Neen in 2013 as she committed to undertaking her midwifery. CareFlight needs nurses who have both midwifery and critical care nursing experience. Because it was difficult to recruit such nurses, they decided to offer a scholarship so that some of their nurses could train accordingly. Working alternately one full week at CareFlight and then one full week at Darwin Private Hospital, Neen also studied fulltime to complete the course in twelve months. While she loved delivering the babies, the year was challenging, and she has enjoyed getting back to fulltime work with CareFlight.

She has no regrets in life. Breaking up with Hawkes was tough, but when her youngest brother, James, was killed in a car accident some years later, she was forced to reassess her priorities. 'No good comes of losing someone,' she says, 'but my brother Peter taught me to be grateful for the wonderful family and friends I have. As he said, I have options. Lots of people don't.'

While life hasn't turned out quite the way she thought it would, she recently turned fifty and is happy with what she has. She loves the Top End, loves her job, loves the team she works with and currently wouldn't change a thing. She thrives on caring for the people who need her, endeavouring always to ensure they are as well looked after as they possibly can be on her watch. When she's not working or catching up on sleep, Neen Hawkes likes nothing better than a good day's fishing. Along with being grateful, she's learnt to worry less about the things she can't do anything about. In fact, the biggest worry she has these days is whether she can land the next big barra.

That and how many crocs are watching . . .

2
INVESTING IN FUTURES
Anna Burley, *Georgetown, Queensland*

Keeping one eye on the sky outside and the other on the Local Disaster checklist, Anna Burley and her staff steadily ticked off the items as they ensured the security of the Savannah Regional Health Service that has been Anna's office space for nearly a decade. It was 2 February 2012, and every half-hour or so, she dialled the number for the Mount Surprise health clinic, 96 kilometres to the east, but no one answered. Outside, a stiff little breeze had picked up and the morning eastern sky was darkening, heralding the arrival of the approaching danger.

For several days, on every radio and television channel, Anna and her colleagues had been hearing about the threat of Cyclone Yasi. They were unsure of its exact path, but preparing for the worst. It's a rare event for a cyclone to roar inland, but everything led them to believe that Yasi was coming and it was coming in a fury.

With the policeman at Mount Surprise away on leave, Officer-In-Charge of the Georgetown police, Grant Wynne-Jones, decided to drive to Mount Surprise early that afternoon, to check on its readiness. Anna grabbed the opportunity and jumped in with him. All morning, she'd been fielding phone calls from Mount Surprise residents asking for advice and direction. Anna recalls one of the calls from someone 'specifically worrying about the older members of the Mount Surprise community, some of whom lived in relatively fragile caravans and cottages. A band of them suggested moving everyone into safer accommodation, which was a great idea and a reflection of the wonderful community spirit brought out by the impending disaster.'

Anna was pleased to be able to hitch a lift down to check that everyone was safe and accounted for. As they drove east, she clearly remembers the overwhelming sense of threat they felt when they caught their first sight of the looming black monster. Even though Yasi was still several hours away, as they drove into the first big drops of rain, Anna says it was like driving into a heavy, dark-grey curtain of water. 'It was suddenly all very real and terrifying,' she recalls. 'The rain was bucketing down by the time we got into Mount Surprise.'

While Anna checked the clinic had been secured and managed to track down the nurse at her home and checked she was safe and prepared for the onslaught, Grant checked that the police station and its adjoining residence were secure. They both checked on the elderly residents who had moved into safe accommodation, drove around town casting an eye over everything they could see in the deluge, then hightailed back to Georgetown to batten down.

Then they all waited . . .

*

Born and bred at Gloucester in the Barrington Tops area on the mid-north coast of New South Wales, Anna Burley's parents' families were all dairy farmers. While her father became a mechanic and had a business in Gloucester, her mother was a telephonist with the Postmaster-General's department, manually connecting telephone calls in the days before Telstra existed. Anna believes she inherited from her mother a streak of rebellion and a very well developed sense of social justice, albeit a little later in life. Quite tall, with dark hair and dark chocolate eyes, nowadays she glows with the kind of bearing and presence that inspires confidence and compels people to listen. After completing all her schooling in Gloucester in 1984, Anna took a gap year, working at home helping her father, before securing a job with the Commonwealth Bank branch in Balmain in Sydney. Firmly convinced that she didn't want to live the rest of her life in Gloucester, Anna spent two years within branch banking before moving across to Westpac, where she worked for their foreign exchange division. Working her way up the corporate ladder, she secured a traineeship on the trading floor in foreign currency options.

She had opportunities to work in both New York and London and should have been thriving on the cut and thrust of high-end finance, but in her early thirties – joking now that she was having an early mid-life crisis – Anna recognised that she was increasingly discontented with the world around her. 'We were buying options at a low price and selling at a high price,' she explains. 'It's not rocket science and, really, it's all just on paper; the only challenge is you've got to be ahead of everyone else to be successful. The high-flyers were making obscene amounts of money and I started to feel uncomfortable with it. I was developing a social conscience and I couldn't see the social value in what I was doing. It certainly wasn't doing anything for the greater good of the community.'

Loading up a backpack, Anna took leave and spent nine months wandering around the UK, Canada and the US, all the while thinking about her options. 'I kept running into nurses and hearing their stories about what they were doing and where they were working. Then when I got back to Australia, I linked up with nursing friends in Sydney who were working in the Neonatal Intensive Care Unit in the King George Hospital for Mothers and Babies at Royal Prince Alfred (RPA). They looked after very tiny babies and they were so obviously contributing something worthwhile to the world. What was I doing that was worthwhile? Nothing that I could see,' she says.

When Anna started to think about it seriously, she decided her career trajectory was wrong and set about putting her money where her mouth was. Fortuitously, thanks to a well-timed restructuring within the bank, she was offered a retrenchment package that enabled her to commit to retraining. Enrolling at Sydney University in 1997, she undertook a fulltime nursing degree.

While she studied, she worked as an usher for the Sydney Cricket Ground Trust and for four hours, every weekday, she worked as the on-ground administrator at a privately sponsored housing complex managed by the Perpetual Trustees. The houses were originally established by Dame Eadith Walker for 'genteel women of limited financial means'. It suited Anna's sensibilities perfectly and enabled her to meet her mortgage repayments. Her budget was tight and the only luxury she allowed herself was Sunday morning breakfast with friends. She completely culled all the social activities that had accompanied her previously 'upwardly mobile' lifestyle.

Anna found that the Sydney University health faculty catered to many areas of allied health. She undertook her first practical blocks at RPA, the Concord Hospital and then, thanks to her friend Jo Laurie (now Fort), a registered nurse, she did a block at the clinic in Birdsville, in far south-west Queensland. Jo, who was working in Birdsville, had known Anna for most of her life and encouraged her to pursue her nursing career and also to consider remote nursing, which she herself loved. Acknowledging it was she who influenced her the most, Anna says with a laugh, 'It's really all Jo's fault I'm a nurse!'

Because Anna had worked autonomously in her previous life in finance, she knew that she would need to be able to establish some semblance of autonomy in nursing. Working at Birdsville with Jo tipped the balance in favour of remote work, but she also knew that she would need much more clinical experience before she headed outback.

Consequently, she did her graduate year at Dubbo in north-west New South Wales, working with a rural program that sent her on rotation to Wellington, Dubbo Base, Coonamble and then Nyngan hospitals. She went home to Gloucester for a couple of years and worked for a while in the casual pool at the nearby Manning Hospital in Taree, and then in their accident & emergency (A&E) department while she studied an external Masters of Rural and Remote Nursing at Sydney Uni through their Broken Hill campus.

In 2004, she decided to travel Australia working for a remote-area nursing agency. She worked in Cape York and at Ayr in North Queensland and then worked for Frontier Services relieving at the Bedourie clinic in the state's far south-west. Getting into Bedourie was an adventure all of its own, since it was raining when Anna flew out there and the plane couldn't land, so she flew into Birdsville, 200-odd kilometres south. There was a huge amount of rain and Anna was told she wouldn't be able to get back to Bedourie until it dried out. However, as luck would have it, the then state governor, Quentin Bryce, was coming to Birdsville for a celebration. The CEO and the mayor of the local shire council were down in Birdsville to meet the governor and offered to get Anna back to Bedourie so she could relieve the incumbent remote area nurse.

'It was a wild ride,' says Anna incredulously, 'totally white knuckle.' There were sheets of water all over the road and, in the pitch dark, slipping and sliding north through the black soil plains of the Channel Country, she admits to thinking, *This is it. We're all going to die!* They did get through though and she liked Bedourie enough to agree to return later in the year after relieving in the north of the state.

Contracted to Frontier Services, Anna really enjoyed the relief work at Bedourie but, at the end of 2004, she was confronted by the changes that happened when the management of the clinics at Birdsville and Bedourie was handed over to the local Diamantina shire and to new administrators. Anna says she experienced a clash of personalities with one of her new colleagues and felt intimidated enough to begin second-guessing her nursing capabilities. Facing changes that she felt were detrimental to the wellbeing of the community, she decided to set her sights elsewhere and returned home to reconsider her future.

Within hours of arriving in Gloucester, she received a phone call from Frontier Services asking if she'd be interested in working directly for them as the primary health care nurse in a new program, the Savannah Regional Health Services (SRHS), based in Georgetown in North Queensland. Hesitating because of the beating her confidence had taken before she left Bedourie, she thought about it for a full two weeks before deciding to back herself and take the job.

When she relocated to Georgetown, the SRHS was still such a new service that there were quite a number of unknowns, so they replicated quite a lot from the Frontier Services model used in Birdsville and Bedourie, as well as from her experiences in other remote communities. During one of her relief stints at Bedourie, Anna, with the help of some of the people in the community, had saved the lives of four young people critically injured in a road accident 80 kilometres from Bedourie and more than 600 kilometres from the nearest Royal Flying Doctor Service base. It was a dramatic and difficult rescue. Reflecting on the incident, Anna says she simply did what she had to do, with the limited resources available at the time. What's more, she says it illustrated that any big accident in a small remote community can be as catastrophic as a bushfire or cyclone.

Up in Georgetown, Anna helped Frontier Services develop strategies to better manage multiple injuries in a remote location as well as weather-related events. And Georgetown is certainly remote. Located about halfway between the base of the Gulf of Carpentaria and the east coast of Queensland, the nearest hospital is at Atherton, about 350 kilometres to the north-east. The only public transport is a bus service that goes through three days a week. Because the SRHS was a federally funded program, one of its central aims was to address community need.

The SRHS covers 70 000 square kilometres of the shires of Etheridge and Croydon in North Queensland. Because of the vastness of the area, many people didn't have access to any services, so Anna set about establishing equity by encouraging partnerships that broadened the access base for the whole region. The initiative was well supported by both the shire councils and the Etheridge Shire Council provided infrastructure in the guise of a new clinic at Einasleigh, extensions to the clinic at Mount Surprise and refurbishment of a room at the Oasis Roadhouse at The Lynd Junction to function as a clinic. The SRHS opened up new outreach services and they continue to keep tabs on what people need. 'We don't have a formal MOU [memorandum of understanding] with the councils; rather, we have a really good relationship and work collaboratively to achieve the best possible outcomes. One way or another, these councils put a lot of money into health,' Anna says.

Community consultation takes place via lots of chats with everybody rather than formal meetings. According to Rosemary Young, the National Director of Frontier Services from 1999 to 2013, Anna has an extraordinary talent for community development and 'almost automatically operates in community-empowerment mode. Nursing is almost secondary. Being the nurse puts her in the right place to achieve a whole lot of other things by virtue of the things she does there. She changes the skill mix that she uses to meet the needs of the community she's in at the time. She's a confident woman who stands her ground and she's well respected. She has presence and she makes things happen,' Rosemary says.

One of the first services people in the region asked for was a hairdresser. 'It makes sense to try and get them out here,' Anna says. Only half joking, she laughs and says that she has always thought, 'A haircut, a facial and an eyebrow wax makes everything right with the world again. When you live at least 300 kilometres from the possibility, it can become a priority and not something to be taken for granted.'

Anna has a talent for professional loitering and says she will go to the opening of an envelope if it gives her access to the people. She goes to all community events providing medical support for sporting events, including races and rodeo, or helping out in whatever way she can to ensure she keeps on top of what's happening in the neighbourhood and what people are thinking about it.

When she first went to Georgetown, Anna says that 'everyone was cruising along pretty nicely but then one disaster after another hit the region.' Ticking an imaginary list on her fingers, she adds: 'The first portent of disaster was Larry, a cyclone that went through in 2006, leaving in his wake a big rain depression and some wind damage but nothing the locals couldn't cope with. Some of them even went down to Innisfail (360 kilometres east) to help that devastated town.'

Marking the global financial crisis of 2007–08 with the next finger, she explains, 'There was a rationalisation of services, but there weren't many services up here anyway, so there was no marked difference really, although there was a tightening on bank loans.'

Flicking up another finger, she continues, 'In late January 2009, Cyclone Charlotte formed in the Gulf of Carpentaria and tracked slowly south-east, turning into a rain depression as it hit the coast. It rained for weeks and Karumba, Normanton and Croydon were inundated and under water for up to fourteen weeks.'

While the initial impact was reported in the press, the area is a long way from anywhere and response times were slow. The stock losses were enormous and the very lifeblood of the land destroyed. 'Thousands and thousands of cattle died,' Anna says. 'Thousands of kilometres of fencing were washed away. All the little animals and reptiles that couldn't climb trees were washed away and all the seed stock was washed away. The long-term effects were enormous.'

As devastating as it was, it was overshadowed a couple of weeks later when Victoria burned. More than 170 people died and more than 400 were injured in the Black Saturday bushfires. It was difficult for the Gulf Savannah people to be recognised by the media for the help they needed and most of them wouldn't ask in the light of the tragedy down south.

Once all the water retreated, people began the long road to recovery. The Northern Gulf Resource Management Group handled fodder drops across the region and stepped in to fight for Exceptional Circumstances funding for graziers and businesses affected by the floods. It took a while to get a response and in the end Noeline Ikin, in her role as CEO of Northern Gulf, dragged the then Federal Minister for Agriculture, Tony Burke, out to see for himself.

Using Queensland Rural Adjustment Authority (QRAA) funding, Savannah Health brought a facilitator up to deliver a two-day workshop providing mental health first-aid training to Northern Gulf staff and some locals. The Department of Primary Industries sent people out to look at grass viability. 'Despite the damage, people were still quite resilient. They were handling it because they expect tough times in the bush and most of them just get up and get going,' says Anna.

Tagging the next finger, she continues: 'Then came Yasi.'

Waiting for Yasi to come on the morning of 3 February 2012, Anna felt the burden of people's fear. It was apparent that the cyclone would be moving inland hard and fast; and people were scared for their lives in the coming twenty-four hours and their livelihoods in the aftermath. 'These people up here are tough, but in the last few years they've just had too much to cope with; one challenge after another,' says Anna.

Glued to their radios and televisions, they all knew Yasi had been upgraded to a Category 5 storm before it had crossed the coast near Mission Beach in the early hours of that morning. They heard it had terrorised the coast; that Tully and Cardwell had suffered major damage; that torrential rain was adding insult to injury; and that it looked like the storm would keep moving steadily south-west. Still, they held their collective breath and waited . . .

When the wind came, it howled in, but it wasn't quite the storm they'd feared. 'Up here it was still pretty scary with a lot of big wind for about twenty hours, but there was not as much rain as expected and none of the anticipated flooding. There were trees knocked over and Mount Surprise copped a pummelling, but it seemed we were okay,' says Anna.

While the Georgetown community counted their blessings, the media and the incumbent state premier kept naming Georgetown as the focus of attention. However, it transpired that Yasi turned slightly south as it cut a swathe through the south of the Tablelands shire and the north of the Charters Towers shire. Rather than Georgetown, it hit Greenvale in the south-east of the Etheridge shire. 'The one good thing Yasi did was pick the path of least population density, but, where the eye cut through, the landscape was completely flattened.'

As the immediate emergency passed, Anna started ringing people in the southern part of the shire and found there was a huge amount of damage everywhere. Mildly confident that, this time, the bush would be included in all the constant media coverage, the first inkling Anna had that there was a problem was when the Local Disaster Management Group was stood down. 'No one had done any proper consultation so they didn't know what damage there was,' she says, her voice reflecting the anger and exasperation she felt then. 'They'd kept saying Georgetown was in the direct path and then reporting that there was no major damage there, so the authorities and rest of Australia seemed to assume that the cyclone had petered out and that there was no significant damage anywhere west of the coast.'

While people on some of the stations were saying that the only roads open were the main ones in to their homesteads, they still couldn't get out into the paddocks by road to check their stock losses and infrastructure damage. In the end, when they were able to tally up the losses, they were enormous. Not only stock losses, which were estimated in the tens of thousands, but fences, windmills, water troughs, stockyards . . . all blown away or smashed to smithereens.

Badgering anyone who'd listen long enough, Anna protested the lack of appropriate recovery services to the area after Yasi. 'We had major problems making anyone understand that the impact here was just as bad. No one was interested. It wasn't population dense enough to warrant attention. Part of the problem is that most urban people don't understand remote Australia. They don't understand the geography or the distances.' As a result of Anna never giving up, gradually the cyclone-damaged area was re-categorised correctly. Eventually there was more support given by the QRAA and Centrelink, but it was a long, slow slog. 'I kept hearing about "economies of scale"!' Anna declares. 'And yet these people were hurting every bit as much as those on the coast. On some stations all of the families do business under one ABN, which meant that instead of each family getting the financial help they were entitled to, they got only one lot between them. And when people ordered their fencing materials, instead of putting the station name on the invoice, the suppliers put partnership names, which muddied the process of successfully submitting claims. They're small details that caused huge financial and emotional complications. Some grazing enterprises didn't even submit claims because the paperwork was too complicated and arduous. Their focus was on the survival of their stock and so on.'

INVESTING IN FUTURES

In the aftermath of Yasi, Anna and the Savannah Regional Health team organised a 'Let's Do Lunch' day down at the Oasis Roadhouse at the Lynd Junction. As the depot for many of the surrounding stations to pick up their supplies, it was a good central location for people to meet. As well as the SRHS, the Frontier Service's Remote Area Family Services team converged on the Roadhouse to provide fun and games for the kids for the day.

Anna had organised experts from the Queensland Mental Health team to come out and talk to people about what to expect from their partners, kids and themselves in the aftermath of the disaster. 'You know, anger, guilt and so on,' she says. But when she rang two days before to confirm it, they said they'd written the wrong date in their diary, so no one would be coming. Anna had a little meltdown and rang Jeanie Brook from Dalrymple Family Support (another Frontier Services program), who happened to have a motivational speaker, Helen Everingham, sitting in her office drinking coffee. Helen juggled her schedule to accommodate the request and offered her services free of charge if they could get her to the Oasis. 'She was fantastic,' enthuses Anna. 'She gave the audience a whole heap of stuff they found helpful. She touched on anger, guilt, self-esteem and what to expect in the days and weeks ahead. Everyone appreciated it and wanted more.'

At the end of the day, everyone had plants to take home to regenerate their gardens. 'The Queensland Country Women's Association provided funding for all the plants. It was such a simple thing to do but they were all so excited. It was something that really helped.'

However, just as the community was making strides with the recovery, the live export of cattle was banned following an ABC *Four Corners* report in May 2011, which exposed cruelty to Australian cattle in Indonesian abattoirs. Joe Ludwig, in his role as Minister for Agriculture, shut the trade down overnight. 'I saw that *Four Corners* report and, along with everyone else, was disgusted by it; but the decision to ban the trade has been catastrophic,' says Anna. Struggling, at the time, to understand the full implications, she went to Northern Gulf for a lesson in export cattle markets. 'There were thousands of cattle waiting to load in northern Australian ports, including Karumba. Not only had the owners of those cattle suddenly lost their market, but they immediately lost that income. And other cattlemen lost proposed incomes. Those cattle are grown for that particular market and sent at a specific weight. Once they're over that weight, they're not suitable for that market. Bringing them home resulted in overstocking and trading elsewhere meant saturating the market and selling at a loss. It has been disastrous for so many people.'

Back in Greenvale, thirty-two people did the mental health first-aid program Anna and her team organised in response to people acknowledging they had issues and didn't know how to handle them. 'It was pretty good because a lot of the people who did the course were dealing with the issues themselves. It bridged people getting access to mental health services by teaching them how to access those services even though they are still not available in the area. It enabled them to ask for the help they needed,' she says.

Meanwhile, a deputation from Northern Gulf met with the minister to plead the case of those in the cattle industry, but to no avail. Even though the ban has since been lifted, many in northern Australia say that they are still feeling the effects.

While some in North Queensland might seem to have reached the end of their endurance, they are, in fact, fighting back. In the Savannah region, Camp Cobbold is a social development program initiated in the area by one of the local mothers. The purpose is to provide families from remote properties in North Queensland with an opportunity to experience support, personal development, social interaction and mental and allied health services for both adults and children.

The Savannah Regional Health Service has been involved in the camp since its first year and, in 2012, provided the funding for North Queensland Royal Life Saving to conduct Learn to Swim and other activities for the adults and children who attended the camp. 'There is a high incidence of drowning deaths for boys under three years on rural properties and this was one way of trying to rectify this,' Anna says. 'It also brings families together in a fun situation and helps to create a sense of community rather than isolation.'

With a bit of creative thinking, after Yasi they were also able to access Helen Everingham for the camp. 'The Georgetown Primary School accessed funding for her to do some sessions for them and she provided extra sessions at Camp Cobbold, on self-esteem and personal development, free of charge. We had a mental health focus and offered psychology appointments and some counselling services,' she says.

One year during the camp, Anna was called away after a woman in the area died tragically. Visiting her family, Anna noticed that none of the photographs in the house included her. 'Not one,' she says, 'because, obviously, she took all the photos.' As a result, in 2012, for the first time, she instigated family photographs for all the camp participants. It's another small thing that has made a big difference.

In the aftermath of Yasi, with grass growing back through all the fallen timber, concern turned to the threat of bushfire. In late 2012, bushfires began and devastated in excess of 5.5 million hectares in the Gulf region, with almost fifty stations having more than half of their country burned. Falling equity and rising debt has brought at least fifty-eight stations in the Gulf to the brink of bankruptcy. Anna says the impact on the whole region has been mentally, physically and spiritually shattering.

While Anna continues her practice of professional loitering and generally keeping an eye on the health and wellbeing of the region, in 2012 she decided it wasn't enough. Sourcing funding from the federal government, she sent Savannah Health's Resource Officer around to every station to provide on-ground counselling and to help fill out forms. 'It was a chance to see how everyone was going. We discovered they were okay, but concerned about the future; about aged care and young people,' she says.

Now she thinks many of them really are at the end of their tether. 'People just aren't recovering. There was no wet season at the beginning of 2012 and drought has gripped the area again. People are trying to destock but for many of them, there's nowhere for their cattle to go. A lot of country has been resumed for National Parks and they're not managed properly, so weeds and fire are always a threat. It's the bureaucratic stuff that's knocking people; decisions being made by people who have no idea what they're talking about,' she says.

And yet, despite the fact that the region is back in drought and many stations have been officially drought declared, there are glimmers of fight still in the station families. 'The fightback is happening,' Anna affirms. 'A group of northern graziers organised a beef crisis meeting in Richmond in May 2013, which was attended by several hundred cattlemen. They're not giving up yet.'

There is also an initiative being pushed in government circles to get tax credits recognised. 'Some of these northern cattlemen have huge tax credits, which, if balanced against their debt with their bank, would improve their equity, thus avoiding foreclosure,' Anna

INVESTING IN FUTURES

explains. The idea was proposed by a northern cattleman, and Anna is lending her finance background to the cause. 'This will be win-win all round if we can get the right model up.'

One of the things that Anna has liked most about working for Frontier Services is the opportunity to create things outside the box that better suit the area she works in. 'Frontier Services does smart, practical things, working from the ground up rather than filtering down from on high, and we can make a real difference. If I see a need, I can start addressing it within a month. That also makes a real difference.'

Some years ago, Anna created a program specifically designed to prepare remote kids for the social, economic and cultural challenges of boarding school. The kids all know they have to go away, but Anna realised they aren't well prepared. 'We teach them about drugs and alcohol, self-esteem, changing negative thinking to positive, how to cope with peer pressure and mental health. We encourage them to ask for help, to look out for their friends and to find help for their mates if they think they need it,' she explains.

Free of charge, the workshop is held in Georgetown and is one of Anna's favourite initiatives. When she thinks about those halcyon days back in finance and compares them to the days she spends helping those remote kids, she knows she really is investing in the futures of everyone around her.

She is concerned about burning out though. 'There will come a time when I have to leave. I might have another midlife crisis! In fact, I always thought I'd like to be a country and western singer,' she says. Grinning, she adds, 'Sadly, I can't sing! This job is all consuming and that has suited me well for many years. When I came here, I could see the development of the services as just a little pimple on the bum of a bigger picture, but I wanted to make it more applicable to the people who live here and I think, together with my staff, I have done that.'

As she looks back on her two very different careers – one investing with other people's money and the other investing in other people's futures – Anna Burley can be justly proud of the work she has been doing for the last sixteen years. Balancing her social justice ledger, she has indeed done a lot for the greater good of the community.

3

TARMACS AND TOOLBOXES

Geri Malone, *Fleurieu Peninsula, South Australia*

Very late one afternoon in 1988, a call came in to the health clinic at the Moomba oil and gas fields, from the doctor at the Royal Flying Doctor Service (RFDS) base at Broken Hill, saying they had received a call from Innamincka Station a few minutes before, requesting urgent assistance for a young stockman who'd been bitten by a snake. The station is located just outside the tiny settlement of Innamincka, which lies about 100 kilometres north-east of Moomba, in the very remote far north-east corner of South Australia. The RFDS plane was on another call-out and couldn't come straight away, so the doctor asked if Moomba clinic could assist.

Geri Malone was the nurse on duty at Moomba who took the call. She'd been told that the stockman – or ringer, as they are called in the outback – had been steadily drinking at the Innamincka

Hotel and, as he wandered home, had decided to try to catch a snake. The area is home to many dangerous snakes, including the inland taipan, one of the deadliest in the world. Time was of the essence. If it turned out to be a taipan, the consequences could be very serious.

Geri immediately alerted the operators of the Moomba oil and gas fields, who approved the use of their helicopter to fly up to the station to retrieve the young man. When they took off it was a very dark outback night and quite windy. The estimated time of arrival was about twenty minutes, so they could soon see the lights of Innamincka and then the station lights blazing like a beacon in the distance. The pilot had radioed ahead and organised the landing point with the station manager, who was waiting to pick them up.

As they circled over the settlement before coming around to land, they were blown a little off-track over the surrounding hills. Suddenly they lost sight of the lights.

Then they crashed . . .

Growing up on a farm near Jamestown in South Australia, Geri Malone was unsure what she wanted to 'do' when she grew up. The one thing she did know for sure was she wanted to go to university. 'Because I really wanted to do some extra subjects that would broaden my education,' she says.

Until 1974, all nurses in South Australia trained in hospitals. However, in 1975, nurse training was introduced into the state tertiary system, just in time for Geri to enrol at the Sturt College of Advanced Education, now Flinders University, as one of that first 'guinea pig' year, to begin her general nursing education. She says she'd probably have done radiography or journalism if she hadn't been able to take up her preferred choice at uni. She acknowledges her eldest sister was a nurse and midwife and a woman she looked up to and admired greatly so, 'maybe, subliminally, that influenced me'.

While she enjoyed it, she found it challenging, even character building. 'It was an interesting time because in the nursing hierarchy, as uni student nurses we were the lowest of the low,' Geri explains. Once she was into it though, she knew she really wanted to be a registered nurse and registered midwife – the whole package. At the end of her three years' training she moved into the hospital system to complete her graduate year before flying to London and then on to Glasgow in Scotland, where she'd enrolled to do her midwifery. 'It was the thing to do in those days,' she explains. 'The joke used to be: "If you trained in Scotland you were a real midwife," ' she adds, with a twinkle in her eye and a half smile.

As soon as she qualified she moved down to London, signed up with a nursing agency and worked short stints as a general nurse wherever she was needed, to make enough money to travel around Europe and the rest of the UK.

Coming home, Geri returned to Jamestown and worked as a very new midwife at the local hospital for a while, but, knowing that she needed to consolidate her midwifery training, she soon applied to work at a private hospital in Adelaide, doing everything from antenatal birthing to postnatal care.

Looking back, Geri reflects that her career path was really quite unplanned. Fairly tall and with excellent posture, on first appearances one might think her reserved until she suddenly bursts into laughter or, very occasionally, swears. In fact, she's very down to earth and her green eyes radiate quiet confidence and composure. More than anything, she looks like someone who knows exactly what she's doing and what needs to be done and yet she believes in serendipity, staying open to opportunities and letting the subsequent pathway unfold.

Thus it was that she took leave from her midwifery job to undertake three months' work relieving an RFDS flight nurse at Port Augusta in 1981. By the end of the contract she knew she had found her niche. She loved the nursing and took to the aviation aspect of her work like a duck to water. Offered the option of staying, she signed onto the RFDS fulltime.

Two years in Port Augusta led to a flight nurse position in Broken Hill in outback New South Wales. Back then, the nurses worked one week on call 24/7 for emergency retrievals, then one week on the routine clinic runs, flying out to pastoral stations and small communities to provide health care. Attracted by the chance to do different things every day, Geri loved the buzz associated with emergency retrievals but equally treasured the opportunity to get to know the people they visited on the clinic runs. Going on the clinic runs often meant going into people's homes, as the stations usually provided a room in their houses for the clinic. The RFDS staff invariably ate smokos and lunch with the family, forming the basis of strong social and medical connections.

In 1986 the New South Wales section of the RFDS was contracted by an energy and exploration company to manage their health clinic in the oil and gas installation of Moomba, located in the Cooper Basin in north-east South Australia. It was one of the first fly-in fly-out 'camps' and an all-male environment when Geri was asked in late 1987 to step in for one of the two male nurse paramedics at the clinic when he had to go on leave. Geri was the first woman to live and work there for the fortnight-on fortnight-off schedule that was normal practice in oil and gas fields in those days.

40

The broad age range of the men working in the Cooper Basin included quite young apprentice-aged men right through to those of retirement age. 'Chivalry was not entirely dead and there were expectations regarding behaviour towards women,' Geri remembers. So much so that the gentlemen running the camp facilities made a new rule upon her arrival: when Geri was in residence, they banned the 'adult movies' occasionally shown on the television system running throughout all the rooms. 'It wasn't an entirely popular directive!' she laughs, but she appreciated that it was a respectful decision.

Despite the inherent paternalism, Geri enjoyed her sojourn at Moomba enough to agree to stay on fulltime when a vacancy came up. It was a change of pace for her to be working on the ground, and everyone on the same rotation got to know each other pretty well.

Although she'd been working for the RFDS for a few years by then and had responded to lots of accidents in hospital situations, her work at Moomba had a very different feel to it because it was happening in what was virtually 'her' very small community. She was more emotionally engaged than she'd felt before because she was living and working among these people.

Geri clearly remembers the first emergency she encountered at Moomba. She and her very experienced nurse/paramedic colleague were called over to the MCG (Moomba cricket ground), where they found one of the older men had collapsed. A couple of men had already started CPR. The nurses took over and continued resuscitating him while directing his transfer onto a stretcher and back to the clinic. In consultation with the doctor at the RFDS base at Broken Hill, they worked on him for some considerable time, but, ultimately, he was pronounced dead.

'It was so sad. He was a manager of one of the teams, very well liked and respected, and his son was also working in the field at the time, so the ripple effect throughout the community was very obvious,' Geri remembers. She acknowledges that her personal connection made it much more confronting than most of her previous experiences.

In the manner of all small communities, everyone looked out for each other and management made a point of looking after the nursing staff. 'It was just such a supportive environment,' she says.

So it was that the whole Moomba community was on high alert when they heard that Geri had not called in to the clinic as expected on her arrival at Innamincka Station to retrieve the ringer who'd grabbed the snake. Meanwhile, the station manager had also raised the alarm when they didn't arrive as expected at the pre-arranged landing site. He'd heard the chopper fly over and then it just vanished.

Geri recalls the last minutes of the flight as abrupt. 'We were coming around to the landing site when suddenly there was no lift, no updraft. We just fell out of the sky. We lost sight of the lights and then *bang*, we hit the ground. There was no time to be terrified. We hit with the front of the skids and tipped over,' she says.

As they tipped over, Geri was on the topside of the aircraft. Her most vivid memory was smelling the fuel. 'The pilot had a helmet on, which was lucky,' Geri says, 'as it had a sizable dent in it. Something came up and hit him in the head but he was okay. Well, he was until I fell on him when I finally got my seatbelt undone!' In reality, they both managed to get out of a hole in the bubble and scramble away from the wreck.

The manager, who Geri knew very well, was driving around looking for the wreck when he heard them yelling. 'When he finally tracked us across country he said he was never more relieved to hear voices,' she recalls.

Assured that they were both basically okay, he drove them back to the homestead. 'You try not to focus on what happened and, in fact, it didn't really sink in straight away,' Geri says. When they got to the homestead, they were met by the manager's wife, who Geri also knew very well. Understandably frustrated with the stupidity of the ringer who shouldn't have been at the pub in the first place, and definitely shouldn't have tried to wrangle the snake, both the manager and his wife were much more concerned with the health of Geri and the pilot.

However, Geri only remembers that all her professional experience kicked in and enabled her to concentrate on assessing the patient. 'He reeked of alcohol and was so drunk it was difficult to tell whether his symptoms were from the grog or snake venom,' she says.

She consulted with the doctor from the RFDS base in Broken Hill, updating him about the accident and providing him with an evaluation of the patient. Normally the RFDS plane would have flown in to meet them at Innamincka, but because of the dark, windy night they decided to land at Moomba and drive the ambulance back down to collect the patient. However, still high on adrenaline, Geri decided she couldn't sit around waiting, so asked the manager if he'd drive them down to meet the ambulance. The pilot had to stay with the aircraft, so they loaded the patient in the back of the station Troop Carrier and the station manager and Geri set down the Strzelecki Track. Geri tried to monitor the patient but it continued to be very difficult because he was so drunk. By the time the ambulance reached them, Geri was apologising to the flying doctor because she hadn't been able to get an IV line into the man; her hands were shaking too much.

The patient appeared not to have any of the usual symptoms of snakebite; however, when they eventually got him to Adelaide, it was established that he had been envenomated by an inland taipan, and he was given antivenin.

Meanwhile, back at Moomba, everyone was most concerned about Geri, who, apart from a rapidly spreading rainbow display of amazing bruises all over, thought she was okay. Everyone agreed that she should go home early for her leave break, but she really wanted to spend the last couple of days of her hitch in the camp while she got her head around the accident. The RFDS doctor checked her out and said she was fine, so she stayed until the usual changeover, getting lots of support from all the Moomba guys who, she quickly realised, just needed to see she was all alright. Likewise the pilot proved to be okay.

Reality hit Geri when she got home on leave. She was very shaken up and spent some time with her family up in Jamestown, coming to terms with her lucky escape. When she got back to Adelaide prior to returning to Moomba, the helicopter company contacted her to see if she'd like to go for another flight. Her father had died by then, but she well remembered his adage about getting back on the horse. She felt it was very important to take them up on their offer and went flying one day with one of the pilots she knew well. 'I just sat in the chopper and we flew around Adelaide. I was a bit leery for a while, even in fixed-wing aircraft, but eventually it felt right to be flying again,' she says.

The incident with the snakebite illustrated very personally for her the stupid, irresponsible things some people do with no concept or consideration for the other people who have to risk their own lives to rescue them.

*

Geri worked at Moomba for a couple of years until the RFDS offered her a role in Central Australia, helping to roll out a new arm of the Flying Doctors. While they had been providing a full service out of their base at Port Augusta, covering most of South Australia, the RFDS had also been providing the aviation side (the planes and pilots) of the Northern Territory Aeromedical Service (NTAS), which operated out of Alice Springs. The nurses who flew with NTAS were employed by the Territory Department of Health.

In 1989 the Health Department decided to extricate itself from the NTAS, and asked RFDS to take over employment and management of the nurses on the flights. Geri was brought on board as the senior flight nurse. Once the details of the changeover were finally sorted out, she moved to Alice Springs and into much more than just a nursing role, as she very diplomatically negotiated the tricky process of merging new nurses into the team of previously government-employed nurses she inherited with the changeover, nurses who already 'owned' the team.

Mindful of the need to be very inclusive with every aspect of the process, Geri says, 'It was one of the more interesting aspects of being an effective manager; slowly, slowly won the war.' The complexities associated with merging the two groups were exacerbated by the lack of aviation experience of the two new staff she engaged, one of whom was Christine Foletti. Neither of the new nurses had been involved in aeromedical nursing before so, while she was confident they had the necessary nursing and clinical skills needed for isolated and remote practice, she knew they had to learn all the aeromedical knowledge and skill the old team had taken for granted.

'The aeromedical context in which they work is an almost "hostile" environment,' Geri explains. 'You're in a small aircraft, and it's mobile and subject to the stresses of flight. At altitude there are situations like a decreased amount of oxygen or pressure variants that do impact on the medical condition. You have to think about gas laws and the effects of deceleration and acceleration; things that impact on staff as well as the patient.'

Consequently, patients must be prepared for flight before they leave the ground because most procedures are best undertaken in a stable environment. Turbulence is an ever-present threat in flight. The nurse, flying with a single pilot, will also be the designated flight crew. Like a stewardess on a commercial flight, he or she will have to instruct the patient and anyone travelling with them about emergency procedures.

While there are rare exceptions, generally flight nurses work strapped into their seats. They wear headphones at all times so they can talk to the pilot even as they're carrying on a second conversation with the patient. All this in the noisy confined space of a small aircraft. 'You have to be really well prepared and work to your environment,' Geri explains. 'There's a bit of a similarity to remote area nursing because it's the context of the environment in which you're working that people generally find most challenging. And until you get used to it, it can be quite fatiguing.'

Geri knows better than most that being a flight nurse appears to be a very glamorous career choice. 'Lots of people think they'd love to be a flight nurse, but don't know they're subject to air sickness until they try it. They don't always realise that, when the plane is in the air, they work in virtual isolation even though they have phone and radio contact with their base. They don't realise how much physical work is entailed and that they need to be quite fit and resilient. There's nothing glamorous about it. On the other hand,' Geri adds, 'the nurses who take to it really love their jobs and the RFDS has excellent staff retention rates. Most staff stay with the organisation for many years.'

As the senior flight nurse in Alice Springs, Geri was also flying a full roster herself. It was a full-on work description and one which allowed her little time for anything other than work. It did, however, lead to her becoming nurse manager of Central Operations, which ultimately led her further down her unplanned pathway to being the nurse manager who established the new flight nurse cohort at a new base in Adelaide.

Originally similar in structure to the Northern Territory service, the aeromedical service out of Adelaide was a collaborative partnership between the RFDS, which provided the planes and pilots, and the South Australian Ambulance, which provided the paramedics on the flights. Unlike in the Territory, however, as paramedics the South Australian staff did not qualify to work as flight nurses with the RFDS as they needed to be both a registered nurse and midwife.

Consequently, Geri had to establish and train the new team in the same building the old team was working out of. Some of the departing staff were not happy with the imposed change to their employment; however, it was to be virtually a walk-in walk-out situation, so the new team had to be ready to step in and take over at the appointed time. Geri brought four experienced flight nurses with her to the new base, so she knew she had a team who could immediately get on the plane and go. However, the other four she needed to engage were new to aeromedical and had to be buddied with one of the experienced nurses for at least two or three weeks, until they could fly solo. It was an incredibly busy time as they seamlessly took over, continued services and supported the new staff. Geri's negotiating skills were honed to an ultrafine edge by the time the last ambulance left and the first of the new teams took off at 8 a.m. on 1 July 1995.

In 1997, after fourteen years as a flight nurse and looking for new challenges and experience, Geri decided to apply to join the International Committee of the Red Cross (ICRC), offering her services to a Third World country. She explained her intentions and negotiated leave with her RFDS manager, did the basic training course and had her name added to a waiting list. In the meantime, she continued to fly. When her call-up to the ICRC came, with three weeks' lead time, the RFDS had a change of mind and would not allow her to take leave. Geri was stunned that she hadn't been supported as promised, despite her fourteen years of dedication to the Flying Doctor Service. Angry and hurt, the usually placid Geri felt forced to resign from her position as nurse manager and flew out to Kenya in northern Africa. It was an opportunity she had no intention of missing. While it took some time for her to come to terms with what she thought was a very unfair decision, in retrospect, she says, 'It was the best thing that happened, as I was compelled to go in a new direction.'

John Lynch is the chief executive officer of the RFDS Central Operations and has been associated with the organisation for nearly three decades. He concedes that the Service did not manage Geri's departure as well as it might have back then because they really didn't want her to go. Acknowledging her impact on the Service in general, he maintains that Geri is one of the most significant characters in its history. 'John Flynn founded the organisation, Clifford Peel suggested aircraft was the way to get medical services around the outback and Alf Traeger invented the pedal radio, and, in my view, the greatest contributor to flight nursing in my time with the RFDS is Geri Malone,' he says. 'The models of service we use in

Alice Springs and Adelaide were hugely influenced by her and she's the one who made those transitions happen. She left a positive legacy with the RFDS which will always be respected.'

When Geri joined her Red Cross team, led by a French doctor, she relocated to Nairobi, in Kenya, and from there flew in and out of war-torn Somalia, a country that had not had a real leader since 1990. The war lords were wreaking havoc across the landscape and, for most Somalis, life was perilous. Geri's team would fly into Mogadishu, and then on to the Juba Valley, west towards Ethiopia. Camping among the ruins of the long-protracted war for three to four days at a time, they lived on local food and dehydrated rations, with no power and no water. Mindful of their value as hostages, every member of the team had a Somali bodyguard armed with an AK-47 and a directive to be very smart about how they did things. 'It was a little daunting having an armed bodyguard,' she admits, 'but I never felt unsafe.'

Their mission was to provide medical support and training to the Somali nurses and midwives trying to cater to the local populace. There were no Somali doctors; they had all left the country. The Red Cross philosophy was to go in and help people help themselves rather than do everything for them. Geri's role was to help them re-establish a sustainable health service. The ICRC paid the salaries of the Somali nurses, and supplied medications and the other resources they needed in their clinics. 'They were very skilled. They didn't need us to tell them how to do things, although they might occasionally consult us,' she reflects. Geri remembers that the whole experience redefined her sense of what was important.

Not long after Geri first went in, while she was still getting a handover from the nurse she was replacing, they got a radio message about a young boy who'd been attacked by a crocodile. He'd poked it in the eye to make it release him but not before it had mauled his arm. Her predecessor knew there were people in the village they had already trained as health workers. They had taught them basic first aid and given them some basic supplies – soap and sterile dressings – and the team was able to organise to get some iron tablets to the boy.

Before Geri and her team could get to the village, the local health workers had acquired some suturing material, pulled the wound together and stitched it up. Unfortunately, it was a very dirty wound and shouldn't have been sutured, and by the time the Red Cross team got there, it was very badly infected and the sutures were tightly embedded in the swollen arm, which was causing the boy great pain. The nurses released the stitches and cleaned the wound. After fashioning a splint for the boy's arm, they gave him antibiotics, pain medicine and more iron tablets, and stressed the importance of keeping it clean and dry.

Not long after the incident, extensive floods overwhelmed the Juba Valley and it was months before the team got back to see the boy. Although he had a terrible scar they were delighted to see he still had his arm and it was functioning. At twelve years of age he was relied upon to work and help feed his family, who were very grateful that he could work effectively.

Watching him smiling as he showed the team how well his arm was moving, Geri could not help but compare him and his family to people back home. 'People in Australia expect so much more than the basic care we were able to provide in Somalia,' she acknowledges. 'It was all so different over there. The people there were very familiar with death and not just from the war,' she adds. 'There were some dreadful diseases there and malaria was endemic.'

During her time there, she also saw some female genital mutilation. 'That was very confronting,' she says, shaking her head. 'The impact on the women when they gave birth and on their long-term health was formidable.'

Geri returned to Australia after eight months with her perspective quite realigned. 'It was very easy to come back here and wonder what on earth people in this country had to complain about,' she says.

When Geri arrived back, she did return to part-time work as a flight nurse with the RFDS and also accepted some part-time work with CRANAplus – the council representing remote area nurses and health professionals. Geri has been a member of CRANAplus since its inception in 1983. The organisation's primary focus is providing education, support and advocacy to health professionals working in remote areas. They have been responsible for establishing a suite of courses specifically created for application in a remote context. Geri helped develop the first two, including the Remote Emergency Care (REC) course back in 1999, and over the years has facilitated many of the courses around Australia. The REC course, in particular, was designed to give health professionals the extra skills and knowledge they need to provide an appropriate emergency response to anyone critically ill or injured in a remote area. The consistent and unique challenge in every instance is 'remote location' and 'professional isolation'.

Mick Lanagan is a volunteer first responder based at the Sandfire Roadhouse, about halfway along the Great Northern Highway between Broome and Port Hedland in north-west Western

Australia. For a couple of hundred kilometres in any direction, he's the man that everyone calls on in an emergency.

'It's different out here,' Mick says. 'You don't have a hospital or medical staff just up the road and because of the distances, it can take hours for an ambulance to turn up. Even the RFDS might take a while if they are already on a call-out somewhere else.' Mick did the REC course a few years ago and says the hands-on skills and knowhow he acquired have enhanced his ability to stabilise and maintain patients for the much longer periods of time associated with responding in a remote area.

In 2011, Geri was appointed as Professional Development Manager for CRANAplus. In between overseeing the education arm of the organisation, Geri's travels the country providing advice on health service delivery in a remote setting to a wide range of people.

While her tertiary qualifications underpin her expertise, her credibility ultimately comes from her professional experience. Over the years, she's been there and done what all those remote nurses are doing, and then some . . .

Her own unplanned career path started in Jamestown in rural South Australia and currently places her south of Adelaide on the Fleurieu Peninsula; not very far as the crow flies. However, she journeyed from one to the other via midwifery training in Glasgow, the wings of the RFDS across half of outback Australia, the oil and gas fields of the Cooper Basin, the war zones of Somalia and back to education echelons of the RFDS. And when that helicopter crashed coming into Innamincka Station, suddenly the boot was on the other foot. Having also been a potential critical care patient in a remote area, Geri is definitely better qualified than most to understand the pressures and challenges that face nurses working in remote Australia.

Though her work schedule these days is hectic, when she can, Geri still enjoys facilitating any one of the many training courses that CRANAplus delivers. Late in 2013, she was standing at the side of a room watching a group of health professionals – on this occasion all nurses and midwives – participating in a REC course in Cooktown in Far North Queensland. Participants had come from all over the Cape as well as from a range of other places outside Queensland and, for most, it was their first REC course.

Geri acknowledges a quiet satisfaction that the courses have been so successful, saying, 'It is very satisfying to think you may have contributed to making the challenges of remote practice a little easier. Whether that's in the development and delivery of the very important courses for upskilling and maintaining skills, or giving support in many different forms, I never get tired of meeting up with these guys, hearing their stories, how they got there and why they stay. They are a unique breed in many ways and the great thing is you meet the most interesting and diverse characters out there, often in adverse conditions, and they tend to be very pragmatic, because they have to be; they show incredible resilience. Ultimately, they're there for the people in the outback. It pleases me to be able to support them doing that.'

4
PUSHING THE BOUNDARIES

Catherine Jurd, *Julia Creek, Queensland*

One evening last year, Catherine Jurd sashayed up to the bar in the Julia Creek Hotel in north-west Queensland and ordered a round of drinks. The barman looked her up and down, raised a skeptical eyebrow and demanded, 'You're going to have to show me some ID, darlin'.'

Catherine sighed, pulled her driver's licence out of her wallet and gently placed it on the bar. 'Okay, right,' he responded, looking at her and back at the ID a couple of times. 'So what did you want again?' he finally asked.

She gave him the order, paid and returned to the friends she'd been sharing rounds with as she enjoyed a night off from her job as a registered nurse at the McKinlay Multi-Purpose Health Service.

Her looks are deceptive. Slightly built with luminous skin and

55

long, wispy chestnut hair, Catherine does look very young, almost delicate even. Whenever she opens her mouth to speak her face lights up like a joyful pixie and her conversation is liberally sprinkled with laughter that hovers right on the edge of giggles. You might even be forgiven for thinking she's a bit of a party girl. However, as she cheerfully bounds through each day with an enthusiasm that is infectious, it quickly becomes obvious that she's about as fragile as a length of eight-gauge fencing wire and her happy-go-lucky demeanour masks an obsessively well-organised and analytical mind.

Catherine acknowledges that looking about sixteen years old has its challenges. 'Sometimes I think people underestimate my ability because I look so young,' she explains.

Her husband, Quinton, just grins and assures her that when they're all old, she'll have the last laugh. But for Catherine, it's no joke. At twenty-five, she'd already gathered up a fair bit of life experience before she'd even started her nursing degree four short years ago.

By the time she rocked up at the Julia Creek Hotel and ordered her drinks at the bar, she was a registered nurse, seven months into her graduate year working in four different hospitals in the North West Hospital and Health Service in north-west Queensland.

Catherine Jurd is on a mission, determined to build a career as a nurse and equally determined to do it in outback Australia, starting in the remote Gulf Country of north Queensland that she and Quinton currently call home.

Growing up on her family's sheep farm at Baynton, north-east of Kyneton in central Victoria, Catherine says she and her siblings – her older brother, Will, younger brother, Tim, and younger sister, Sarah – are all committed to doing something worthwhile with their lives. One of the many things they admire most about their parents is their work ethic. Catherine's father, Gerard Ryan, runs the farm, while her teacher mother, Belinda, is the deputy principal at the local Catholic primary school. 'They're always busy,' Catherine says, 'either on the farm or helping with something or other in the community.'

For all the years that Catherine was a university student, she spent most of her holidays either helping out at home or working as a roustabout with a local shearing contractor. Long weeks spent penning up sheep, picking up shorn fleeces and throwing them on the wool table, helping the wool classer skirt fleeces and keeping the floor swept clean around the shearers, apparently did little to build up her physique, but it did confirm her reputation as a hard worker.

Strong-minded, even as a small child, Catherine's pressure valve has always been running. Showing early signs of the indomitable resolve that would mark her progress through later life, in Year Three she lobbied the sports teacher ceaselessly until she let her join the Year Four long-distance running squad. Back at home on the farm, she used bits of baling twine tied to the fence to mark off their front lane at 100-metre intervals so she could plan each day's training schedule.

In her early years at high school in Kyneton, Catherine had designs on going to Genazzano FCJ College in Melbourne to complete her education. Established in 1889, the college included a small boarding house for about fifty girls from Year Nine up. She'd heard about it from a friend and, although her eldest brother, Will, had completed his education in Kyneton, Catherine decided she was going to get herself into the school of her choice. With classic single-mindedness, she put her head down, worked hard and won a scholarship for the last three years of her schooling.

Barely able to contain her excitement, right from the first day, Catherine loved everything about boarding and the new friends she made – friends she's still closely connected with. She happily immersed herself in her schoolwork, taking time out only to indulge in her favourite discipline, long-distance running. Unsurprisingly, she thrived. In going to Genazzano, she broke the mould for her younger two siblings, Tim and Sarah, who also went to boarding school.

Having achieved her goal of getting into Genazzano, Catherine then set her very high sights on university. 'I've always wanted to be the best at what I did and, because I was interested in health, doing medicine seemed the obvious choice,' she explains. Hell-bent on being a doctor come what may, she put her head down and studied hard. Dedicated to the cause, often when her friends were off enjoying extracurricular activities, she'd be studying. Long-distance running was her one concession. She ran to relieve the pressure she put on herself to succeed.

With an impressive Australian tertiary admission ranking of 97.6, Catherine won a place in biomedicine at the University of Melbourne and also a place of residence at Queen's College. Biomedicine relates to humans' biological and physiological ability to cope with environmental stress. To Catherine it seemed like a perfect undergraduate conduit into her chosen field. However, having committed so heavily to her studies in Year Twelve, she decided to defer her entrance to biomed and take a gap year before she started studying again.

Having heard tales of the Gulf Country in north Queensland, Catherine submitted an application to work in a stock camp up there. Although she was a farm girl, she had to tick 'no' to many of the questions on the online application form. Consequently, she didn't really expect to get a response. Imagine her surprise and delight a couple of weeks later when she received a phone call from John Stafford, manager of Miranda Downs – one of the Stanbroke Pastoral Company's cattle stations – offering her a job. Within a week she was on a plane flying north to Cairns.

When Catherine first got off the plane she thought the intense heat must have had something to do with the jet engines, but soon realised it was just bloody hot. Almost due west of Cairns, Miranda Downs is about two hours east of Karumba, up in crocodile country. When she got off the next plane at Normanton, the temperature had climbed even higher. 'It was just so incredibly hot and humid. It was at the end of the wet season and I could not believe that it could possibly be that hot,' she says.

Arriving late in the afternoon, she was sent straight out to work the next day, repairing flood fencing. Now laughing at the memory, Catherine admits that all she managed to do for that first day was carry around a pair of pliers. 'I just could not do anything more,' she recalls. Fortunately, she knew it could only get cooler – eventually – so with typical resolve, she stuck it out and soon acclimatised.

Hardwired as she is to be positive, Catherine loved her year at Miranda Downs. She respected the people she was working with and felt valued in return. 'There again,' she says, 'because I was only eighteen and looked about twelve, everyone looked after me. The whole crew was fantastic!' She spent most of the year in a stock saddle learning about cattle and life, camping out in a swag on occasion and growing up fast.

Also new to the camp that year was a young Tenterfield man, Quinton Jurd. A few years older than Catherine, Quinton had done his butcher's apprenticeship back in Tenterfield before taking off to the racetracks to work with horses. Being too big to be a jockey, however, the attraction soon wore thin and, like Catherine, he succumbed to the lure of the Gulf Country he'd heard so much about. He and Catherine became firm friends. The stock camp spent the year working and playing hard and Quinton introduced Catherine to the rodeos that are his passion outside work. An accomplished bareback and saddle bronc rider, Quinton has competed in rodeos all over the country and his name regularly appears in the top placings. When they parted company at the end of 2007 – she to head south and he to join a contract mustering team working their way across the Gulf Country and the Northern Territory – they pledged to keep in touch, as all good mates do.

Basking in the glow of a year well finished, Catherine went home to Victoria, convinced that she would return to the Gulf. In the meantime, she moved into Queen's College and into the first year of biomedicine. Predictably, she enjoyed everything about living in college and going to university, however, she soon began to question her career path. First to admit that once she gets an idea in her head, she's like the proverbial dog, it took her a while to acknowledge to herself that, after all her hard work, she may have made a mistake in choosing biomedicine as a conduit into medicine.

Hating not to finish something she'd started, Catherine worked right through until the middle of her second year before she finally admitted to herself and everyone else that she wanted out. Pulling the pin, she took the rest of the year off and moved north to the Riverina district in south-western New South Wales to work as a jillaroo at Tupra, a sheep station north-east of Balranald. She relished being back in the bush and used the time to soothe her battered ego.

Having reconsidered her options but still determined to be a doctor, upon her return Catherine elected to enrol in nursing at the

Australian Catholic University (ACU). 'Dad always said I should be a nurse,' she admits, eyes twinkling. It was a viable undergraduate choice – she knew she could get good marks and she knew that once she qualified she'd be able to work as a nurse to support herself while she studied medicine.

Much to her delight, a week into the course, she fell in love with the possibility of nursing people, really looking after them instead of just 'treating' them. 'We had fantastic lecturers who really inspired me to pursue this career.' She hadn't been able to get any credits for the units she had undertaken in biomedicine but looking back, she says it was better that she did the whole course from scratch. Realising that nursing would enable her to really care for people – to connect with them and to advocate on their behalf – Catherine switched gears completely and relinquished her aspirations to be a doctor.

In the course of her university program, she did her practice (prac) blocks in various places. Her favourite was working between the trauma unit (multi-system and torso injuries) and plastics unit (plastic and reconstructive surgery) at Royal Melbourne, which she did in the first semester of her third year. 'We had a great educator there and the nurses were all doing more study, loved their work and were so skilled at what they were doing that you couldn't help but be inspired,' Catherine explains. The educator regularly pulled each of the students aside and challenged them about the condition of different patients, making them do full head-to-toe assessments.

When Catherine was at Melbourne Uni doing biomedicine, she had joined the Rural Health Club. When she left, she never officially resigned. By a quirk of fate she was able to stay a member of the club even after she enrolled at ACU. In fact, she chaired the body for a while. She was also a member of the National Rural

Health Students' Network (NRHSN), which was established to provide opportunities and support for students to experience rural and remote health and to advocate on behalf of students and communities. With a vision of the Gulf Country still clear in her memory, it was right up Catherine's alley. Keen to promote her belief that rural and remote locations were feasible options for professional practice in all fields of health, she quickly became an active participant. She firmly believed that it should be possible to work, study and learn in an outback or far-flung location to acquire and consolidate the experience and skills that one needed to continue to work.

Although she was already busy, in her second year she committed herself to a leadership role by undertaking the position of secretary of the Student Network. While the year was very full-on, she likes pushing herself and had no regrets about taking on the extra workload. As a result of her contribution, she was one of five nurses chosen each year to join the Emerging Nurse Leaders Program. The initiative provides participants with access to experienced mentors and supports them through a program of personal and professional development for a period of three years. Catherine embraced the opportunity with her usual enthusiasm and committed to make the most of it.

Meanwhile, she and Quinton had recognised the possibilities of romance built on the foundations of their long friendship and promptly established themselves as a couple, albeit a long-distance one. They still only ever saw each other if one of them travelled the thousands of kilometres in between. Communicating mostly via long letters posted and delivered by the helicopter musterers who flew in and out of the camps Quinton worked in, they only occasionally spoke on the phone and even that was not without its frustrations. Quinton once drove an hour and a half into a station homestead to ring her but she didn't have her phone with her and didn't get the call. Blissfully ignorant, Catherine didn't know about it until she got his next letter some weeks later. She eventually made up for it by getting on a long-haul bus and travelling to see him while he was mustering out on the western side of Queensland and Northern Territory border.

When Quinton accepted a job as head stockman at Canobie, an Australian Agricultural Company cattle station two hours north-west of Julia Creek, their relationship became a bit easier to manage. While they continued to enjoy writing letters to each other, they were also able to talk on the phone a little more often because the stock camp mostly stayed in at the station quarters instead of camping out.

After she and Quinton announced their engagement at Easter in 2012, Catherine applied to do her second semester prac at the Mount Isa Hospital in north-west Queensland. It was an opportunity for her to trial her theory about remote nursing and to spend all her days off at Canobie, only three hours away. The Mount Isa Centre for Rural & Remote Health provided orientation and cultural awareness training for Catherine before she began her placement on the surgical ward. While she had imagined it would be different from working in a metropolitan hospital, in the end, she found there were plenty of similarities. 'Sick people are still sick people needing care and attention, wherever they are,' she says.

Having thoroughly enjoyed her experience in Mount Isa, Catherine was even more convinced that it would be possible for a nurse to gain her required skills and knowledge away from an urban medical environment. With her graduation imminent, she listened to the many people who advised her that she should undertake her graduate year in the emergency department of a big-city hospital, especially if she was going to head for the outback. Ultimately, she decided to put her money where her mouth was and see if she could prove her theory. Underpinning her decision was the knowledge that she could apply to work in a metropolitan emergency department if her quest failed.

Geri Malone is the Professional Development Manager with CRANAplus, the council that represents remote area nurses across Australia. She has come to know Catherine over the last couple of years through their mutual association with the NRHSN. She thinks it's entirely possible for new graduates to gain the skills and knowledge they need in a graduate year in a non-urban location. She believes that the quality of their experience depends on their support networks, the diversity of work they undertake and, most importantly, the professional and personal resilience of the individual nurse. 'It really depends on the individual,' Geri iterates. 'Catherine knows what she is doing and understands her own professional capacity very well. The program she is doing is well supported and, for her, it was always going to work. She's very focused, capable, has a good understanding of the remote context and she knows how to make it work.'

Having had an incredibly positive prac experience at Mount Isa paved the way for her to apply and be accepted into the North West Hospital and Health Service 2013 graduate nurse program. The one piece of advice she took without question was from Nicole Baines, the coordinator of the ENL program, who told her not to study during her graduate year, but rather just to do the work and, the rest of the time, just enjoy being married and at home with Quinton. Catherine admits it has been good for her as she has learnt to relax and maybe not always be such a perfectionist.

When she finished uni, Catherine went home to the family farm to prepare for her wedding in February 2013. As was her habit, she jumped back into the shearing sheds as a roustabout for a couple of months, enjoying the opportunity to catch up with old friends and to work with sheep and wool for the last time before she moved permanently north into cattle country.

After their wedding in the Catholic church at Kyneton, a reception in her parents' garden and a week's honeymoon, Catherine and Quinton moved into the head stockman's house at Canobie and Catherine headed straight to Cloncurry Hospital to begin her graduate year with North West.

Catherine says she really enjoyed her three months at Cloncurry, as the nurses there took her under their collective wings. 'I think the fact that I was newly married and living at Canobie appealed to them and they were keen to help me settle in. It was a lovely beginning to my graduate year,' she says.

She drove home to Quinton on her days off, seeing him either at home or out in the stock camp. Two of their wedding presents, from two of their close mates, were horses. One was a buckjumper for Quinton to compete with in the rodeos and the other a young paint filly for Catherine. Quinton broke the filly in and keeps her handy so that when Catherine's at home on days off, she can sling a saddle on her and go mustering with him. As the year progressed, they quickly settled into their dual lives.

After her happy and productive three-month block at Cloncurry, Catherine moved west to Mount Isa. Looking forward to returning to familiar territory, she settled back into the bigger hospital. Unfortunately, socially, Mount Isa was not such a happy experience. One night, after work hours, when she was returning from dinner with friends, Catherine was approached by two men in the carpark near the nurses' quarters. She was on the phone talking to Quinton when one of them grabbed her. She thrashed and yelled and apparently frightened them off. As it happened, the police and a security guard were nearby, yet the perpetrators were never caught.

While she wasn't physically hurt, it scared the hell out of her and tarnished an otherwise good professional experience. However, it didn't shake her determination to follow her dream.

A week later she rolled her car driving home to Canobie; all this on top of Quinton breaking his ankle a few weeks before. Counting on the old adage about bad things coming in threes, Catherine put her head down, refused to be rattled and steadily worked out the rest of her placement at Mount Isa and then gratefully retreated to Julia Creek, delighted to be back in a small community.

At Julia Creek, Catherine was surprised to encounter team nursing for the first time. Instead of allocating patients to individual nurses, the two nurses on duty each shift look after everyone together. At the end of a shift they divvy up the patient charts to write up the notes. Used to having complete control over the care of her allocated patients, Catherine has found the team approach invigorating. 'You always have to be communicating with each other,' she says. 'You have to share what's happening and really work as a team because, all the time, you both need to know what's happening with every single patient throughout the shift. You have to plan the day together and then you have to fit in the other jobs as well, like one of you assisting the doctor or maybe one off admitting a patient. Then you have to catch up again with what's going on.'

Generally, as a graduate, there are some procedures Catherine can't perform because they are not yet within her approved clinical scope of practice, even though she may have done them during

PUSHING THE BOUNDARIES

her practical training sessions. She finds that a little frustrating but concedes it's part of the rite of passage and the supervised process of developing her clinical skills. While she acknowledges that she still has a lot to learn, one thing that challenges her is people underestimating her either because she is 'only a graduate' or because she looks so young.

'Most senior nurses are terrific and have made every effort to be inclusive but some are less helpful,' she says. 'I know I need to consolidate my training and I know I have a lot to learn, but sometimes a nurse won't let me do something because they assume I don't have enough experience or don't know how. That's actually the bit that's frustrating; the assumption that I won't know what to do or how to respond. Maybe I won't, but I'd like to learn. When that happens, it feels as though I am missing opportunities to learn or practise.' Conscious of the need to keep it all in perspective, she has put a positive slant on those occasions, using them to clarify in her own mind just how she hopes she will behave when she's a senior nurse.

Back at Canobie, sitting at home on her front verandah, cuddling puppies, Catherine Jurd looks every bit like the sixteen-year-old people think she is until they get to know her. She has no regrets about resisting all the well-meant advice about working in city emergency departments and she's clearly convinced that she can follow her nursing dream wherever it takes her. Generally she thinks she'll be happy to follow Quinton wherever he goes, safe in the knowledge that he will support her decision to return to nursing somewhere else if she needs the experience to advance her career. As they both say, they've really only ever known a long-distance relationship and being apart for periods doesn't discourage them from pursuing their goals. It's as though they have two lives sometimes; but lately they've been lucky enough to spend a lot of time together. As Catherine says with pure joy in her voice, 'It's been fabulous because we've seen each at least once a week, sometimes for two or three days at a time.'

Having taken the year off from study, she looks back upon the year appreciating the professional support she's had, as well as the fun she had being at home at Canobie. But, as the year draws to a close, she is already dusting off her books. She's a girl with a vision and now she's ready to launch into the next phase of learning to be the nurse she knows she can be out in the remote areas she has come to love so well.

5

A PATH LESS TRAVELLED

Christine Foletti, Cocos-Keeling Islands, Indian Ocean

Cyclone season is over and the south-west trade winds have brought cooler weather, migratory birds and asylum seekers to the tiny Cocos-Keeling Islands in the middle of the Indian Ocean. Over the coming weeks more boats will arrive in the lagoon, crowded with men, women and children who have spent weeks at sea in perilous conditions. The area comprises twenty-seven islands of which only two, Home Island and West Island, are inhabited. Located nearly 3000 kilometres north-west of Perth, they lie roughly midway between Sri Lanka and Australia and are one of the nation's most far-flung territories. Home Island is also the current workplace and residence of Australian nurse and midwife Christine Foletti.

As more boats arrive in the lagoon they are moored in a brightly coloured row, slowly clunking and bobbing in the breeze. Ultimately, these boats will go on one final voyage when they are towed out to sea behind Horsburgh Island to be burnt and sunk. The asylum seekers who have arrived on these boats are lucky their journeys have had a safe ending. Word has just filtered through of another boat capsizing off Christmas Island, 950 kilometres to the east of the Cocos; 144 people have been rescued but four have died and two are missing. Days before, another nine died, including a baby.

A couple of years earlier, while working on Christmas Island, Christine had witnessed another asylum seeker boat that had lost power, being pounded by churning seas as it edged dangerously towards the cliff face. Christmas Islanders desperately threw life jackets and tried to make human chains to rescue the survivors, but 3-metre swells, strong winds and razor-sharp rocks made it almost impossible to do anything.

The navy spent all day searching, plucking men, women and children from the dangerous waters. Many were saved but some were not so fortunate. Triage sites were established at Ethel Beach and local volunteers ferried the injured and the survivors to the hospital where they were stabilised. Some were evacuated to Perth by the Royal Flying Doctor Service (RFDS). The smell of diesel permeated everything and survivors were stunned and inconsolable. Men and women wept at the memory of loved ones drowning before their eyes, while others rejoiced at being reunited with those they thought were lost.

Asylum seekers arriving on the Cocos-Keeling Islands spend only a short time at the old quarantine station on West Island, where they are processed prior to being transferred to Christmas Island. For every boat that safely lands, one wonders how many don't make it . . .

A PATH LESS TRAVELLED

*

Growing up in the western suburbs of Sydney, Christine had no real idea what career she wanted to pursue when she left school. A scholarship to do primary teaching gave her a taste of what she *didn't* want to do with the rest of her life. Coupled with a short stint working for the public service, teacher training left her no clearer on what direction to take. Finally, her mother showed her an advertisement for general nurse training; it gave her the nudge she needed. She completed the training in 1982, then worked for a couple of years before undertaking her midwifery training at the Royal Hospital for Women in 1986.

She wasn't very confident socially and was, in fact, very shy. Even today, she is quiet and reserved, very much a reluctant centre of attention, despite her adventurous life. 'Nursing was the right choice for me because it gave me structure and as soon as I put on that uniform I became a nurse. I could be professionally confident,' she concedes.

After five years working as a midwife in Sydney, Christine ventured abroad undertaking a three-month contract at a hospital in Saudi Arabia. It was her first foray into nursing outside Australia and ignited her interest in overseas work, though her future destinations were to be much more challenging.

Upon her return home, she applied for three jobs. One on Thursday Island, at the tip of Cape York in Queensland, one on Palm Island, 65 kilometres north of Townsville, and one in Warburton in the eastern desert country of Western Australia, 1500 kilometres form Perth. Despite putting the wrong applications in the right envelopes, she got offered all three jobs. 'I chose Palm Island simply because it was close to Townsville,' she says.

71

Palm Island was named by Captain Cook in 1770 and established as a community in 1918 after Hull River Mission near Tully was demolished by a cyclone. The ninety survivors of the cyclone were transferred to Palm Island and over the next two decades people from many different Aboriginal and Torres Strait Islander groups were relocated there. Ultimately, the people became known as the Bwgcolman people, which translates as 'many tribes, one people'.

On arrival at Palm Island in early 1990, Christine quickly realised she was way outside her comfort zone of suburban midwifery, and stepped onto a very steep learning curve. 'Having worked exclusively in midwifery for several years, I had little experience in paediatrics, A&E [accident & emergency] and no experience in Indigenous health.' There was an environment of extreme violence, HIV rates were among the highest in the country and suicide was common.

Midwifery on the island provided her with new challenges as many of the pregnant women suffered complex medical problems which, combined with poor living conditions, were a dangerous mix. Good midwifery outcomes were never a given. Patients experienced varying levels of antenatal care and sometimes none. On one occasion a woman turned up at the clinic complaining of a 'gut's ache' and then gave a big push – as Christine got her up onto the bed and examined her, a tiny head appeared and within minutes a healthy baby boy was born. 'I'd been working in midwifery for quite a while, but I felt like I learnt more there on Palm Island doing a handful of deliveries than I learnt in all the years working in a busy delivery suite in Sydney,' she says.

While she learnt a lot from the local doctors, she also learnt much from the enrolled nurses and Aboriginal health workers who had been there for years. 'I had no experience with the management and treatment of nits or scabies and I had no idea what "failure to thrive" meant,' she says. 'I knew next to nothing about tropical diseases. At the time, there were a couple of old Palm Islanders who had been disfigured by Hansen's disease [leprosy], who been patients at the leprosarium on nearby Fantome Island until 1973. I was stunned and shocked that a rich country like Australia had people with diseases that you would normally only see in the developing world.'

'I probably did a lot of things wrong in those early days,' she says. 'It's very easy in remote communities to get very involved with the people and their lives, and probably their expectations are higher than in the usual nurse/patient relationship in a suburban setting because you don't just go home at the end of the shift; you live in the community. I think when I left Palm Island I was shell-shocked at what I had seen and experienced and it took me quite a while to process.'

Learning that self-care was integral to survival, Christine realised she needed to keep a little distance, to put some self-preservation strategies in place to avoid getting burnt out. 'Some nurses work in communities and get very involved with people; they'll help people do their banking, fill out forms, sort their passports, every little thing. I decided I would teach them how to do those things, but I'm not going to do it for them.'

When she left Palm Island, she went up to Cape York to do a short stint relieving at Pormpuraaw and Kowanyama, until she saw a job advertised with the RFDS in Alice Springs. Christine had dreamed of working with the RFDS when she did her general training, but doubted she would ever have the skills or opportunity. Despite her uncertainty, she decided to give it a go.

Until late 1990, the RFDS had flown out of Alice with staff from the Alice Springs Hospital. However, in early 1991, they decided to employ their own staff, and having appointed Geri Malone as Flight Nurse Manager for Central Australia, tasked her with the job of recruiting staff. So it was that Geri interviewed Christine for a job, which she got. Although, Geri says, she nearly didn't employ her. 'Christine was very well qualified with a broad range of experience, but she was obviously very shy and lacking confidence. RFDS is very team-oriented and everyone has to connect and work well together. Christine was so shy she wouldn't look people in the eye. Despite any misgivings, my gut instinct was to give her the job, so I did. I never regretted it and in fact employed her again a few years later.'

Back then, as now, RFDS nurses flew about three-quarters of flights without a doctor, so they had to be able to manage whatever situation they were in. Christine found that working for the flying doctors created a different set of challenges from her previous postings, as she hadn't been exposed to that level of acuity, especially with children. By its very nature, in those days, RFDS saw a high level of serious medical or surgical emergencies, though the introduction of vaccinations improved those statistics, particularly among children. Nowadays, RFDS provides a broad range of primary health care services across inland Australia, as well as undertaking retrievals and evacuations.

Working with a small team of nurses, doctors and pilots was a great team-building experience. She learnt to communicate more easily by encouraging people to talk about themselves. Asked how it is that she can appear so confident professionally and yet be so shy socially, again she credits the uniform. 'When I'm in uniform, I am the nurse. I'm not particularly gregarious by nature, but that does have some advantages, as I think I observe quite a lot.'

After three and a half years with the RFDS, Christine was on holidays in Kenya when she saw a job advertisement seeking a midwife to work in Sudan with an American company, International Medical Corps. They phoned and said they didn't have a job for her in Sudan, but asked if she would go to Rwanda. Aware that a civil war had broken out, her only question was, 'Is it going to be like a *M*A*S*H* unit?' On reflection she shakes her head, laughing ruefully, and adds, 'I really did not have a clue.'

Her preparation for her first deployment into a war zone was a visit to the travel doctor for a health check. Then she received an airfreight mailbag in the post containing a t-shirt, a bum bag and an airline ticket, and off she went.

Initially employed to work as a midwife, within a couple of weeks Christine was given the role of Primary Health Care Coordinator responsible for facilitating the re-establishment of eight primary health care clinics and about eighty staff in the south of Rwanda. Tens of thousands of people were on the move, escaping the devastation of the war. Communicable diseases like diarrhoea and measles were causing many deaths, especially among young children. It was an intense training ground and taught Christine a great deal. 'Very often it's not the big things that save people's lives,' she reflects. 'Access to safe water supplies and access to childhood vaccinations can have the greatest impact on a large proportion of a vulnerable population. I saw many children die of measles, so the fact that you can vaccinate a child and give them something that can't be taken away from them can really make a huge difference. You can't guarantee their personal safety, and there was always the possibility they might lose their home, but a vaccination is something you can give them that can't be taken away.'

After six months in Rwanda she returned to midwifery in Sydney and was on a bit of a high for a while, having not yet lost the adrenaline rush that came from the kind of work she was doing in Rwanda. However, she soon realised she was missing something. 'There's no place for autonomy in a big-city hospital and I missed that,' she says. 'Geri told me she needed a community health nurse out of Port Augusta, so I went back to RFDS for a year and loved it. It was a fantastic job because I got to go bush three days a week doing clinics.'

In the vast expanse of inland South Australia, she found a new challenge working in Aboriginal communities, remote railway sidings, mine sites and sheep and cattle stations. 'The rural recession of the time and the closing of railway communities had a huge impact on the lives of people living in remote areas. Schools and health clinics were closing and many people living in remote areas were struggling to provide the basics for their families. The pressures of family and work were increasingly being felt by the rural women who were teaching their children, keeping house, nursing people, helping run the family business and doing stock work,' she says.

Having identified that the greatest challenge for people at that time appeared to be mental health – due to the strains and stresses associated with managing the economic downturn, isolated from appropriate support networks – Christine set about improving access to counselling services for families living and working in remote areas of the state. In a twofold attack, she explained the situation to the appropriate services, ensuring they understood the challenges faced by the women of the outback, and then she educated the women about the processes involved in accessing the services. 'People were honest and made it known that they didn't want any more surveys but, rather, something concrete to assist them and their families. Many services were already available but just needed to be more user-friendly for people living and working in remote areas and also people just need to be linked with services,' she says.

Over the next year, the counselling services set up for rural women adjusted their hours to allow women to use them, which made a huge difference. A woman found Christine at a remote airstrip later in the year and thanked her. She told her how she had contacted the rural hotline and described the difference it had made to her life and to her relationship with her husband. For Christine, it reiterated the theme that it's often the little things that make a real difference.

At the end of that contract, Christine and a couple of friends from the RFDS applied to work for the International Committee of Red Cross (ICRC). Her first mission was in Sierra Leone on the west coast of Africa. 'It was very isolated, eight hours up country by rough road from the capital, Freetown,' she says.

Working out of a small building with three other delegates, Christine was the only one of the team with a health background. The hospital was barely functioning and as the war unfolded it became increasingly difficult for staff and wounded to access it. As the conflict escalated and moved closer to town, more and more patients were presenting to their office as movement to and from the hospital became impossible. As the local Red Cross volunteers donned their tabards and went out to collect the wounded, Christine set up a triage area on the verandah outside to treat those that arrived. As numbers increased, the decision was made to perform surgery on the most acute cases. An office was set up as an operating theatre, a conference table was the operating table and bedside lamps were used for lighting. A local Sierra Leonean surgeon and his staff tended to at least ten people with minimal equipment and material and great skill and ingenuity. 'It was amazing to see what could be done with so little with such great impact,' Christine says.

'It was a bit like something out of a movie; almost unbelievable except that it was real.'

The experience in Sierra Leone had a huge professional and personal impact on Christine and influenced the course of her career for a number of years to come. She says it's hard to describe the way of life in a war zone to those who have not experienced it. 'You live in a very intense way. You live right in the moment. There is an instant of fear when you question, "Can I do this?" You get this adrenaline rush and you constantly feel intensely alive, because you're surrounded by such extreme challenges,' she says.

As the conflict escalated in Sierra Leone, it became extremely unsafe and the ICRC team was ordered to evacuate with only a few hours to get ready. 'The one thing that it highlighted for me was that, as expatriates, we can always leave, but local people don't have that luxury,' Christine says. The local surgeon who had trained in the Ukraine and worked in the United Kingdom prior to returning home to Sierra Leone was one of them. 'You've got to get used to it; this is what happens,' he told Christine when she tearfully went to say goodbye. He would stay on doing what he could with the little he had.

Leaving Sierra Leone confirmed Christine's perspective that 'it's a delusion to think that what you're doing is more important than what anyone else is doing. The people who are special are the people who are there every day, who live there, who can't leave.'

On arriving back in Australia she applied for a job on Hayman Island as a senior registered nurse (RN). When interviewed she was asked if she was used to dealing with difficult people. She recalls saying, 'Well, it doesn't matter if people are paying $2000 a night or they're a child soldier, high on coke with a gun in their hand. They can all be difficult. You have to manage them in the same way.'

In fact Christine found the transition, from war zone to five-star resort, a bit odd to say the least. Having dealt with people managing in the most difficult circumstances surrounded by war and deprivation, she found herself catering to a clientele who were a world apart. 'People's expectations on Hayman were very high,' she says. Having dealt with war-wounded patients and people with illnesses due to lack of any kind of health service at all, she found herself confronted by indulgence. With people suffering sunburn, marine stings and the occasional diving-related injuries, she found that no matter how trivial some of the problems might be, some people still demanded careful and immediate attention. 'The expectations of some people can be equally taxing, whether they're paying $2000 a night or they're the kid with the gun,' she says. Despite the different challenges it was a respite and an interlude she enjoyed, even though she would never go back.

A year later, lured by the challenge of work in conflict areas, Christine returned to Africa, this time to the ICRC hospital in Lokichogio in a dry, dusty corner of northern Kenya. With 500 beds, all in large makeshift tent-like structures, it was the biggest hospital for war-wounded patients in the world.

When Christine arrived in 1999, the civil war in neighbouring Sudan between the central government and the People's Liberation Army had been raging for several years. In the course of the twenty-two-year war, four million people in southern Sudan were displaced at least once and the civilian death toll was one of the highest of any conflict since World War II. The situation was too unstable to have a hospital in South Sudan, so planes would fly in and pick up the war-wounded and take them back over the border to operate on them in the ICRC hospital. Christine's new role as the senior flight nurse involved coordinating and attending their aeromedical evacuation out of South Sudan and back to Lokichogio.

The operating theatres were constantly busy with an international team of surgeons, nurses and technicians working long hours to keep on top of the endless list of surgical procedures. Made up of Kenyan, German, Swiss, French, Australian, New Zealand, Finnish and Norwegian staff, the teams were truly multinational.

Although she was back in planes, Christine found it starkly different from her days with the RFDS. 'In Australia the golden rule is "stabilise the patient first"; get them in the best possible condition before transfer and then you have the added bonus of all the necessary high-tech equipment that is available,' she says. 'Flying into South Sudan was a completely different story, as we flew with the bare minimum in terms of equipment and often the plane was completely gutted to ensure we could evacuate as many people as possible. Rubber mattresses were laid on the floor and the wounded and ill would be laid sardine-style to get as many in as possible. A tiny plane would sometimes have eighteen people on board, with IVs hanging from every available spot. It was incredible.'

Security was the other major concern, as different areas in South Sudan were under the control of different military factions but would often change hands. A nurse and some pilots from the ICRC had previously been taken hostage when they flew into an area that had been taken over by a rival group. Christine spent a lot of time speaking to relevant people to ensure that they were clear about where they going and exactly what their role was, to ensure their own safety as well as the safety of the wounded.

One day they flew in a plane the size of a Caribou aircraft to an area in the north to evacuate around twenty casualties. They landed on a small bush strip and opened the cargo doors to see an almost biblical scene. Figures distorted by the shimmering heat were moving across the claypan towards them, carrying their wounded on homemade litters over their heads. It had taken many of them two days of walking to bring their wounded to the pickup point. Christine and the pilots worked quickly, mindful all the time of everyone's security.

'I rapidly triaged and the pilots quickly loaded the twenty severely injured civilians and soldiers,' she says. 'Despite the number of casualties and the terrible injuries, it was eerily quiet – everyone was acutely aware of time, fading light and the need to get out of there quickly. As the cargo doors closed, the propellers churned up the dust and we took off; there was a collective groan of relief from everyone. Now we just needed to get home safe.' Meanwhile, the casualty-bearers melted back into the landscape, returning from whence they came.

Though Christine provided IV fluids, pain relief and basic stabilisation on the flight, she was very aware of how inadequate it may have been for many of the injured. 'We did not have the luxury of high-tech equipment or doctors. This was literally snatch-and-grab management; all the golden rules I had learnt at home went out the window,' she says. One man died of his injuries in flight, but the rest made it safely back to be treated at the ICRC hospital in Lokichogio.

As the wounded recovered, the next challenge was to try to get them back home again. This could sometimes takes weeks or months to organise. Christine started going around the other agencies, begging a lift to get people back. She'd get one on here and two on there, hitching lifts on trucks, planes or any vehicle that was heading into an appropriate area of Sudan.

Sometimes flights were organised to repatriate wounded back

home but often things did not go to plan due to changes in security or weather. On one such day, as they flew over the area, the pilots ruled that they could not land at the agreed spot but could land at a village 20 kilometres away. Christine told the group they could take them back to Lokichogio or they could get out at the other village. 'They said, "Yes, yes, we have family in this village and we'll walk back".'

Reflecting on them, she says, 'I'll never forget them because most of these were people who'd lost limbs, so they were all wearing their artificial limbs and were all wearing the white t-shirt and blue shorts that the hospital had given them on discharge. They got out, put their belongings on their heads, crutches over their shoulder and moved off into the marshes. I remember thinking, *Wow, can you imagine anybody at home doing this?* People over there are extremely resilient and tough.'

Christine stayed in Kenya for about eight months, which was enough. 'I had a great time and really felt we had achieved something,' she says. Then she flew home and went to Townsville and got a job in sexual health for a year. Again, it was a complete change, but she worked with a great team of colleagues who included RNs she had worked with in the Northern Territory and another girl who'd just come back from working for the Red Cross in Tanzania. Their shared experience ensured an easier transition and productive work environment.

Responsible for assessing and providing clinical care and counselling to people with sexually transmitted diseases and blood-borne viruses, Christine found the work required the development of some new skills. She enjoyed working with the young people she came in contact with. Most of them suffered from a combination of problems related to sex, drugs and alcohol, and had little or no respect for themselves. In her new role, Christine provided them with strategies to help themselves, encouraging them always to value their bodies as their most important possession. She also provided education and support to other health care providers, as well as working with young people in schools and the justice system.

Having established a balance between her work in Australia and the lure of work in developing countries, Christine spent the next eight years travelling to and from conflict areas under the banner of the ICRC.

In Myanmar (formerly Burma) she visited prisons and labour camps, assessing the health of inmates in an effort to help improve their living conditions. 'A lot of detainees were extremely brave talking to us. Later we would register them so that we could make sure they didn't just disappear,' she says.

There followed stints in Dafur, in Sudan, in Pakistan and Belize in Central America, interspersed between contracts in rural and regional New South Wales, the last of which was a two-year block working as the Refugee Health Nurse for the Hunter New England Health Services. The newly developed role was implemented to ensure that all recently arrived refugees had access to health assessments. Christine also provided support and education on refugee health issues to health service providers, educators and community groups.

Prior to moving to Home Island in 2011, Christine spent a couple of years working on Christmas Island, where the permanent population is about 1500 and made up of Chinese, Malay and Australians, and the main industries are phosphate mining and tourism, as well as the detention centre.

Since moving to Home Island, where the population of 600 is predominantly Cocos Malay, Christine has grown to love both the islands and the people who live there. It is a remote and very beautiful tropical setting and one in which she feels very happy to be living and working. The Cocos Malays have a unique culture and traditions born of living for so long in isolation. Having voted for full integration with the Australian mainland as recently as the 1980s, it is only since then that they were granted the same rights and responsibilities as mainland citizens. However, they still retain a distinct culture. As an outsider, Christine is interested in learning the culture and language but, as always, says, 'I know that I am a visitor and that my time here will be brief in terms of the life of the community.'

Her nursing role in the islands focuses on diabetes education and management. While generally the Cocos Malays don't drink or smoke, everything revolves around eating, and, as access to processed food from the mainland has become easier, the incidence of diabetes has risen. That and greater reliance on vehicles have resulted in higher rates of obesity. 'Much is currently being done in relation to encouraging healthy choices and chronic disease management,' says Christine. 'Mind you, I can encourage people to eat well and walk everywhere but, like everyone else, in the end, they must make their own decisions.'

Christine's parents and extended family live in the Newcastle area of New South Wales. They like having her 'safely' back in Australia even though she's as far away as she can be while still in the country. She does try to get home to spend time with them all as often as possible. Having discovered a talent for art while living on the islands, she looks forward, one day, to retiring to the Newcastle area and pursuing some of the other interests she has acquired over the years.

Meanwhile, nursing turned out to be a career choice that Christine has really enjoyed and she cheerfully maintains there have been very few days when she didn't look forward to going to work. 'A lot of people have jobs or careers that they don't particularly like,' she says. 'Nursing is very diverse and I've had lots of opportunity to travel all around the world. I love being a nurse but I do think we're too focused on the technical side of things and how much we can do and what we're allowed to do. We forget that what makes us good at what we do is just being human. It's how we connect with others that sometimes has the greatest impact on people's lives.'

It has been a journey of extremes and, sitting quietly, several years later, Christine seems a little alert, a little watchful, not quite completely relaxed. Having managed the chaos and challenge of working in some of the most isolated and dangerous places on the planet, she murmurs, 'It was an incredible time of my life. I really feel very privileged.'

6

HEART OF THE TERRITORY

Margie McLean, *Victoria River and Barkly Regions, Northern Territory*

Margie McLean is a registered nurse and midwife but, these days, she's also a farmer's wife. She lives with her husband, Lindsay, on their farm in the Wide Bay–Burnett region of Queensland. She claims to be sixty-seven years old, although her wavy, honey-streaked hair and glowing face deny it. She adores spending time with her granddaughters, Josie and Katie, and she loves gardening, quilting and relearning the Italian language of her youth. On the face of it, she seems like a lady who's enjoyed a pretty nice life until you look into wise brown eyes and see the soul of someone who's cared more for other people than she has for herself, who's put herself on the line to advocate for those less fortunate and who, more than once, has felt the hair stand up on the back of her neck during the four decades she spent nursing in the changing health landscape that is the Northern Territory.

Margie well remembers the day in 1985 when she was driving to Tennant Creek Hospital with Aboriginal health worker Oscar Wilson. They were chatting idly to pass the time, when she thought to ask him about an incident that had occurred fifteen years before, when she was first working at the health clinic on Victoria River Downs (VRD), a cattle station 360 kilometres south-west of Katherine in the Northern Territory.

She said to him, 'Oscar, back in 1970 when I was working on VRD, I was called out to see an old Aboriginal man who was said to have died, whose name was Kumanjay Newcastle. Did you know him?'

While Margie had assessed that he'd had a stroke, she always wondered if that was what really happened to him.

Thinking back today, Margie runs her hands up her arms to soothe a cool slither of goose bumps. She remembers Oscar saying quietly, 'Oh, yes, Margie, I knew that old man. He was sung.'

Margie had been working in the health clinic on VRD for two weeks in September 1970 when, late one evening, she was asked by the station manager, Ian Michael, and the assistant manager, Hugh Petherick, to accompany them down to the old and abandoned Wimmera hospital building, located on the side of the station airstrip. They had been called because it was believed that an old man had died down there.

It was a dark night and, as they arrived, they could see light from an open fire flickering ghostly images across the old walls of the building. Taking up the story, Margie says quietly, 'There were many countrymen inside the building and we could see faces peeping out from the shadows. Out on the back verandah, there were several men sitting near a large pile of canvas swags and in the fire light I could see what looked like an arm convulsing from among the heap. Ian quickly asked the men to remove the swags and there was the man and he was still alive.'

The old man appeared to have had a stroke. Noticing his pill bottles, Margie realised that he had been on medication for high blood pressure. She asked his family how long it was since he had taken his tablets. 'Him finish little bit long time,' someone said. She told them that he needed to go back to the clinic. No one argued with her and they all went with her. Margie looked after the old man for forty-eight hours while his family roamed around the hospital and garden waiting. Then he died. The family told her not to touch him. They took him away and that was the end of it, but she had always wondered . . .

Talking to Oscar years later, she had the opportunity to ask him why they took him away after he died.

'What did they do, Oscar?'

He told her that when they prepared him for his first resting place they put rocks in with him. When they collected his bones for his final burial the rocks had changed colour. Then they knew who had sung him.

In the immediate aftermath of the Second World War, Margie Favaloro and her three younger sisters, Gaye, Anne and Elizabeth, were encouraged to appreciate the diversity of culture around them. They were the daughters of an Italian-born pastry cook, Bartolomeo Favaloro, who had migrated to Australia as a teenager, and his

Australian wife, Elizabeth, a nurse of Irish and German descent. When he was just fourteen, Margie's father and his eleven-year-old brother migrated from Italy in the care of fellow countrymen. Although he became naturalised and served in the Australian Army, because of his Italian heritage he was treated with suspicion after the war; discrimination against migrant 'aliens' at that time was widespread. Consequently, they were taught to consider those less fortunate than themselves.

Reminiscing, Margie says, 'Our mother also told us stories about growing up in country Victoria during the Depression, when my grandfather would arrive home with people who were down on their luck. She said they'd often have extra people at the table for dinner and sometimes they'd wake up to find strangers sleeping on their verandah.'

Margie spent her first years in country Victoria, but when she was thirteen, the family moved to Melbourne where prospects for a good education without boarding were better. Her father believed that a good education was the best thing parents could give their children since his own was limited. He opened his bakery in Bentleigh East and enrolled the girls at the Lady of the Sacred Heart College.

'The nuns at Sacred Heart were strong women of a missionary order,' Margie says of the women who were also her teachers. 'Many of the nuns had worked in Daly River and the Tiwi Islands in the Northern Territory, as well as Third World countries overseas, so, as students, we were exposed to the idea of advocating for and helping others.'

In 1965, Margie commenced her general nursing training at St Vincent's Hospital in Melbourne. 'It was very tough as the hospital was located in the backyard of Fitzroy, where we were exposed to people with lifestyles that most of us had never known – prostitutes, drug addicts and homeless people,' she says. 'The strict discipline that underpinned our training helped us face some pretty challenging situations on a daily basis and to learn to deal with them. The Mother Rectress [the head of the Sisters of Charity who owned and operated St Vincent's], who ran the hospital, informed our parents that graduates from St Vincent's would not require a written reference, as successful completion of one's training was its own reference!'

Once qualified, she went to Launceston with three of her St Vincent's colleagues, to do midwifery. Meanwhile, her sister Gaye completed her general nursing training at St Vincent's. Once Margie completed her midwifery, she applied to join Australian Volunteers Abroad with a view to going to the Solomon Islands. However, in the interim, in 1970, she and Gaye moved north to Darwin to work.

While she waited for the call to go to the Solomons, Margie spent three months in the paediatric ward of the old Darwin Hospital, where many of the patients were Aboriginal children with illnesses that she had not previously experienced. There were several young Aboriginal girls from the Tiwi Islands who helped on the wards and who, Margie says, 'were possibly the forerunners' to the Aboriginal health workers that exist today.

At the same time, one of Margie's nursing colleagues, Liz Brady, was a member of a team of community health nurses based in Darwin who travelled to remote communities screening for leprosy and providing support and assistance to remote area nurses. They would visit the mining camps, missions and cattle stations in the north-west quadrant of the Northern Territory every four to six weeks.

Victoria River Downs was one such station, owned at the time by the Hooker Corporation. VRD had been without a resident nurse for a couple of years and the station manager's wife attended to health matters when and as she could. Because there was no privacy on the open airwaves of their only communication system, Liz sent Margie a cryptic message via HF two-way radio telling her there was a job opening for a 'Sister in Charge' at VRD and that she needed to make a decision within a week. Still awaiting the call to Volunteers Abroad, Margie decided it might be an interesting interlude and accepted. It was a life-changing decision.

She laughs as she remembers the tongue-in-cheek orientation information she received ahead of her arrival. 'The night before departure, I was informed that "the R has dropped out of VRD again, so we'll send speculums and penicillin on the plane with you",' she says, recalling their reference to venereal disease. 'I was also given the "bush book", a lever-arch folder with a range of recipes for treating anaemia, hookworm and leprosy, and how to insert an intraperitoneal tube into an abdominal cavity to provide babies with fluids for gastro.'

Back then, prior to Northern Territory self-government, nurses working in remote locations were subsidised in part at a federal level. Their salary was calculated on the number of residents in the community they serviced and the balance was paid by the mine, station or mission who employed them. At that time, the VRD clinic tended to a population of almost 500 Aboriginals. Margie recalls her pay was quite a bit less than her hospital salary; however, since she didn't expect to be there for very long, it was not one of her considerations.

The day she flew to VRD, there were seven passengers on the Connellan Airways flight and a lot of freight. 'We took off at 0700 hours and we were each handed a cardboard box containing our lunch. There was no refrigeration or eskies on the plane in those days and the temperature reached about 35 degrees,' she says. 'On board was a young child from VRD who was mentally challenged, who was flying home from the Darwin Hospital unaccompanied, so I became his escort by proxy. At midday we landed at Kununurra, where the lad took off down the airstrip in the heat. I had to run after him and get him back on the plane. It was a pretty eventful day! VRD was the second-last of fourteen stops and we finally arrived there at 4 p.m.'

The ladies of the local Country Women's Association branch were meeting that day at the station. When Margie stepped out of the plane dressed Melbourne-style in her white stockings and mini-skirt, she was quickly aware of the scrutiny of the ladies from nearby stations. These ladies were to become close friends who she would love and respect but, at the time, she did wonder whether there was really meant to be a meeting that day or whether they just wanted to meet the new nurse.

Jumping straight into her new role, among Margie's first patients were some young Aboriginal women whose partners were the people she'd been warned to expect, who might be suffering from venereal disease. Upon learning that a new young nurse had arrived, the men had reportedly cleared out to Katherine for treatment so she wouldn't find out they'd had VD.

On that first morning she also had a call from the station bookkeeper, who told her that there was a really sick man out in one of the cattle-mustering stock camps based at the station. The man had had vomiting and diarrhoea for three days. The helicopter was going to bring him in by lunchtime. When the patient had not arrived by early afternoon, Margie was getting worried, as it was quite hot. She had little in the way of resources and equipment, as the clinic had been unmanned for a couple of years, and she was concerned he would be severely dehydrated. She started to wonder if he had died and no one had told her.

93

Eventually, when a young man turned up at her doorstep freshly showered and shampooed and smartly dressed with his hair slicked back, she inquired as to his needs. 'I'm the fellow they rang y'about,' he responded. Surprised and not a little shocked, she gave him a thorough check over and quickly realised there was nothing wrong with him. The whole episode had been a ruse cooked up in the stock camp to get someone in to check out the new nurse. Apparently this man had a certain reputation for being a ladies' man. Margie gave him short shrift and sent him on his way. 'He was a malingerer!' she says now.

When he returned to the stock camp, his description of the new nurse was, 'She's a death adder!' Knowing nothing of the customs or rules of station life, Margie wasn't aware of the lengths that people would go to to entertain themselves, often at her expense. However, as time passed, she became great friends with everyone and generally got her own back amid much laughter and good cheer.

Margie's accommodation at VRD was a Sidney Williams hut – a corrugated iron hut much favoured by the armed forces in the Territory during World War II because it could be flat-packed and erected easily on site – with gauze screening and roll-up bamboo blinds on three sides and the fourth side shared with the hospital. 'There was a kitchen not much bigger than a toilet and a tiny bathroom, with a small bedroom in the centre of the building,' she recalls now, from the luxury of a well-padded chair. 'The hospital, a corrugated iron structure with fibro ceilings, had four beds and a central clinic area with none of the trappings or equipment that one would expect to find in any modern health centre in remote communities today. It was very cold in winter and very hot in summer!'

Her first suturing job on VRD was on a man from the main roads camp based in Timber Creek who came in with a deep laceration in his thigh. 'Have you done this before?' he asked suspiciously.

'Of course,' she declared, 'and if you're not happy, you can drive to Katherine!' She successfully completed the job, which was well-timed practice, since her first major incident at VRD was a tribal fight three days later after someone had smuggled alcohol into the Aboriginal camp.

There were several severe injuries, as the protagonists were apparently bashing each other with nulla-nullas. 'I'd not seen injuries like that since my days working in casualty at St Vincent's,' Margie says. 'Quite a few stitches were required and there were a couple of broken bones. Naturally, of course, it all happened at night! Generally people were very reluctant to go anywhere; they'd rather put up with pain. I had to splint the breaks as well as I could with minimal resources and then medivac the patients out on the plane the next day. Because there had been no nurse there for so long, the clinic was barely equipped and I had little to work with.' Margie did admit to wondering whether she'd made the right choice in going to VRD, but reassured herself that it wasn't for long. Surely not much else could happen before she left for the Solomon's?

Late one afternoon towards the end of her third week, a very pregnant young Aboriginal woman came into the clinic in labour. She was a Gurindji woman, originally from Wave Hill Station, and a long way from her own family. She'd had no antenatal care and she'd been in labour for some time when she turned up at the clinic. 'By 11 p.m. her cervix was fully dilated and I could feel the baby was positioned in a transverse presentation,' she explains, meaning that the baby was lying across the woman's abdomen instead of head-down. Despite frequently pressing the emergency button on the radiotelephone, it took an hour and a half to raise Darwin. Dr Charles Gurd, who was on call that night, reassured her that she had done all that she could to assist the distraught woman, but she would probably lose the mother and baby because they could not get a plane into VRD until daylight, as there were no night-landing facilities at the station.

Being quite alone out there, but not prepared to lose two of her patients if she could help it, she acted on impulse and sought unconventional advice. She went down to the camp in the dark and found a couple of Aboriginal women to help her. She brought them back to the clinic; however, the distressed young mother was climbing the walls and wailing and it quickly became obvious that they were not helping the situation. So she returned to the camp to see if there were any Gurindji women available. Two elderly ladies returned with her. These women guided the young mother to the floor and settled her, singing and soothing her. With a small shake of her head even now, Margie describes their remarkable accomplishment. 'I watched them somehow turn that baby. They sang and turned and pushed and massaged and eventually the baby was safely delivered. It was extraordinary,' she says.

While Margie delivered the afterbirth, the women breathed on the baby. The whole event took several hours. Margie knew that she had witnessed an exceptional event; one that challenged Western medical beliefs. Over time the baby grew into a healthy child, although the right arm and leg were slightly thinner than their opposites. 'Those first three incidents in my first three weeks – the fight, the old man dying and the birthing – were the first of many experiences involving the skills and knowledge of ancient Indigenous culture that I was privileged to witness during my years working in remote health in the Northern Territory. The Aboriginal culture was strong and a daily way of life for the people back then,' she says.

By her fourth week, Margie began to settle into some sort of routine at the VRD clinic, though she struggled for many months with minimal resources and equipment. After her first few months, she went home to Melbourne for a break. Everyone at the station looked for her assurance that she would be back. She still hadn't heard from Volunteers Abroad and she was growing to like the lifestyle and people on the station, including one Lindsay McLean, who was running one of the stock camps. Despite her parents' reservations, she returned more confidently, knowing that she was contributing to primary health care for the people of the VRD.

However, she still faced many challenges. Oxygen was of particular concern since she had none. She kept ordering it and kept getting fobbed off with excuses: it's too expensive, they couldn't bring it on the freight truck, the roads were too rough (despite the fact they were bringing in oxyacetylene for the workshop). Finally, after eighteen months, she was really fired up, and the opportunity arose for her to do something about it.

Annually, all of the nurses working remotely in the Northern Territory gathered together in either Darwin or Alice Springs for what was called the Summer School. Margie headed to Darwin that year with a plan of action. One of the community nurses had made the appointment for Margie to see the Territory administrator for Aboriginal affairs about the lack of oxygen on VRD. She'd been warned that the gentleman was known to be charming and persuasive but, never one to be intimidated by authority, Margie sizzled off to meet the man in the old Leichardt building, determined not to be charmed and equally committed to winning her case.

Margie described the issues as they related to the population of VRD. Knowing he was very familiar with the station, she explained in detail the fate of people with no access to oxygen, including people dying from an asthma attack because they had no oxygen; people dying of heart failure due to of a lack of oxygen; and newborn babies dying because they couldn't be resuscitated without oxygen. Drawing herself up to her full 162 centimetres, she challenged the administrator, saying, 'The price of oxygen is $9 per cylinder. We have a moral obligation to save lives and I would expect and trust that a cylinder is delivered to VRD by the end of the week when I return!' There were three oxygen cylinders at the station when she got back and she never had that particular problem again.

The incident cemented one other decision in her mind. At about the same time, she finally heard from Volunteers Abroad offering her a posting to the Solomons. However, by then she was firmly committed to the station community and so she declined the offer. 'Why go to a Third World country when there was so much I could do right there at VRD?' she asks.

One of her many challenges was facilitating the doctor's visits to VRD every six to eight weeks for about three hours. Half the people who needed to see the doctor would leave without consultation. Part of the problem was the very short timeframe available; however, a more significant complication was the practice of avoidance where – due to cultural traditions – certain people cannot be in the same room as certain other people. Fascinated by the intricacies of the skin groups and relationships within the Aboriginal community, Margie spent many evenings recording everyone's skin groups and family names so that she could understand each person's relationships and obligations. By understanding their skin groups, she was eventually able to plan and prioritise the doctor's clinics more effectively.

The nursing director of remote health services based in Darwin flew in to the clinic once a year on her rounds to spend an hour or so with remote staff, and the pharmacist came once a year to check pharmacy supplies. However, Margie's main support was provided by the community nurses on their visits every four to six weeks. As well as providing moral and professional support, they would always bring goodies, including books and any fresh fruit and vegetables that would not spoil on their journey around the outback. 'These nurses were our friends and lifeline and so much loved and appreciated,' Margie says. She also had access to twice-daily radio schedules on the HF two-way radio with the doctors in Darwin when there was a need to discuss any problems. 'The station folk really did appreciate having a nurse around,' she adds with a smile. 'I was on call 24/7. The Aboriginal people were wonderful and considerably healthier than their children and grandchildren are today. I was never judged, even when I made mistakes. I was able to learn about bush tucker, bush medicine, and the importance to the people of the seasons.'

Meanwhile, she was slowly getting to know young Lindsay McLean, who was the head stockman of the stock camp based on VRD. They met up every week on movie nights when the station showed whatever reels turned up on a custom-built screen set up out under the stars. Laughing, she remembers, 'It was not unusual to watch a film only to find one of the reels had been left in Katherine or elsewhere!' Encouraged by the stock camp cook, Lindsay proposed to her more than once before she finally said 'Yes!'

In 1972, they married at Victoria River Downs surrounded by all the station staff as well as all the residents of the Aboriginal community. Their families, friends and colleagues from neighbouring stations, Katherine, Darwin and interstate flew in for the nuptials. 'It was a great celebration and everyone on the station bought new clothes from the station store especially for the event.'

The festivities lasted for a week, with Margie working right up to the day of the wedding, when she delivered a baby a couple of hours before the ceremony. The night before, as she was on her way to the hens' night, she stitched the ear (that was hanging by the ear lobe) back on one of Lindsay's mates after he rolled a car bringing beer back from Top Springs for the bucks' night. 'Suffice to say,' she laughs, 'he did not require any anaesthetic and, as I stitched, he kept saying, "Just cut the bastard off!"'

An old friend, a priest from Melbourne, officiated along with the priest from Katherine. Her father delighted in baking his eldest daughter's wedding cake and carefully transported it by road all the way from Melbourne for the occasion. She laughs again as she remembers how astonished her parents were about everything to do with her new life. 'But they had experiences they would not have otherwise enjoyed,' she adds.

In 1973, Lindsay was offered management of Moolooloo, an outstation of VRD. Margie was pregnant with their eldest child, Mac, but she ran a clinic for the community at Moolooloo and continued to assist the new single-certificate nurse at VRD. During 1974 there were management changes at VRD as well as within the cattle industry. When Ian Michael became manager of Scott Creek Station, 40 kilometres from Katherine, he offered Lindsay the cattle manager's position there. Lindsay took it, and he and Margie relocated there until April 1975, when they moved to Queensland, where they had bought a cattle property near Biggenden. Their daughter, Fiona, was born just after the move.

Margie continued to work, returning, for the first time in years, to a hospital environment when she got a part-time job as night supervisor for surgical wards at the Maryborough Hospital and then a year later at the Biggenden Hospital. While they missed the north and she missed the autonomy that went with her work as a remote area nurse, they all enjoyed the advantages of living less remotely.

When Lindsay was offered the job of head stockman at Newcastle Waters Station in 1985, Margie transferred to the Northern Territory health department in Elliott, 27 kilometres south of Newcastle Waters on the Stuart Highway. This Barkly Tableland community is located about halfway between Darwin and Alice Springs and, back then, had a population of about 600 people, who were predominantly Aboriginal. The couple lived at the station and Mac and Fiona went to the school there.

Over the years, Margie worked with many nurses who were special in their own ways and from whom she continued to learn, but the most significant partnership was at the Elliott Health Centre where she worked with an English registered nurse (RN), Wendy Dow, who'd come out as a ten-pound Pom. Their partnership lasted ten years and thanks to the education programs that had been running in the Territory at that time, there were six Aboriginal health workers (AHWs) on staff. Subsequently, the clinic functioned very well. During the '80s and into the '90s most of the health centres had lots of AHWs who were the culture brokers of the communities, who also provided health care and liaised between the RNs, the Aboriginal patients and the community at large.

These days, according to Margie, there are considerably fewer AHWs, due in part to the change in the model of training and in part to the transient nature of fly-in fly-out nursing staff. 'Continuity of care is fundamental for the provision of ongoing support in a community and the fly-in fly-out model doesn't ensure the same level of continuity and ongoing support that is required,' she comments. 'The nature of changes taking place in communities has also been a factor.'

Located on the Stuart Highway, 780 kilometres north of Alice Springs and 700 kilometres south of Darwin, the staff at the Elliott Health Centre were, and are, frequently called to attend to road accidents and station accidents as well as providing primary health care to the people of the district. Health service delivery entailed working with and coordinating multidisciplinary teams, including a visiting medical officer, a few days every three or four weeks, as well as visiting allied health professionals who worked with the local community council, school and police to reinforce good health messages for health promotion and disease prevention.

Margie and Wendy worked well together, complementing and balancing each other with their different personalities and strengths. While Wendy did everything to the letter of the law, Margie would push the boundaries to gain better outcomes for their clients. Wendy was calm and methodical while Margie was more passionate and creative. Both of them had years of experience and reams of common sense and had managed and treated horrific injuries and extreme illnesses in harrowing circumstances.

In October 1993, Margie, who was on call, received a phone call from the Elliott police informing her that an eight-year-old boy, Clinton Liebelt, had gone missing from his home at the Dunmarra roadhouse. The police had been called to a problem at another location, but said they would go to Dunmarra as soon as possible. In the meantime, Margie packed an overnight bag and drove up to the roadhouse to comfort his parents and to be on hand when Clinton was found. Nothing could have prepared any of them for the days ahead . . .

The Elliott nurses were very familiar with Dunmarra. It was one of the regular stops on their clinic runs around their particular part of the Territory and it encompassed 30 000 square kilometres between Daly Waters and Renner Springs. The area includes seven

102

cattle stations and two roadhouses. Margie and Wendy knew the Liebelts both professionally and socially.

Steve and Adele Liebelt had bought the roadhouse at Dunmarra in 1988 in partnership with friends they later bought out. At the time, their two sons, Greg and Clinton, were aged five and three respectively, and settled into their new life easily. In due course, Adele's brother Glenn, his wife Lu and their son Daniel moved to Dunmarra and the three boys were great mates. As they grew up, their parents had a handful of strict rules to ensure their safety, the most important being that they were not to go out of the back paddock where Steve had graded some tracks for them to ride around on their pushbikes (and later motorbikes). Another was that they should never, *ever* cross the highway unless they were accompanied by an adult. Steve also taught them, if they were lost, to follow the sun; as long as they didn't cross the highway, it would bring them home.

On that hot day in October 1993, a couple passing through Dunmarra had stopped for a break and off-loaded two horses. Just as they were coming off the float, a truck roared past with its horn blaring. One of the horses spooked and took off. Despite a search, the horse was not found. By lunchtime the next day, Steve and Glenn decided to give them a hand. They took Greg and Daniel with them, thinking Clinton was with his mother. When Clinton found they had gone, he decided to go for a ride on his small BMX motorbike. Adele assumed he had gone with Steve. When Steve returned several hours later they realised Clinton was missing. The men searched well into the evening looking for the young boy, returning to the roadhouse to be told that he had been seen crossing the highway . . .

Early the next morning the search began again, with several black trackers from Elliott, staff from the surrounding stations on horses and a couple of station helicopters and fixed-wing planes. The motorbike was soon spotted but there was no sign of Clinton. Police arrived from Darwin and set up command at the roadhouse, where the search plan was established. They drew up a grid pattern and carefully plotted the area.

Many hundreds of people from all walks of life left their cars, caravans and motorcycles to join all the locals, including many of the people from the Elliott community, in the search for this child. Margie's one night turned into several as she set up a makeshift clinic in one of the motel rooms, with supplies brought up by Wendy and health workers from Elliott, who helped as much as possible between running the clinic at Elliott, and extra supplies delivered from Katherine on the Greyhound bus.

Before daylight Margie would attend to dressings on blistered feet, reinforcing them for the long hot day ahead. Water bottles were filled with Gastrolyte rehydration mixture to be left for people out on the search lines. As the days passed, the sadness and quiet of the searches became more distressing. Over the course of the ten days of the search, 260 people were treated for sunburn, dehydration, dizziness, vomiting, chest infections, twisted ankles, blistered feet, cuts and abrasions, with some being evacuated to Katherine. Ultimately, Margie says, she knew after the second day that it would be unlikely that Clinton would be found alive.

On the third day, pieces of his clothing were sighted and they assumed Clinton would soon be found, so Margie and Adele prepared to go to the site as soon as word came. 'It was close to last light and suddenly the news came in that a search helicopter at the site had crashed,' Margie recalls. 'I was flown out, not to Clinton as we'd all hoped, but to the crash site where two men were badly injured and needed to be medivaced to Katherine. This major event would normally have had a team of paramedics fully equipped to manage such an accident; instead we had a basic drug kit, the open floor of Lloyd's search and rescue chopper and the dark . . .' Margie went to Katherine with them and after a couple of hours' sleep, returned with fresh medical supplies.

One of Margie's clearest memories is of the Jingili Aboriginal women elders telling Clinton's mother, Adele, about the womens' country where the female spirits of their people went after death. 'They told her that the spirit women were looking after Clinton, protecting him until he was found. This appeared to comfort Adele and helped sustain her throughout the nightmare. She always knew that Clinton would be found.'

On the tenth day, when the search had been scaled down, some of the local stockmen who had been frustrated by the methodical nature of the grid search, set out on their horses, heading due west as the trackers had initially advised. By late morning as most people had left the roadhouse and the emergency services teams were packing up to leave, they finally found Clinton's helmet. Shortly after, they found Clinton's dead body lying beside a log, untouched by the usual feral scavengers of the outback. 'It seemed the Aboriginal women had been right,' Margie says. 'The spirits of their long dead women had watched over him.'

Until now, twenty years after the search and discovery of Clinton's little body, Margie has been unable to read *The Lost Boy*, a book written about the tragedy by journalist Robert Wainwright. She recalls that particular tragedy as the most challenging incident of her nursing life.

'As a mother, whose children [Mac and Fiona] were involved in the search, the loss of a child can only be imagined,' she reflects. 'To remain positive while witnessing those ten days of increasing stress and sadness, knowing that eventually the outcome would not be good, was a harrowing experience. Steve and Adele were our friends and, as a family, they accessed our clinics. Because the roadhouse was also the centre for the search planning, the family had no real privacy to grieve and ultimately the toll on them was considerable.'

'We roller-coasted between the highs when Clinton's bike and clothes were found, to the lows of dashed expectations when the buses would return on nightfall with the emotionally drained, tired and distressed and sometimes injured searchers bearing no results,' Margie says. 'There was sadness and empathy for the parents etched on every face and the frustration of failure was constantly noted.

'As a health team we felt quite isolated. The health management of the day in Alice Springs could not comprehend the scale of what was taking place at Dunmarra, although they sent counsellors and some assistance towards the end of the search. In recent times this area of remote nursing has been considerably improved and health management policies reflect the importance of supporting the needs of staff working in remote practice and in the challenging situations they often face,' she says.

Looking back over her career, Margie says she really went to the outback more than forty years ago with no orientation, no remote bush experience and no knowledge of Aboriginal culture, and was armed only with confidence (unfounded, she claims in retrospect) and a licence to learn. 'I was fortunate and privileged to have worked with so many people within both the circles of Western medicine and the Aboriginal body, land and spirit world; people who have been my mentors, friends and teachers, who have given freely to my education and experience,' she says. 'They provided me with the knowledge that is fundamental to my understanding and acceptance of the differences and the similarities we all share, enabling me to see the "big picture".'

Having seen many mysterious and sometimes spine-tingling things in her long career in remote communities of the Northern Territory, Margie says she never, ever felt afraid for herself or her family. She readily acknowledges that the Aboriginal people of the VRD and Elliott communities were particularly generous in spirit. 'In the beginning I was such a new chum and over the years I continued to learn but they never judged me even if I did the wrong thing,' she says.

Margie continued to dispense care and attention to the Elliott community until 1997, when she was seconded to Darwin to work with remote health practitioners across the Territory, managing the development and implementation of a primary care information system.

Much loved by the Elliott community and district, she was welcomed back to the Elliott clinic in 2005, when she accepted the role of Clinic Manager. In 2009 she moved to Tennant Creek to manage the Barkly Area health services, a role she continued until her retirement early in 2012.

From her home in Queensland, she reflects on four decades of nursing service to the people of the Victoria River and Barkly regions and considers herself fortunate to have had the life she's had, working with the people she's worked with and caring for the people she's cared for. 'I got so much satisfaction out of working with the amazingly gifted, skilled colleagues I've known over the years. I've experienced a remarkable lifestyle, known some extraordinary people and been privileged to work with another culture,' she says.

NURSES OF THE OUTBACK

One of the things Margie misses most is the vast outback landscape, the glorious colours of the day and the big, clear, blue-black nights sprinkled with blazing stars. 'That gave me a great perspective on understanding the big picture,' she says. 'I miss the people and the unique way of life. I wouldn't have been able to do what I did had it not been for the wonderful support of my family, colleagues and friends,' she says. 'It has been a very humbling experience.'

7

THE MAGIC OF MOOMBA

Chris Belshaw, *Moomba Oil and Gas Field, South Australia*

With the edges of his Irish brogue slightly flattened by years of living in the outback, Chris Belshaw answered the phone at the Moomba health clinic at 4.30 in the afternoon. The nurse practitioner and team leader of the Royal Flying Doctor Service (RFDS) Cooper Basin health centres was told that a young ringer (outback stockman) had been out teaching a Pommy jackaroo how to ride a motorbike. The ringer was riding about 100 metres ahead of the other bike when he looked back over his shoulder to see how the Pommy was going. With his head turned back, he never even saw the fence before he hit it. It was his eighteenth birthday.

Thrown off headfirst, the ringer banged his head very hard. By the time the Pommy pulled up he was groggy but seemed okay. However, when he went to get back on his bike, he was all over the place. The Englishman left him and went for help.

The accident happened on a cattle station about 150 kilometres down the Birdsville Track from the Moomba oil and gas fields in the Cooper Basin in the far north-eastern corner of South Australia.

The station overseer slipped out in a vehicle to pick up the ringer and by the time they got back to the shed, the injured man was dazed and confused. They called 000 and were transferred through to MedStar, the organisation that manages all retrievals out of Adelaide. Deciding it would take too long to get a helicopter up from Adelaide, Medstar contacted Santos, the company that owns the Moomba oil and gas field. Santos referred it to their clinic, which is staffed and managed by the RFDS. That late in the afternoon was deemed too late to safely fly in and out in the Santos chopper, so Chris requested the use of their ambulance instead. He and a designated driver travelled the two hours south as speedily as possible, across the rain-ruined roads.

By the time they arrived, the ringer's condition had deteriorated significantly. He appeared to have no other significant injuries apart from the obvious head trauma, but he was slurring monosyllabic answers to questions and his pupils were responding sluggishly. Suspecting major internal bleeding inside his skull, Chris intubated him, and got him loaded into the ambulance and on the road back to Moomba as quickly as possible. He deteriorated so quickly that Chris was relieved and a little surprised that he was still alive when the RFDS team from Broken Hill retrieved him and flew him out to Adelaide.

Chris doubted he would survive the journey.

In any number of ways, Chris Belshaw has been preparing for his whole life to have an opinion about that head injury. Born in 1965 and raised in Holywood, about 5 kilometres out of Belfast in Northern Ireland, he came into the world just a few short years ahead of three decades of 'The Troubles', the name given to the years of violence between elements of the region's Irish nationalist and pro-British unionist communities, during which more than 3600 people were killed and many more injured.

The youngest of four siblings, Chris's first real memory is of Neil Armstrong walking on the moon in 1969. Though one thing had nothing to do with the other, he remembers everything changed after that and life in Northern Ireland became hazardous. There was a lot of sectarian violence involving bombings and shootings. His father was a policeman, an added danger in an already unsafe environment; but Chris doesn't recall ever feeling unsafe at home, even though he well remembers the shotgun that rested in the hallstand by their steel-plated front door. A row of cartridges stood ready on the hallstand shelf, just in case.

Historically, Ireland is very family-oriented and, culturally, most families look after their elders. The Belshaws were no exception. Chris's grandparents lived with them and his mother also fostered pre-adoption babies. As a youngster, he always helped out with the babies; he knew how to feed them, change their nappies and entertain them. Chris remembers his whole extended family congregating around the big kitchen stove. 'It's where the family meets and greets and it was where the heat was,' he recalls. 'It was the heart of the house. In some ways our upbringing was quite remote, as we didn't have the technology or comforts that are available these days. We didn't have an inside toilet. We didn't even have running water in the house. It was all outside.'

Even though his father's Protestant family were all loyalists and 'Orangemen', Chris says that his dad always taught his children to ignore sectarian divides. 'He encouraged us to make our own friends and not let political or religious denomination sway our views,' Chris says. 'As such, my best and oldest friends are all Catholic. I really think that this is where I got my strong belief in the need for social justice. I could see how minority groups were treated and the inequalities that were so widespread, and it really took a while for proportional representation in Ireland to kick in.'

Despite the violence surrounding the Belshaws, Chris remembers a happy childhood. 'We had a little bit of land and we were pretty self-sufficient. We had ducks, geese, chooks and turkeys and we kept a big vegetable garden. We actually had a really nice family upbringing despite the pressure my parents were constantly under.'

Chris's aunt was the matron of a hospital in Belfast and, although she retired when he was young, he had an awareness of and interest in what she did. In his early teens his grandmother had a stroke and, as the biggest and strongest in the family (despite being the youngest), he was integral to her ongoing care. He was the only one big enough to carry her around. He would help her up in the morning, help get her showered and carry her to her chair. In the evenings, he was the one who assisted her back to bed. Being a carer was just a normal part of life for him.

As a student at the local grammar school, Chris excelled at sport and particularly loved rugby, although he says he struggled academically and had to work very hard to achieve good results. He thought about joining the British army for a while but, when his father told him he'd shoot him himself if he did, he decided to pursue nursing as a career.

On the morning of a job interview at the Ulster Hospital for his first nursing role, chance dealt him a wildcard when he was offered a place at the University of Wales to study sports science. He felt he'd had a really good interview at the hospital, but when he asked them what would happen next, they said their policy was to let everyone know after the interviews were completed. Hedging his bets, he told them about the offer from University of Wales, saying he would take the nursing job if he was offered it, but he needed to know straight away. They were so amazed that anyone would give up a university degree to become a nurse that they hired him then and there.

Chris says Ulster Hospital was a wonderful learning environment. 'It was an incredible training experience because, in the height of The Troubles, we got exposure to everything, including bomb wounds, gunshot injuries and severe burns,' he says. 'The hospital had a great burns unit and an excellent plastic surgery department and they looked after all Northern Ireland.' They did lots of plastic surgery and facial maxilla surgery – anything to do with the face, jaw, neck and hard or soft tissues of the mouth – so Chris got extraordinarily good practical experience treating the victims of conflict. It was also a very rural and agricultural area, so there were also lots of farming and industrial accidents being brought in to Ulster. 'It was the whole gamut of possibilities and because it was hospital-based training, we were there every day covering all the shifts and we really did learn hands on,' he says.

Still, there were a few obstacles on his chosen career path. One was maternity. He loved it and would have happily been a midwife. The charge sister of maternity recommended that he pursue it, but in those days men could work as, but not actually train as, a midwife in Northern Ireland. His only option would have been to train somewhere like Scotland, for instance, before returning home to deliver babies. Looking back, he says regretfully, 'Discrimination does not always work in the obvious ways.'

Chris and his siblings were all urged by their parents to get a good education and to get out of Ireland, as they believed it would not be a good place to live any time soon. He had two sisters, who emigrated to the US, where one is now a teacher in New York and the other an obstetric nurse in Utah. His brother is a business executive in south England. Following their daughters, his parents moved to America in 1994, although his mother has returned to Ireland to live since his father died in 1997. Chris himself finished his training in Ulster on a Thursday and by the following Sunday he was in London. He'd bought a one-way ticket and he arrived with a rucksack, a sleeping bag and his certificate. It was 1988 and he was already a very grown-up twenty-three.

First thing Monday morning, he visited the UK consul and registered with them, enabling him to work anywhere in the UK. He then joined the British Nursing Agency and registered to work for them. They said they'd be in touch. Never one to let the grass grow under his feet, by mid-afternoon he'd found himself a job. With the same charm and obvious talent that saw him talk his way into nursing in the first place, he had called around at Brompton Hospital where one of his three London-based nursing friends recommended him to the nursing coordinator. She asked him about his training and experience and within twenty minutes he was in uniform on a paediatric thoracic ward, nursing children suffering a wide range of problems related to the chest cavity.

Chance continued to play a part in Chris's life when his father rang him a couple of months later to say he'd received a phone call from Charing Cross Hospital, asking if Chris was interested in having an interview with them. The hospital had done a recruiting drive in Belfast some months before Chris left and, never one to ignore an opportunity, he had filled out the forms. Owning neither a coat nor a tie, he had to borrow both from a mate to dress correctly for the interview and, until he was in the interview, he actually had no idea exactly what job he was going for.

Walking through the appropriate ward on his way to the meeting, he recalls it looked a bit like a battlefield. 'Everyone had heavily bandaged heads and lots of tubes everywhere,' he says. In the interview he was asked why he wanted to work in neurosurgery. He replied that he didn't, he had just put in a general application and this was what came up. Asked what he knew about neurosurgery, he replied, 'Not much, but I'm willing to learn.' He got the job.

Like a duck to water, he loved it. Chris worked with patients who'd suffered cerebral aneurysms (a weakness in the wall of a vein or artery in the head that causes a ballooning in the blood vessel), acute strokes, multiple sclerosis, spinal cord injuries, skull base tumours and central nervous system infections, among a broad range of conditions related to neurology. The ward incorporated seven high-dependency beds, generally fully filled with intubated, totally dependent patients. Building on the foundations of his quality training at Ulster, he found he just had to add the required knowledge and skills for each new speciality. The basic nursing care didn't change.

Like many other hospital-trained nurses, Chris believes university-trained nurses lack the benefits of immersion in 'hands-on' nursing. 'University-trained nurses tend to be less clinically orientated. Because of their limited practice time during training, they are often busy doing assignments and case studies and miss the opportunity to learn that good basic nursing care starts with knowing exactly what the patient needs or wants,' he says.

His catch-cry has always been, 'What the patient needs is good-quality care.' That and 'The mark 1 eyeball is the most valuable tool in nursing,' referring to nurses using their eyes to assess the patient instead of relying too much on technology.

He's watched staff come onto a shift, particularly in intensive care, look at the charts, check the monitors and note the readings on the machines, before finally looking at the person in the bed. Given that his nursing ethos is firmly embedded in his background caring for his elders and the babies his mother fostered, Chris is unimpressed. 'You need to eyeball the patient first thing. You look at them, at their colour, at their body language, and you talk to them. Then you check the technology,' he states. He believes in talking to families, and building relationships with both the patient and their support crew, so that everyone is on the same page. 'Families need to be engaged and included in the care; they need to understand fully what's happening.'

From Charing Cross, he moved around gaining as much practical experience as he could, before moving to Wakefield in Yorkshire to work at Pinderfields Hospital while undertaking a neuro-medical and neuroscience course. Wakefield had an added attraction for him in that he was able to join the rugby club. The England captain and many of the internationals were playing there at the time, so he had a really happy year working, studying and playing rugby.

At the end of the course, he had to do a presentation as part of his assessment. Generally half a dozen people attend what's normally a pretty straightforward process. When Chris presented his 10 000-word paper on acoustic neuroma – a benign, often fast-growing tumour that originates in the canal connecting the brain to the inner ear – a couple of hundred people turned up, including several consultant neurosurgeons. It is the only benign tumour that can be deadly since, if it advances enough before diagnosis, it can put fatal pressure on the brain stem. Chris was delighted with the response, even if a little daunted by the turn-out. It was one of his favourite topics and he got the same excellent marks for the presentation that he got for all his studies. Despite that, he still maintains he wasn't academically smart enough to do medicine.

With rollicking laughter, he suddenly remembers a faux pas of his own making when he was on rotation in maternity during his training. 'In Belfast you rarely saw anyone who was not Caucasian. One day a girl came in and they said, "She's going to have a really big baby." I asked the midwives how they knew. They said her husband was Jamaican. I asked, "Who's Jim Aitken? Is he someone famous?"'

Seriousness restored, he continues, 'I've always really liked the practical learning and application that goes with nursing. Whenever I did assignments I would just relate it to people I'd nursed and write about their situation, treatment and nursing care.'

Leaving Wakefield in pursuit of unrequited love, Chris spent some time working in intensive and coronary care on Jersey and the Channel Isles, but he quickly realised he wanted to enhance his training and experience with more learning. He returned to London to undertake a graduate diploma of intensive care nursing at Harefield Hospital. Once again, it was a fateful decision.

On the first day, in a general class that encompassed various courses, one girl arrived a few minutes late. He thought she looked really lovely and set about getting to know her. Heather Mason hailed from mid-north South Australia and was in London broadening her nursing experience by working at the heart transplant unit. Having acknowledged mutual admiration, Chris and Heather soon established themselves as a couple. Once they finished their respective courses, they worked in London for a couple of years until Heather finally felt a hankering to return home. Chris decided to apply for a visa and South Australian nursing registration and move with her. They arrived in Australia in July 1994 and married in April the following year.

Australia was a revelation to Chris. He was a little apprehensive about meeting Heather's parents and her nine siblings – in particular her seven brothers – for the first time at Adelaide airport, but found that bonhomie was quickly established. Being so positive by nature, Chris was always going to find things to like about his new country, and he has loved it from day one. Heather's family took him for a cook's tour of Adelaide before driving north through the Clare Valley to Jamestown, where the Masons hail from. 'Everything about it was fantastic,' he recalls. 'Adelaide had such a nice feel to it and the Valley is just beautiful. It's a gorgeous country and it just felt like home.'

In fact, Chris was and is so enamoured with Australia, he chooses to spend vacations seeing more of this country rather than any other. He has only returned to Ireland once since leaving it in 1994, and that was for the funeral of his sister Jennifer's husband, Andrew Grene, in 2010. Andrew was Special Assistant to the Special Representative (USA) with the United Nations in Haiti, and was killed in the earthquake in 2010.

Having unpacked their bags to settle in Adelaide, Chris signed up with a nursing agency in Adelaide. He well remembers waving his way into the office through the cloud of smoke that perpetually surrounded Val, the agency owner and manager. 'With one hand holding a fag and the other on the phone, she'd peer up at you through glasses as thick as a Coke bottle. She was a tough old bird, but she had an absolute heart of gold,' he says.

She quickly ascertained that he'd cheerfully do anything and go anywhere, including country postings, so she sent him off to Port

THE MAGIC OF MOOMBA

Augusta for three months. With his usual enthusiasm, he loved everything about it. He continued to roam wherever Val sent him until one day she asked him had he ever done any mine work. 'No,' he said, 'but I've half a mind to try.' Ushering him out the door, she advised him, 'Be at the airport at 8 a.m. tomorrow and you'll need steel-capped boots.'

He managed to find a pair of boots at short notice and duly presented at the airport next morning to find he was going to a place called Moomba somewhere up in the north of South Australia. Sitting next to a fellow called Vince Kaminsky, who worked for Santos at Moomba, Chris heard his first descriptions of the destination ahead, but none of it prepared him for the reality.

'As we circled before coming in to land, I could see this huge refinery belching smoke out in the middle of nowhere,' he says. 'The horizon stretched endlessly. When we landed and they opened the door of the plane, all the air was instantly sucked out and replaced by the November inferno.' Even the swarm of flies, which turned the white t-shirt in front of him black, fascinated him. He says he later realised 'that's why old bushies talk out of the side of their mouths'.

In the terminal he was met by one of the RFDS nurses, who handed him a set of keys for the bongo van (similar to a kombi), a mud map to find the clinic and a final 'good luck' as she boarded the departing plane. Out in the carpark, he was perplexed to find the bongo van had three pedals but no gear stick. He'd never seen a column shift before, so that took a bit of sleuthing, before he headed off to meet the fate chance had dealt him this time.

Lisa Duffield was the RFDS nurse he worked with in that first week out in the Cooper Basin on the edge of the Simpson Desert. He says Lisa was a really good educator who helped him quickly work out what he could do. He knew, right from that first week, that this was a posting where he could apply all the skill and knowledge he had accumulated over the years. Despite the heat, the flies and the isolation, Chris felt like he had landed in his perfect job. He loved everything about it and, on his return to Adelaide, he told Val he'd go to oil and gas fields any time, regardless of what else he was offered. For the next nine months he flew back and forth to Moomba, relieving any time they needed him.

Then, suddenly, two of the nurses at Moomba were leaving the RFDS and their positions were vacant. For the first time fate dealt him a dodgy hand when he realised he couldn't apply for the job. It didn't matter that he wasn't a midwife while he was relieving under the employ of the agency, but all RFDS-employed flight nurses were required to be. He thought back to when he did his training in Northern Ireland and the fact that he hadn't been allowed to train as a midwife and thought regretfully, 'If only I'd gone to Scotland . . .' So it was that he missed the opportunity. He quickly determined that he would not miss the next one. He really, really wanted to work permanently at Moomba.

Back in Adelaide he discussed his dilemma with Heather. She supported him doing his midwifery training, so he researched his options. He particularly wanted to do hospital-based training so he phoned each of the state nurses' boards and steadily compiled a list of the possibilities. Then he got a map and plotted the relevant dots across Australia. Collectively, Queensland had the best options. However, the Queensland nurses' board told him not to bother applying to do hospital-based midwifery training in Queensland if he didn't live there as, without exception, they gave first preference to Queenslanders; they had too many internal applicants not to. Needing to establish an address in that state, he phoned Townsville Hospital and asked to speak to the manager of the intensive care unit (ICU). Introducing himself, he explained his qualifications and asked her if she had any jobs available. She asked when he could start. He then asked to be put through to operating theatres since Heather would also be looking for work. He spoke to the theatre manager and organised to transfer all their appropriate paperwork, and two weeks later they were driving to Townsville to start their new jobs.

Chris remembers a really good, caring, compassionate crew working in the ICU and settled in quickly and easily. Within a few weeks, notification came around about the next course for midwifery. He put in an application despite all the girls around him telling him not to bother as they had only ever accepted one male trainee in the ten years it had been available. But he never considered not applying, and as he filled out the 140-odd pages of the application, he researched and answered the questions carefully. Before he handed it in, he got one of the midwives to check it. She was surprised to discover he had found the answer to a question none of the previous applicants had been able to find, so he was confident of being one of the top twenty who would be granted an interview for one of the twelve available places. He was invited in for an interview and, by the end of it, they told him he was definitely in but that he couldn't tell anyone until they had finished the process. His impossibly wide grin as he departed the interview should have been a dead giveaway.

The course started in the following March and, as always, he embraced it enthusiastically mostly, he says, because one of the midwives, an Indigenous nurse with a big heart and a gentle hand, took him under her wing and taught him how best to care for a woman about to deliver a baby. 'She was an Aboriginal lady and I was a white Anglo-Saxon man but, on the first day I worked with her, we got talking and somehow we connected. She mothered me through the course; she was one of the kindest midwives I ever worked with,' he says.

By the time Chris sat his state exam at the end of the course, Heather was pregnant with their first child and keen to return to be nearer to her family. Chris got a job as a midwife in Adelaide and found he could apply all his intensive care skills to the task at hand.

Then, as luck would have it, one day while he was out running errands, he ran into Lisa Duffield and Sue Rayson, the RFDS flight nurses from Moomba. They told him there was a job going at the Moomba clinic, as Lisa was taking a year off. He immediately applied and got the posting, which, after a year, just confirmed that it was his absolute dream job. When Lisa returned he went back to midwifery in Adelaide and waited for someone to retire or die, such is the fantastic retention rate within the RFDS! Eventually Lisa did decide to relocate to Kununurra and Sue announced she would be leaving as well. Chris applied specifically for Moomba and started as permanent staff at the clinic in 2003.

The Moomba clinic offers services first and foremost to the Santos staff and other oil and gas personnel working in the Cooper Basin. However, as the only available medical service, they also provide care to the people who live on the cattle stations in the surrounding area and to passing tourists.

When Chris started there permanently, he decided he needed to do some more training. He consulted Angie Parker, a midwife and educator he'd met previously, who challenged nurses to understand why they did what they did rather than just doing it because that's what they'd always done. She was one of the first nurses he had met in Australia with a passion to drive evidence-based nursing and she encouraged Chris in his pursuit of further knowledge. He enrolled externally at Charles Sturt University to do a Bachelor of Health Science in Nursing. He'd work in the clinic throughout the day and then study until midnight each night. He knocked it over in a year.

He took a break and just worked for a while, challenged initially by his promotion in 2005 to the Team Leader of the Cooper Basin Health Centres, which services both Moomba and Ballera, the Santos oil and gas fields across the border in far south-west Queensland. However, he soon became frustrated with the processes involved in providing optimum care. Sometimes they would have patients from the cattle stations who'd drive several hours to get to the clinic, who'd then have to wait because the doctor at the RFDS base at Broken Hill would be tied up with something and not be able to prescribe whatever drugs they needed for some hours. Then they'd still have the long drive home. Chris felt it was unfair so he decided to investigate nurse practitioner (NP) training. It appealed to him as NPs are able to work on their own to assess, manage and refer patients to other health professionals, and can also prescribe certain medications and order specific diagnostic investigations.

Chris phoned Olwyn Johnson, who was the first nurse practitioner to be endorsed in Australia. Ollie – as her friends know her – was working at Goodooga and strongly encouraged him to do the training. Chris recalls she told him, 'You've got to do it for yourself. Plus, you've got to do it for your patients because they deserve the best care and you've got to do it for those coming after you.'

Initially, Chris put a business proposal to RFDS, which approved the idea and endorsed his plan. He did his Masters of Nursing Science (Nurse Practitioner), again externally, at the University of

South Australia. Julie Farrelly, one of the casual nurses relieving at Moomba, had completed the study to be an NP, although she had not yet done her candidacy and qualified. Julie mentored Chris through his training and helped him to establish a network of other NPs. It was incredibly hard work but he knew he could make a very real difference at the end. As soon as he graduated, he applied successfully for official endorsement as a rural and remote emergency nurse practitioner.

While as the team leader he is generally based at Moomba, he does occasionally relieve over at Ballera, a situation that highlights some of the hurdles related to working in this particular environment. Chris got his pharmacology endorsement to accompany his NP qualification, but there's a different drug law in every state in Australia, so he has to prescribe differently in South Australia from how he prescribes when he goes across the border to Ballera. 'Eventually,' he says, 'they will have to have one national standard for drug administration.' It's just one of the unique challenges that Chris faces in his job.

The Moomba clinic is open from 7 a.m. until 5 p.m. and the nurses are on call for the remaining hours of the day, seven days a week. Like most remote community clinics, more than ninety per cent of their workload is primary health care. In the course of a normal day, the nursing staff routinely assess and treat all manner of ailments, from minor through to serious, for Santos personnel as well as those of the other oil and gas companies working in the Cooper Basin and the surrounding cattle stations. They run education sessions and generally keep a weather eye on everyone. Although all staff fly in and out of Moomba at the beginning and end of their hitch and have done for the forty-plus years of its existence, the majority of the personnel return regularly, creating a sense of permanency less often seen in fly-in fly-out locations.

Most often, the major incidents are related to the tourists. Chris says these accidents can be frustrating because many of them are avoidable. 'Some of them retire, buy a big 4WD and a big flash caravan and head for the outback. Too many of them have never been off the bitumen or further west than Ipswich and they drive too fast for the conditions. They get caught, especially on the dirt, and over they go. A lot of our call-outs are to road accidents. Occasionally tourists get stranded by rain and run out of medication, but that's okay. We'll be called upon to top up their medications.'

And then sometimes, as with the young ringer they brought into the clinic after he hit the fence on his motorbike, the major incidents are related to the stations. Chris remembers that one well because he didn't expect the ringer to survive the journey back to Moomba, much less Adelaide. The next day, Chris rang for an update still expecting the worst and was astonished to hear the lad was out of ICU and up on the ward. He was told that the surgeon in Adelaide had performed a craniotomy and, as Chris had anticipated, had found a big extradural haematoma – where a build-up of blood occurs between the skull and the outer layer of the tough protective membrane that surrounds the brain and spinal cord. Typically, there will be a period of lucidity followed by rapid deterioration, leading to loss of consciousness and respiratory arrest. Luckily the stockman was treated in time and made a good recovery. When Chris finished his two-week hitch and returned to Adelaide himself, he went to see the young ringer. 'When I saw him, I just had to touch him. I couldn't believe he was alive.'

There are other stories that illustrate even more just how

efficient the RFDS is. For instance, they had a call one day from a rig, run by one of the other companies in the Cooper Basin, saying that a man's hand had almost been amputated. Chris advised them to pressure bandage the wound and elevate the arm until he could get there. He requested that the RFDS in Broken Hill send a plane, then requested the use of the Santos helicopter and pilot and flew out to the rig. They loaded the man on a stretcher and into the chopper and flew him straight back to Moomba, where the RFDS arrived fifteen minutes later. The retrieval team then took him to Adelaide and he went straight to surgery. It was less than six hours from the time he sustained the injury to the time he arrived in the theatre in Adelaide for surgery. He spent twelve hours on the operating table and they saved his hand.

Outcomes like that one, and the young ringer's, just serve to enhance Chris Belshaw's commitment to Moomba. All of his years growing up, caring for his grandmother and foster siblings, doing his nursing training during the conflict and violence that plagued Northern Ireland, training in neurosurgical nursing and intensive and coronary care, and training as a midwife, all of it led to this job in one of the most remote and sometimes inhospitable areas of outback Australia – and he couldn't be happier. He says that it gives him the best opportunity to apply all of the knowledge and skills he has acquired over the years.

Given he's not yet fifty years old, it seems likely he has many years ahead of him out in the Cooper Basin, but he wouldn't have it any other way. It isn't easy being away from home all the time and he acknowledges that it's much harder for Heather and their four children. 'I work two weeks on, two off, so I'm away for six months of the year. That's particularly tough on Heather, but the upside is that when I'm home, I'm a fulltime parent,' he says.

Despite the obvious challenges it's still his dream job and he loves every minute of it. He loves the sense of community at Moomba and the outback itself. In fact, he really thinks it's the best job in the world, and anyone waiting to step into his role is just going to have to wait . . . and wait . . . and then probably wait some more . . .

LEFT: Neen Hawkes faced the ultimate test when called upon to save the life of her neighbour and good friend after a motorbike accident on his cattle station in central-west Queensland.

ABOVE AND LEFT: Anna Burley swapped the corporate world for nursing and has made a difference in Georgetown, Queensland, doing everything from teaching kids about sugar levels in soft drink (above), to managing emergency plans as the ominous clouds of Cyclone Yasi approached (left).

ABOVE: Catherine Jurd from Julia Creek in Queensland may look delicate at first glance, but she's about as fragile as a length of eight-gauge fencing. Catherine also appears on the front cover.

RIGHT: Geri Malone thrived on the buzz of emergency work with the Flying Doctors, but says there's nothing glamorous about being a flight nurse: 'When the plane is in the air, you work in virtual isolation.' (Courtesy of Rosey Boehm Photography)

ABOVE: Christine Foletti's remarkable career has included working with the Royal Flying Doctor Service in Australia and emergency rescues in African war zones.

LEFT: Christine now works far off the West Australian coast on the Cocos-Keeling Islands. *(Courtesy of Rosey Boehm Photography)*

RIGHT: Margie McLean was busy delivering a baby just hours before her wedding ceremony at Victoria River Downs in the Northern Territory in 1972.

ABOVE: Chris Belshaw's nursing career has taken him from the sectarian violence of his former home of Northern Ireland, to the unique demands of the Moomba oil and gas fields in South Australia.

ABOVE: A dust storm rolling in to Moomba.
RIGHT: Moomba workers unwind.

ABOVE: Aggie Harpham was drawn back to Kununurra in Western Australia by fond childhood memories: 'The power would go out and we'd sit on the verandah watching these huge storms lash across the sky.'

RIGHT: Nurse, midwife, mum, fundraiser and crisis-solver Maureen Ker (left) was thrilled to receive a Medal of the Order of Australia from New South Wales Governor Marie Bashir. *(Courtesy of Rob Tuckwell Photography)*

LEFT: Aboriginal health practitioner Jo Appoo never planned on being a nurse, but loves getting out of bed every morning to work at the Elliott Health Centre in the Northern Territory.

ABOVE: Timeworn locomotives stand beside the railway tracks that once carried the Old Ghan through Marree in South Australia.

LEFT: When nurse and midwife June Andrew roared into Marree in her Ford Laser in 1982 to run the local clinic, she zapped the community alight. *(Courtesy of RFDS Central Section)*

ABOVE: Karen Schnitzerling from the foggy west coast of Tasmania has nerves of steel and infinite staying power.

LEFT: Fred Miegel, pictured here near Alice Springs with fellow nurse Emma Corcoran, knows what it takes to stick it out in remote palliative care: 'Plenty of people who come into rural and remote areas…talk the talk but never walk the walk. They don't stay long.'

LEFT: Shamiso Muchando faced a difficult transition moving from Zimbabwe to remote Western Australia, but she loves her new home country. *(Courtesy of Kimberley Visions Photography)*

ABOVE: Sue Stewart works in Bidyadanga in north-west Western Australia, where the local Aboriginal diet includes bush turkey, kangaroo and turtle. *(Courtesy of Tony Wells, Rural Health Workforce Australia)*

8

LOST AND FOUND

Aggie Harpham, *Kununurra, Western Australia*

At thirty-three years of age, Aggie Harpham is in the best place in her life. Tall and slim with honey-blonde hair, sparkling hazel eyes and a beaming smile, she's healthy, happy and spiritually whole. There was a time when she plummeted into the depths of despair but, with sheer guts and determination and the support of a handful of very dear friends, she hauled herself up and turned herself around. Aggie's come full circle in more ways than one, returning to her roots in the Kimberley region of Western Australia to undertake a nursing role she loves, working with Child and Adolescent Mental Health (CAMHs) to help people she values.

Aggie Harpham was once exceedingly lost but now she's very much found.

When Aggie was young, driven by an early desire to help others and a good dose of romanticism, she dreamed of working in

Africa. While that fantasy has long since been retired, she's found a perfect compromise. 'The Kimberley is my African dream,' she says. 'It has the wide-open space, the grandeur and the richness of one of the oldest cultures in the world. Like all remote areas and particularly Indigenous communities, it also has social injustices and people that need help.' Focusing on children and working mostly with the families in the Kununurra, Warmun and Halls Creek areas, Aggie says she loves working with the families and the challenge of trying to see the world through a different lens from her own.

One way or another, without intending to, Aggie has been preparing for this role for the last fifteen years. Having been on the glugging end of binge drinking in her younger years and having had her emotional wheels fall off once or twice along the way, she's better placed than many to understand the challenges facing young, unsupported people. Since then, she's trained as a nurse and, most recently, undertaken a Masters of Mental Health, training that will help her give young people the help she so sorely needed when her future looked anything but clear and positive.

Aggie was born in the Kununurra Hospital in 1981. Her parents managed Carlton Hill Station north of Kununurra for LJ Hooker. She has no true recollections of station life back then, other than the memory of a story about a king brown snake wrapped around the rails of her cot and the terror of those charged with getting her out of it. She has another anecdotal memory of when the bishop was flown in to officiate her bush christening. However, her first tangible reminiscences centre on and around Leichhardt Street in Kununurra.

Carlton Hill was sold when Aggie was still very young and her family moved into town, to Leichhardt Street. She recalls most readily the huge electrical storms. 'The power would go out and we'd sit on the verandah watching these huge storms lash across the sky,' she says.

She remembers swimming in the Ord River, watching the catfish from a boat and a seaplane landing on the water. It is a montage of snapshots that revolve around her memory of Nancy Ogilvie, a big, comfortable Aboriginal woman who babysat her and her younger sister, Sarah.

When she was six, her parents' marriage broke down irrevocably. Her mother packed the two girls up and moved to Toogoolawah in Queensland's Brisbane Valley, to be nearer to her own family. Her father eventually returned to his homeland, England. Aggie remembers begging to know when the family was going back to Kununurra, but despite her pleading, the move was permanent and her mother later remarried. Aggie talked about the Kimberleys and tried to hang on to the images but gradually they faded. She clung to her memories of her father, who she saw once in Grade Three and once in Grade Nine. He wrote for their birthdays and Christmas, but otherwise Aggie didn't see him again until she was aged twenty-two.

Around the time she turned fifteen, her mother's second marriage folded and things started falling apart at home after the departure of her stepfather. As the oldest child, Aggie found herself on an emotional seesaw trying to balance her life as a boarder at school in Toowoomba with the need to support her mother and help hold things together at home.

Having already tasted her first alcohol at the end of Grade Nine, by the following year Aggie and her friends were plotting how to get booze for their next binge-drinking session on their boarders' weekends or during the holidays. For Aggie, it was a form of escaping the horrors at home and an attempt to fit in and feel like a normal teenager. She also loved getting away to the bush with other boarder friends going home for the holidays and soon discovered that social culture out there revolved around alcohol. At the end of the day, and certainly at parties, most people seemed to be drinking something, usually rum.

On those visits Aggie was delighted to rediscover smells and images from her childhood that resonated with her. Some of her best memories are of long weeks spent with the Cannon family at Rutland Plains Station up on Cape York Peninsula in Queensland. She found being in the outback with the Cannons was restorative. They provided a level of stability in her life as well as a lot of fun; it was the kind of family life she longed for but didn't have. Julia Cannon was a formidable mother figure for Aggie and provided the kind of supervision she felt she had been missing. Julia was a tireless fundraiser for the Royal Flying Doctor Service, which meant everyone pitched in, including Aggie. She loved it.

Not everyone in her life was as supportive though and there came a time when her trust was shockingly abused by other people close to her. It was a shattering experience, but one that she locked away as well as she could while trying to get on with her life.

Looking towards her future, Aggie began to think about studying medicine. Influenced by her grandfather, Dr Keith Shaw, a GP in rural Queensland, her dreams of Africa revolved around a career as a doctor. She worked hard at school and study was never a problem for her; she enjoyed learning.

Despite the binge-drinking sessions she and her friends indulged in whenever possible, and in spite of memories of betrayal lurking just below the surface of her consciousness, she managed to score well enough to get into the University of Queensland to study science as a precursor to medicine. However, a few short weeks into the semester, she realised she was not ready for uni. Much to the disapproval of her family, she decided to defer. She took a year off and went contract mustering up in the Gulf country of North Queensland.

It was a tough year camping out and spending long days in a saddle or the kitchen. Aggie was the only girl on the crew, apart from the contractor's wife, and although she enjoyed certain aspects of the lifestyle, in the end she failed to return one weekend after arguing she wanted an extra day off. Some weeks before she'd met a boy, Pete, who was also working in the area, and she felt for the first time that someone was there just for her. She got a job at the Gidgee Inn Motel in Cloncurry and saw him as often as possible until uni resumed the following year.

Pete moved home to southern Queensland and he and his family became the stable force in Aggie's life for the next couple of years. They extended their hand of friendship to her sister, Sarah, as well, enabling the pair to enjoy a semblance of family. Having had no real home life or parental control since her mother's second marriage breakdown, she appreciated the caring adults who kept an eye on her and Sarah. Despite that, she still never really felt the presence of a responsible adult to pull her up and ask her what she thought she was doing.

She returned to university and managed to get through her first year. In fact, she did so well, she was awarded with a Dean's commendation at the end of the year. She spent the long summer holidays working in the cotton fields with Pete's farming family and went into her second year of study ready to work. As the year wore on, though, Aggie began to unravel around the edges and her relationship with Pete started to deteriorate. She was crying a lot and simply not managing well. Pete recognised that she had problems and that she was drinking way too much, and encouraged her to get help. However, she couldn't deal with the issues he was drawing attention to and, in the end, she told him to go away. He went back up north to work. They got back together for a while but Aggie says it was a disaster and that afterwards it was over for good. Reminiscing, she says that Pete tried very hard to help her and their relationship was the one good thing in her life at the time, but she just wasn't ready to admit that she was in trouble.

Later in second year she started failing subjects. Sometimes she didn't even go to lectures, although she says her friends were pretty responsible and would drag her along. She was working several jobs to help support herself, as well as studying. Her father had said he would pay her college fees but he never did and, while her very supportive college warden helped her get a scholarship, she still had a big college debt. She planned to move out at the end of second year and study externally.

Having just made that decision, Aggie then discovered an accelerated nursing course at Charles Darwin University in the Northern Territory, and decided to switch over. The course was two years and she felt it would help her when she was eventually accepted into medicine. Certain that she would be better if she moved back to the Kimberley, she applied for a job at Carlton Hill but then, over the summer holidays, changed her mind yet again and decided to go to Sydney. Then news came that an old friend was tragically killed in an accident in the Territory. After his funeral back in south-west Queensland, she decided to head north after all.

The bush had always been the most healing place for Aggie. She applied for and got a job governessing at Legune, a station up near

Joseph Bonaparte Gulf in the Northern Territory. She loved the kids but hated teaching and found the station very lonely. With her emotional wheels increasingly wobbly, after a few months she left and got a job at the Timber Creek Hotel on the Victoria Highway in the Territory, about halfway between Katherine and Kununurra.

By then Aggie was feeling her life was out of control. Years of trying to cope with the scattered remnants of her family life, of being the grown-up in her family, of being abused by someone she had trusted, of trying to keep everything together, all finally caught up with her.

'In hindsight,' she muses, 'I think having an adult taking responsibility for me would have helped. Maybe there were adults who had been trying, but I had been so independent from such a young age that maybe I wasn't receptive to help. Independent teenagers are often hard to help. You can't control them but you've got to try and guide them. In 2003, at uni, there were people I'd been involved with socially who were very supportive and kept an eye on me between them, but then, when I went up north, I didn't seem to have that. I knew some people up there but when I was drunk and crying at the pub, not one of them came up and asked, "Hey, Aggs, are you all right?" It took a long time to find a bit of kindness.'

She felt quite powerless to stop the roller-coaster her life had become and she'd regularly go into Kununurra and write herself off with alcohol. Desperate to be saved, she had several 'relationships' while searching for someone to love her. Looking back she says, 'I felt so worthless. This time, crying throughout, I allowed myself to be abused because I had no sense that I was worth anything better.'

She spent those days feeling as though she was almost detached from her own body, unable to get a grip on anything. Finally, one weekend in July, she and Sarah went to the Katherine Show and

Aggie reached the absolute low point of her existence. She completely wrote herself off, missed a shift at the pub and experienced horror coming off the grog afterwards.

A few days later she and Sarah went into Kununurra for their days off and wandering around town she came across the Anglicare counselling service. Timing is everything and on the spur of the moment she wandered in and asked if there was anyone she could talk to.

It was the beginning of her recovery.

She committed to getting help for as long as it would take and while she continued to work at Timber Creek, every week she drove the 200 kilometres in to Kununurra to attend an hour-long counselling session. 'I was in a pretty bad place. I talked to the same counsellor every week for almost two years. It was really tough but it changed everything. Something shifted and it turned everything around for me; that and later moving to Newry Station to work for Rod and Alison McColm,' she says.

Rod and Alison managed Newry, about two-thirds of the way along the road from Timber Creek to Kununurra. Aggie had friends working there and she often overnighted at the station on her way back from the counselling sessions. Towards the end of the year, Alison asked her if she could come and work as camp cook for a few months to finish the cattle mustering season, which runs from about March to November, depending on the wet season. She grasped the opportunity gladly and moved to Newry for the rest of the year.

Having enrolled in the Charles Darwin nursing course earlier in the year as planned, Aggie had failed to do the first semester; she just wrote it off. When she went to Newry she managed to complete the first assignments and passed, juggling study around her job in the camp kitchen. As a result, she went to Darwin for her first prac block. She felt incredibly alone and terrified. She rang her counsellor who told her, 'Get yourself together, Aggie. You can do this. Get through the prac block, then get those last assignments done and get them in.'

At the end of the year, however, she remembers the lecturer saying to her, 'Listen kiddo, whatever you're doing, stop, give up, you can't do it.' Aggie was horrified but walking away was never an option. She knew she could do it. She knew she could study. She knew she was smart. She also knew she was distracted by the issues she was dealing with.

Looking back, she says, 'When you're stressed, when you have all this stuff going on in your life, you can't function properly. I was not functional and that year I sometimes felt so judged by people because, when you're mentally unstable, you're acting out and you don't have control and your stuff is owning you.' At the time, her self-esteem was shattered but, although it sometimes all seemed a bit hopeless, she knew if she just kept slogging away, she could do it.

Aggie stayed enrolled and Alison and Rod asked her to come back for the following season as station cook feeding fourteen to twenty-two people at any given meal in at the homestead complex and, when needed, eight out in the stock camp. The McColms' backing and encouragement were integral to Aggie's success. They gave her the adult supervision and support she'd been missing, the kindness she'd been wishing for and the flexibility to meet her course needs. She had to be very, very organised but she managed it by planning ahead. 'The Newry stock camp usually works from home base each day instead of camping out like a lot of other stations do, so most of my job was in the kitchen at the homestead complex,' she explains. 'That made it a bit easier to manage but I couldn't have done it without the support of Alison and Rod.'

She'd get up early, organise breakfast and pack the smokos and lunches to go out for the day. Once she'd cleaned up, she'd have time to study until she organised dinner later in the day. When the stock camp did camp away from the homestead complex, she'd go with them, pitching in if they needed her to get on a horse and muster but otherwise managing her study between preparing meals. Powered by a generator, she worked on her laptop, steadily finishing her coursework. 'I don't think I failed another assignment after that,' she says.

It did, however, take her another three years to complete the course. In her third year she did every muster in the first round, as well as cooking, meaning that she cooked breakfast, organised smokos and lunches, then jumped on a horse and went mustering before coming back to organise dinner later in the day.

Over the three years, Aggie planned her prac blocks to fit in with the mustering rounds, opting to do the pracs during the wet season. Her first was at the Kununurra Hospital. 'I did three to four weeks' general ward nursing and loved it all!' she says. 'I remember a little girl about fifteen years old came in to have her baby. Her boyfriend brought her in sitting on the handlebars of his bicycle. She was about 7 centimetres dilated at the time. I got to assist with that birth, which was just great; it was such a breeze for her and great to be a part of her delivery. The staff really looked after me so well, as it was my first time in a hospital. They were just fabulous and made sure I was a part of things. Everyone was just so fantastic and I fell in love with practical nursing.'

On another placement she got to work with Sister Lex at Kalumburu, an isolated Aboriginal community up on the coast at the very north of the Kimberley. 'I learnt more there in two weeks than I did everywhere else,' she says.

138

Finally, in 2007, Aggie graduated from Charles Darwin with good grades and put in an application to register as a nurse in Western Australia. For her graduate year she applied to work at the Kununurra Hospital, where she was rotated, as is the rule, through the general ward, aged care, paediatrics, casualty and theatre. Because mental health wasn't included in the usual rotations and because it was her specific area of interest, she requested a prac block with the mental health unit. Acknowledging Aggie's commitment, the professional development nurse organised for her to do it.

When she finished the year and with her life apparently back on track, Aggie took off overseas for some months. Because she has a British passport, thanks to her father, she tried to organise her nursing registration in England, but somehow the stars just didn't line up and, while she did a bit of assistant nursing over there, eventually she came home and returned to the Kimberley. She worked short contracts in Halls Creek, Derby and Broome while she refilled her financial coffers.

Prior to leaving for Europe, Aggie had enrolled in a counselling course. Though she didn't make much progress while she was away, she knew it was the direction she wanted to take. News that Sarah was getting married took her back to Queensland, where she joined a nursing agency. Having one last weekend of fun before heading off to a job at Bamaga, she went to the Roma Races in south-west Queensland. There she met Emile Seiler, an engineer based in Charleville who was working for the Great Artesian Basin Sustainability Initiative. They hit it off straight away and at the end of the weekend he asked her for her phone number, but she said, 'Don't bother, I'm off to Bamaga.' However, bother he did, and they kept in touch, building the first tenuous links in their relationship over the phone. When she came back down for Sarah's wedding she took a few extra days to go to Charleville and see Emile.

She arrived to see him in February 2010, just hours ahead of one of Charleville's worst floods. With the town devastated yet again by floodwater, the serious cases from the hospital and nursing home were evacuated to Brisbane, while everyone else was sent up to the local showgrounds to be billeted in the pavilions. Being a Queensland summer, it was also very hot. 'You could see the oldies just suffering in the heat. As a trained nurse, I volunteered to help out and Queensland Health put me on their casual books,' says Aggie.

Aggie decided to stay in Charleville and continued to work casually at the hospital once everything got back to normal. However, she refused to be tied to a contract as her goal was to work with young people. She worked as a clinic nurse for a while with the Charleville and Western Areas Aboriginal and Torres Strait Islander Community Health.

In the meantime, she heard about a rural family counsellor position at Lifeline in Charleville. 'I was plodding away with my study and this opportunity came up. It was not a nursing thing at all. I spent twenty months driving around, visiting people all over south-west Queensland. I loved it. However, I didn't want to lose my nursing skills so I had to rethink my pathway.'

By then, she and Emile were living together and, early in 2012, while Aggie was still doing fulltime graduate studies in mental health nursing and working fulltime for Lifeline, Emile took over running their home. 'He was so supportive. I just worked and studied and he did the rest!'

A few months later, she arranged to do a prac up in Broome for five weeks with the Adult Mental Health team. It was exactly the kind of professional break she'd been looking for. While she was there, she got to go out with the CAMHs team. Because of that, when a vacancy came up for someone to take over the child and adolescent mental health role in Kununurra, they contacted her and asked her to apply. Reflecting on the turns her life has recently taken, she says, 'The counselling work with Lifeline was just enough to get my foot in the door professionally. After that, things just started falling into place.'

Leaving Emile behind in Charleville, Aggie moved back up to Kununurra in late 2012 to start the job, which has proved to be everything she hoped for. 'The most challenging thing about working with the kids with CAMHs is staying professional about it,' she says. 'Even while, on some level, you might be wishing you could take them home and look after them, you have to develop a high level of emotional awareness and responsibility. Reflective supervision is integral to maintaining that awareness of the boundaries. That's where I've found nursing helps because, as a nurse, you're trained to acknowledge boundaries; you have to step away and hand over at the end of a shift.'

The work of CAMHs can only progress when the families want to commit to the process. The team's job is to provide opportunities for them and to walk along beside them and guide them to change things for themselves. 'There has to be a decision to change and, of course, with kids, the decisions are made by their parents or guardians. We can teach the kids some skills but they're locked into this bigger family system that's not always supportive of them,' she says.

A lot of things have changed in the north, even since Aggie was there last. She was working in Halls Creek a few years ago when the grog laws changed. 'Back then, for instance, there was a sea of green cans all over the place. Now there are hardly any. Now there are services to support people recovering from chronic alcoholism. It's all still complex though and there are no easy answers,' she says.

While she's never felt unsafe living in Kununurra, she says there is a slight feeling of intensity in the atmosphere that wasn't there a few years ago. There are still challenges and complexities bubbling away there that haven't been resolved. 'You just need to use your common sense about where you go and what you do.'

Aggie's father came back to Australia when she was twenty-two and over the years they have worked at building a relationship. 'It is what it is,' she says with a shrug. When she returned to Kununurra, she asked him for a list of all the Aboriginal stockmen who ever worked for him on stations in the Kimberley in the past, so she can talk about them with the old people. It's helped her establish some links with them and the local history and, in turn, bolstered her credibility. 'It's a challenge being a white government worker in what is, predominantly, an Indigenous program. We're called *kartiya*. History dictates fear and suspicion [towards whites] but I'm slowly building meaningful relationships.'

The young people are not so easy to connect with and, while some are willing to engage, others are distrustful. Referrals come from schools or other agencies, but CAMHs workers still have to have parent permission to intervene. 'Some parents are looking for help while others will say, "Yeah, righto", but the commitment is not there,' she says. 'For those kids, often, nothing really changes. But there are success stories. One mother asked for help and her son, who was smoking gunja all the time and seemed completely hopeless, joined a program where they go out and learn station work. He loved it and now he's on track. Another man was a chronic alcoholic until his wife died. He is now clean and looking after their two sons. He is reflective and engaged in talking about the family's grief and the issues facing his sons. There are great outcomes that make the CAMHs team feel their support work is definitely worthwhile.'

LOST AND FOUND

*

While Aggie admits to being a dreamer with an overdeveloped sense of social justice, her own experience has made her realistic and pragmatic about her own contribution. 'You can only walk beside other people and offer them guidance. They have to want to change things,' she says. She loves to learn and study but she no longer wants to do medicine. One of the positives of her erratic pathway was falling into nursing. She absolutely loves it and she loves helping young people. She is doing her Master of Mental Health at the same time as she builds her experience in the field. She'd like to finish it by the end of the year, but, she says, 'You never know what life will bring.'

'Mental health is not scary, but it still confronts most people. I've been on the receiving end of gossip and judgment in the past when I just wanted someone to give me a lifeline. People with mental health illnesses are just people suffering and I want to help them, particularly younger ones. My ultimate dream is to have a place in the bush where people could come and feel safe and supported while they learn the skills and strategies to help get themselves back on track,' she says.

While her job with CAMHs is considered a nursing role, she doesn't actually undertake any clinical nursing, so she'll try and organise a couple of weeks' prac experience during the year to keep her skills updated. Her mother, grandmother and aunt were all nurses and it's a tradition she's proud of. 'There are so many pathways in nursing. That's one of the beauties of it; there are so many choices.' While she was working at Derby Hospital a few years ago, her grandfather wrote to her telling her how proud he was of her decision to nurse and for doing good work for people who needed it. It was an endorsement she values more than most.

Early in 2013, Emile asked her to marry him. He also moved to Kununurra so she can follow her dream. His family are farmers in Queensland and she knows there may come a time when he wants to go home to the family farm, but for the time being he knew this was an opportunity she couldn't miss. Surrounded by a small group of their nearest and dearest family and friends, they committed to each other on the banks of the Ord River in late 2013.

These days Aggie Harpham is at peace in her own skin. She feels confident and secure. While she says she owes her nursing qualifications and her recovery and stability to Alison and Rod McColm, she still did the hard yards herself. She made the decisions and did the work that transformed her life. Now she'd like to support others to give them that same opportunity.

9

BEYOND THE BLACK STUMP

Maureen Ker, OAM, *White Cliffs, New South Wales*

Many years ago, Maureen Ker, a registered nurse and midwife, had not long opened up for Saturday-morning clinic at the White Cliffs Health Clinic, in far north-west New South Wales, when she heard a commotion at the front door. A handful of the local yahoos, still half plastered from a very long Friday night in the pub, were helping their mate Mick negotiate the doorway.

'Quick, Sssister. Mick's been bitten by a sssnake!' one of them drunkenly slurred.

'Oh?' Maureen questioned very calmly and took hold of Mick's hand to have a look. Sure enough there were two distinct fang marks on the tip of his finger. While his mates cracked snake jokes and giggled among themselves, she quickly sat him down, immobilised the arm from shoulder to fingertip with a splint and bandages, then rang the on-call doctor at the Royal Flying Doctor Service (RFDS) base in Broken Hill.

After she explained the situation, the doctor asked her if they had the snake.

'Have you got the snake?' Maureen asked the group.

'No, Ssister, but we'll go and get it,' one replied.

And they all staggered out the door, including Mick.

While telling the doctor that they'd gone to get the snake, Maureen decided not to tell him that the patient had gone too! She remembers thinking, *Oh my God, I hope he doesn't drop dead while he's gone*. Ten minutes later they rushed back in the door, gleefully, if groggily, telling Maureen, 'We goddit! It was in Mick's suitcase.'

Grinning from ear to ear, Mick stepped right up to Maureen, plunged his hand into the hat he had balanced on his upturned, bandaged hand, and triumphantly held up the very small but live and wriggly brown snake. She carefully backed away and watched its bobbing head, thinking, *Oh my God, it's going to bite him again and then he's going to drop it on me*. She sternly said to Mick, 'You'll have to take it to Broken Hill with you and you can't take it alive! You'll have to kill it.'

'I can't kill the poor thing,' said Mick, holding it at arm's length. But he took it out and bashed it on the head while Maureen called the doctor with an update. All snakebites were routinely flown out, and despite Mick arguing that he'd been bitten eight times before and only needed antivenin once and therefore didn't need to go, Maureen got him loaded on a plane and away to Broken Hill.

Recalling the incident with a shudder, she laughs and says, 'I was so sure he was going to get bitten again and drop that snake right on me. There are a few unusual people out here!'

Despite her seventy-three years of life, Maureen Ker looks much younger, and despite her initial reaction to the snake, she is actually unflappable. She doesn't 'do' panic or fear and she looks as though she knows exactly what to do in any given situation; a perfect demeanour for a nurse. In addition, she has a delicious sense of humour.

Seeing the funny side of most things is the strength that has supported Maureen through more than fifty years of nursing, thirty-eight of them in White Cliffs, well beyond the proverbial black stump. Juggling her job with supporting her husband on their remote sheep station, raising three children, fundraising for charity and attending to almost every crisis that happens in the community, Maureen embodies the spirit of the quintessential bush nurse.

Born in 1940, Maureen grew up on a farm around Albany in southern Western Australia. She trained at the Mount Hospital in Perth and then moved across the country to undertake her midwifery training at Royal North Shore in Sydney. Fully qualified, she returned to the north of Western Australia and worked as relief staff around the Pilbara. She was relieving at the hospital at Roebourne, just south of Karratha, when she had the opportunity to work with the RFDS on a couple of clinic runs, providing the Salk vaccine, which was formerly used to prevent polio, to the children of the region. It was her first taste of working with the RFDS and she liked the experience.

Drawn back to the east coast, she worked for a nursing agency in Sydney for a while, filling in as a relief nurse at whichever hospital or nursing facility the company directed her to each day. While she didn't mind working in the city, ultimately she was exposed to one germ too many and got very sick with the flu. Deciding she needed to get out of town, she asked the agency to send her as far from Sydney as she could be without leaving the state.

They sent her to Wilcannia, 950 kilometres to the north-west.

While many might consider a posting to such a far-flung location a punishment, Maureen loved the town. 'When I went to Wilcannia in the mid '60s it was such a beautiful place; it was quite a thriving little town,' she says. 'There was a large community of Barkindji people living there, some of whom worked on the stations and some of whom worked at fruit picking and other seasonal work.'

The only challenge, as she saw it, was that some of the Aboriginal babies suffered from dehydration in the summer and died. 'However, just after I arrived, the Sisters of Mercy came to town and established a mission. They started a program providing all the young mothers with glucose water for their babies and more of them survived. It was a wonderful thing.'

Back then, as it does now, the RFDS flew to Wilcannia to operate clinics three days a week. There was a full-scale hospital with maternity rooms, wards for children and the elderly, and a medical ward. 'We did deliver babies when we were sure they were going to be trouble-free, but all first deliveries and any out of the ordinary went to Broken Hill or to wherever the mother had family to stay with.'

The matron and five registered nurses, including Maureen, did all the nursing work, while ward maids did domestic and kitchen duties. 'We had an ambulance, which was just a 4WD Toyota utility with a canvas cover over the back,' she says. 'We rarely got called out of town though because, back then, the roads were so bad there was very little traffic, so road accidents were pretty rare.' However, sometimes Maureen flew out to the stations with the flying doctor to bring patients in to the Wilcannia Hospital or occasionally she flew with them to Broken Hill when a patient needed to be transferred

148

there because there were no flight nurses with them then.

They did have regular call-outs to the Aboriginal camp, where people would silently point them to wherever the prospective patient was. Negotiating the way in and out of the camps was not without hazard. Early one morning, when Maureen was in charge and on call because the matron was away, she had just settled into bed after spending half the night delivering a baby when she was called out to go down to the camp. She thought it was a joke, but got up anyway, threw an overcoat over her pyjamas and drove to the camp. 'People pointed me along the river to a little house and there was a young, very pregnant woman lying on a bench, already in labour. It was still half dark. I said to her, "Come on, get up, we've got to get you down to the hospital. You can't have your baby here." She got up and walked out, and as I walked behind her my foot went through a hole in the floorboards. They'd pulled up the floorboards to use for firewood.'

Laughing, she says, 'I can remember thinking, *That's all I need. No sleep, another baby to deliver and now a broken leg*. Luckily I could always see the funny side of things.'

Although the nurses all worked long hours, they took advantage of an excellent social life around Wilcannia. 'There were always parties and sporting events happening,' says Maureen. One night, at a wedding anniversary party, she met a young man named Bruce Ker. A grazier who lived on Tarella Station, about 75 kilometres up the White Cliffs road, Bruce had come home when he was just nineteen years old to help run the family property. Bruce and Maureen were just friends for quite a long while. 'He used to come in every weekend to play cricket but I was usually at work, and when I got time off, I went waterskiing. It was much more fun than boring old cricket!' Eventually, however, their romance blossomed and, in

November 1966, when Maureen was twenty-six, they were married in the garden at Tarella.

Swapping her nurse's veil for a broad-brimmed hat, Maureen gave up nursing and settled with Bruce at Tarella, where she became a jack-of-all-trades, helping with various work on the station. Meanwhile, throughout the late '60s, drought strangled the life out of most of the eastern states, and life around Wilcannia and White Cliffs reflected the hardship endured across the country. At Tarella, they had sold off most of their sheep before the drought worsened. The thing Maureen remembers most clearly is the enormous dust storms and the thick bulldust on the road to town.

In Wilcannia, the shire council decided to establish a program of relief work for anyone who needed it. Along with the local Barkindji people, Maureen remembers a lot of Aborigines from other areas being drawn to Wilcannia by the offer of work. When the drought broke and things picked up, many of them stayed.

In 1968, Bruce won a land ballot for country resumed from a very large sheep station in the Quilpie area of south-west Queensland. The Kers moved up to Quilpie and set about meeting the strict development requirements of the ballot. In 1972, their daughter, Sarah, was born without fuss.

When Bruce's father died in 1973, leaving Tarella to him and his brother, Colin, he and Maureen decided to sell up in Queensland and return to White Cliffs where they bought Colin out and settled down to run the family business. Although she had relieved at the Quilpie Hospital for a couple of months during the years she was away, Maureen hadn't officially nursed for some time when she was asked, in 1974, if she would relieve at the White Cliffs Health Clinic. Given she had always loved nursing, she decided to accept the offer and spent a week at the Wilcannia Hospital refreshing her skills. A week before Maureen was to commence the six-week relief block, the previous nurse announced she wouldn't be coming back.

The policy in those days was to employ any qualified local woman on the grounds that they were less likely to leave, so Maureen was offered a fulltime job. Unsure about a long-term commitment because she had a toddler, she agreed to trial it for twelve months.

When Maureen first went back to nursing, part of the reason she accepted was because she had hurt her back waterskiing one weekend down at Wilcannia. She couldn't do any heavy-lifting work, which meant she couldn't help Bruce on Tarella, so she figured if she could make enough money nursing to pay a man to work for them and still have a little left over, it would be a worthwhile exercise. She found she could and she enjoyed the return to nursing. It was an arrangement that suited everyone in the district.

The clinic at White Cliffs operated out of a house and included a room for the surgery at one end of the front verandah and a hospital room at the other end. Over the years, the nurses spent plenty of time running between the two rooms. Maureen was able to keep her daughter, Sarah, with her at the house while she ran the clinic – although on doctor's days she organised someone to care for Sarah if Bruce was unable to keep her at home. Initially she was expected to stay in town fulltime, but since she only lived 20 kilometres out of town, she asked to be allowed to go home at night. Her employer agreed on the proviso that she still be on call. The authorities were reluctant to agree to this until the Nurses Union backed Maureen and declared that if she was to live at the clinic on twenty-four-hour call, she should be paid accordingly. 'That fixed it. They let me go home at night,' she says.

A doctor from the RFDS flew in to White Cliffs once a month to provide a medical clinic, although the town wasn't as big then as it is now. 'Back when I first worked there, there were more families on the properties but less in town,' she says. As the clinic got busier, the flying doctor service came every two weeks. In the modern White Cliffs, there is an RFDS clinic every week.

Comfortably settling in to the routine of five days a week in town, in 1976, Maureen organised a relief nurse for six months while she took maternity leave and gave birth to her son, Jack. Returning to the fray, she kept both her children with her at the clinic house until Sarah started school.

Although the White Cliffs district was connected to a manual telephone exchange that closed from 10 p.m. until 7 a.m., the telephonist always left Tarella, the pub, the hospital and the town phone box switched directly through to Wilcannia overnight. Consequently, if anyone needed Maureen, she was always accessible. 'If it rained or if someone was very sick, I always stayed up at the clinic.'

One such occasion was after she had retrieved a man from the bottom of a mine shaft. He had been standing near the top of it when he blacked out and fell about 6 metres to the bottom. No one knew he was there until his dog started barking at the top of the mine late in the afternoon. By then the man was conscious but unable to climb the ladder beside him. Alerted by the dog, his neighbours called Maureen. Taking the hospital bag and a stretcher, a very light bamboo construction specially designed for use in spaces with limited access, she climbed down the ladder to assess his situation. 'He kept saying, "Thank God you're here," ' Maureen remembers.

He'd hurt his hip, so she secured him as well as she could and then, with the help of another miner, managed to pull him up onto the stretcher and get him winched up. While she wasn't at all claustrophobic, she was a little rattled when a rock was accidentally knocked down from above. It landed in her medical bag but might just as easily have fallen on her head. It made her realise just how badly they needed a trained rescue team in the town.

Consequently, she applied to go on a two-week rescue course in Mount Macedon. Leaving Sarah with a friend and Jack at home with Bruce, she arranged to do the course on her own time because the Wilcannia Hospital Board, which overarched White Cliffs Clinic, didn't approve of her going. She was encouraged by the local SES coordinator though and also by the Health Department.

Maureen and a young lady from Victoria were the first women in Australia to undertake the course, which focused on major disaster rescue. She learnt how to manage rescues from burning buildings, collapsed bridges, derailed trains, gas explosions, mine shafts and major accident sites, without further endangering life.

While she found the course physically strenuous and the hours long as they worked all day and then returned to the classroom at night for a couple of hours, she did enjoy the experience. Laughing at the memory, she says the men were all lovely and on the weekend, in the middle of the course, they taught her how to sing lots of football songs.

Returning to White Cliffs, Maureen formed a mine rescue team. One of the mines at Broken Hill sent them some ropes, slings and a stretcher, and one of their staff came up to teach them all how to use that specific equipment. Maureen organised practice days three times a year and encouraged all the miners to participate because, 'When there's an accident, it'll be the bloke in the mine next to you who'll be there first to help you.' Maureen's team continued providing this vital service until the SES established their own teams some years later.

Acknowledging that six months hadn't really been long enough when she had Jack, in 1980 she took another twelve months off to have her next child, Callum.

Planning to go to Adelaide to give birth, Maureen was shocked when she went into labour early. On a hot March night, the very night before she was due to leave for South Australia, she and the children were sleeping on the living room floor, under their only air conditioner. She woke in the night to a twinge of pain and the idea that she might have a urinary tract infection. She went to wake Bruce and just as she pulled the light switch cord, her waters broke.

While Bruce rapidly got the older children organised and into the car, Maureen tried without success to ring the nurse at the clinic. Finally she rang the publican and asked him to go and warn the nurse that she was on her way into town. The nurse and the publican met Maureen on the road, but she was in a hurry and didn't bother to switch vehicles. Callum arrived just as she staggered in the clinic door. They tried to wake the Wilcannia exchange to put them through to the hospital to get help but couldn't raise them either, so the nurse went and woke the local telephone exchange lady, Anne, who lived at the post office next door to the clinic. It was Anne who managed to help with an emergency alarm. Just to add to the excitement, Anne then came to see if she could help. 'Here, you can hold the baby,' the nurse said, but when she saw the blood where Maureen was lying on the floor, she went pale and became faint, and had to be directed onto the verandah to sit with her head between her knees. Ultimately, Maureen and Callum were retrieved by the RFDS and flown out to Broken Hill, where Callum spent his first few days in a humidicrib. Thirty-plus years later, he's a happy, healthy engineer.

With the boot on the other foot for once, Maureen says it spurred her to encourage all her antenatal patients to leave the district for elsewhere at least three weeks before their deliveries. 'Whether they were going to Broken Hill, Adelaide or Sydney, I would tell them to plan well in advance and get out of town in good time.'

When Maureen returned to work, the clinic continued to open from nine to five on Tuesday through to Saturday. The children went in with her every day, Sarah to school and Jack and Callum to the house part of the clinic. The only drawback was that when she went to town on Mondays specifically to take Sarah, and later her other two, to school, she'd find patients waiting for her. The same thing would happen when she went back in the afternoon to collect them; so basically she worked six days a week. With no timesheets, always being on call and on a salary only, she worked many extra hours for a flat rate of pay. Then there was her other hat. 'It was and is a town without a police station, so any time anything went wrong, they'd call me, even if it wasn't medical!' she says.

For many years, White Cliffs didn't have an ambulance, so Maureen used to take people around in her own car. She was paid 11 cents a kilometre and one of her regular travel jobs was ferrying the RFDS staff to and from the plane on their clinic days or any time they came in to retrieve a patient. She also did home visits, including, at one stage, regular weekly visits to a station about 70 kilometres out of town. 'In the beginning I did everything – the nursing, the gardening, the cleaning,' she recalls.

One of her funniest memories is taking four old fellows down to Wilcannia to see Fred Hollows when one of his mobile eye clinics was in town. One of the old men, another Fred, had been doing the yard work at the pub but was going blind and couldn't do his job. However, social security told him he couldn't have the old-aged pension because he was blind. They didn't tell him that he had applied for the wrong pension. Maureen rang them and gave them a blast upon discovering that he should have been applying for a disability pension. She was taking him down to Fred Hollows to get supporting documentation as well as appropriate treatment. The other three men had varying stages of diminishing eyesight, so she made appointments for them and set off early in the morning to get them to the clinic.

'They were all drinkers and as soon as each of them finished at the clinic they headed off down to the nearest pub or club and settled in,' she recalls. 'When I finished at the clinic with the last one, we went down to pick up the other three and the fun began. I found the first one and by the time I got back to the car, the one I'd brought with me had disappeared. I then went off to find him and the other two. I found those two and brought them back and the second old man had disappeared. So it went. It was hilarious. I spent the whole afternoon rounding them up.'

In 1989 the White Cliffs Clinic finally got its first ambulance. Although it was a reject from a nearby town, Maureen was happy to have it. She took it down to Broken Hill, had a metal floor put in it so they could roll a trolley stretcher into it, and rallied her local community to raise the money to equip it. 'The Health Department maintained the vehicle but White Cliffs is the end of the line, so the community got little assistance from the government.'

They did get some much-needed help though. When a children's charity went through White Cliffs one year, they called in at the school and asked if they could do anything to help. Someone suggested that they go to the clinic. Maureen made up a list hoping they might find something on it they could help them with but, much to her amazement, 'They gave us everything on it and they did it twice. It was well over $30 000 worth of vital equipment.'

Through various endeavours of their own, the White Cliffs community has managed to acquire other much-needed equipment. 'The Lions Club at Cobar holds a bash each year and they have helped us in recent years with a new ECG [electrocardiograph] machine and also supplied us with two electric beds, which they delivered to the clinic. They were second-hand ones but they work perfectly well. That was wonderful, too,' she says.

Settling into her busy routine of running the clinic, attending to the needs of the community and supporting Bruce as and when she could, Maureen says she only recalls a single occasion of being afraid. She was staying in town one night because it had rained. 'A man had a fight with his de facto and went off his head. He took to his car with an axe and then set his caravan alight. Typically, the locals rang me!' Maureen rang the Wilcannia police, but because there were long stretches of water on the road between White Cliffs and Wilcannia, they anticipated taking a long time to arrive. While waiting, Maureen went down to find the man crouching in shrubbery in the school grounds. When the locals heard the police were coming, they all upped and went to the pub, leaving her alone with the man.

Laughing at the memory, she says, 'I was sitting on my own in the schoolyard with this crazy man when someone came back from the pub and suggested I take him over to the hospital. I was just starting to say, "I'm not taking him over there," when out of the grass this deep voice said, "No, she won't want to take me over there. I might be dangerous!"'

Eventually the police turned up, restrained him and moved him

NURSES OF THE OUTBACK

to the hospital. The police camped on the floor and the next morning they took him back to Wilcannia and charged him.

'The thing was, I knew the man but I didn't know that he was capable of doing what he'd done, and therefore I didn't know that he wouldn't do something else,' Maureen says.

In 1994, a young nurse was sexually assaulted and murdered in Walgett, about 450 kilometres east of Wilcannia. While the perpetrators were quickly apprehended and jailed for life, it sent a collective ripple of fear through the region. As a consequence, the powers that be in that region ruled that nurses couldn't be on duty on their own. 'Someone rang me and said I couldn't see another patient until there were two of us working at the clinic at all times,' says Maureen. 'Linda, the cleaner employed at the clinic, was in fact an enrolled nurse (EN). I rang her and offered her a job as security person, which worked well until someone official came to Wilcannia, realised she was qualified and got her employed as an EN. That was even better.' Then they hired a new cleaner. If Maureen was called out and neither was available to accompany her, either the publican or Bruce would always fill in as volunteers.

Maureen says that most of the time, she left work at work. When she went home, she was too busy helping Bruce and bringing up three children to worry too much about what had happened at work. If something happened that she needed to talk through, she would go to Father Peter, a Catholic priest who lived in Wilcannia, who used to visit the White Cliffs community providing Ecumenical Church services. 'He was lovely and if something really awful happened I would go and talk to him and he would just listen. Then I'd be right. Mostly I managed really well on my own though.'

Sometimes, though, the accidents were particularly grim.

Maureen got a phone call from the RFDS one night, asking her

158

to go out to an accident 110 kilometres north-west of White Cliffs. Two men had been severely injured in a helicopter crash and the nearest airstrip was at the Pack Saddle Roadhouse, 100 kilometres south-west of the accident. Seconding the publican, Graham, to drive the ambulance, Maureen travelled as quickly as possible out to the station. The clinic's enrolled nurse, Belinda, travelled behind them in a second vehicle from the SES, driven by her husband. 'Someone had gone through and left all the gates open for us so we didn't have to stop, though we did have to keep a sharp eye out for cattle on the road,' Maureen recalls.

The helicopter had crashed late in the afternoon when the pilot, flying low on his way home to land, lost sight of the skyline, became disoriented and came down in heavily timbered country not far from his homestead. He was talking to people on the ground via radio when he crashed and they had seen the chopper bounce and the subsequent fire. By the time Maureen got there, the station people had cleared a road into the site and set up a generator for light. When the chopper bounced on impact, the pilot was apparently thrown out but his passenger managed to drag himself away from the aircraft before it exploded. While both were conscious when the first people reached them, the pilot died soon after.

'We arrived not that far ahead of the RFDS, who'd been brought across from Pack Saddle. It was horrific. I can remember being able to step over the ashen remains of the helicopter. Somehow the passenger had dragged himself out with two very badly smashed legs before it caught fire. He was conscious and as I got an IV line into him, he said he was about five on a pain scale of one to ten, but it must have been much worse than that. He had some burns on his face.'

The RFDS team established intensive care status, intubated

him and sedated him, before pulling his legs carefully together and splinting them to immobilise them. 'They were so badly smashed it was thought he might lose them both. It was so awful that, in a situation like that, it's easy for people to get flustered in the urgency of it all but you have to stay calm. It helped that the RFDS doctor and flight nurse were wonderful . . . so efficient.'

Loading him in the ambulance, the RFDS doctor and flight nurse monitored him in the back while Graham drove and Maureen sat up front. They took the patient, as quickly as possible, back to the plane at Pack Saddle while Belinda and her husband followed in the SES vehicle. They got back to White Cliffs at about 7 a.m. in the morning.

'The man did lose one leg but they saved the other,' Maureen says. 'When he recovered he came back to thank everyone. I didn't know him or his family well, but I knew who they were. It's always a little bit harder when you know them.'

For many years, as a lone nurse, Maureen's arrangement had always been to let the RFDS know if she wasn't going to be there. She'd long since organised for an RFDS medical kit to be located at the pub so that if she wasn't available, people could ring the RFDS and access medications. If she was going to be away, she'd leave the keys for the ambulance at the pub in case anyone needed it.

One day, a few years ago, there was a big accident out of town with a lot of kids involved. Maureen was away for the day at a funeral in Broken Hill. She had advised the RFDS of her plans and left the keys for the ambulance at the pub. On her way home from Broken Hill, someone rang her and asked where the keys were. She said she'd left them at the pub but apparently they couldn't find them and the owner was also away at the funeral. A nurse who worked in Wilcannia was up there on her days off and when they eventually located the keys, she went out to the accident.

In the tragic circumstances, given that a death had occurred, the response time was called into question. In the review that followed, it was ruled that someone had to be on call 24/7 in the community. The nurses' union got involved and said Maureen couldn't be on call around the clock for fifty-two weeks of the year and that she had to have every second weekend off. Wilcannia Hospital was duly instructed to send someone to relieve her every fortnight. 'It worked well for about six weeks and then they said they couldn't find anyone to relieve me. Although I was able to organise relief occasionally, it came at the expense of my rostered days off.'

In 2011, at the age of seventy-one, Maureen finally decided to call it a day and handed in her resignation. 'It was time and I got sick of being on call. I just decided I'd worked long enough,' she says.

While she was initially only going to run the White Cliffs Health Clinic for twelve months, Maureen ended up doing it for the larger part of thirty-eight years. She was registered as a nurse practitioner (NP) in 2005, at about the same time as a new clinic was built. White Cliffs is now designated as an NP appointment. They have a constant rotation of relievers sent there but no one permanent. 'The town has changed quite a lot and there are many more people living in the town,' Maureen says. 'Mind you, there are far fewer families on the properties, many of which have become national parks. A lot of creative people live in White Cliffs now; it's a bit bohemian, which adds an interesting artistic perspective to the community.'

Retiring from nursing was hard and Maureen admits to missing most parts of the job, although she doesn't miss the unseen urban bureaucrats who make decisions and issue directives from afar without any real understanding of the challenges of remote nursing. 'It was a wonderful job though, and I loved it,' she says. 'I'd love to see someone permanent come there and enjoy it as much as I did.'

In acknowledgment of her enormous contribution to the community, she was nominated for the 2013 Queen's Birthday Honours List and was overwhelmed to receive a Medal of the Order of Australia, which was presented at Government House in Sydney by the Governor of New South Wales, Professor Marie Bashir.

Sitting beside a doctor waiting for their presentation, Maureen says, 'I got a little emotional and felt a pain in my chest. I thought I was going to have a heart attack there and then.' Her sense of humour firmly in tact, she laughs and says, 'At least I was sitting next to the right person!'

10

NURSE ON A MISSION

Karen Schnitzerling, *St Helens, Tasmania*

When Karen Schnitzerling got a phone call from the West Coast District Hospital in Queenstown, Tasmania, at 3.40 a.m. in 2010, she just knew it was going to be trouble. At that hour, it always is.

The nurse on duty said a lady had arrived at the hospital, twenty-seven weeks pregnant with twins and with her waters broken. The babies were on their way. At the time the nurse unit manager had already been called in to help a man with head injuries and the only other midwife was on annual leave. The doctor was already there so Karen, as the director of nursing (DON), checked that the retrieval team had been called, then got her skates on and arrived shortly after.

The young woman had been seeing a private obstetrician and hadn't started coming to the regular midwife clinics, so she'd had no practical preparation for delivery, and the staff had no knowledge of her history. When Karen arrived the woman was in labour, and was 6 to 8 centimetres dilated, and said she had to 'poo'. Karen explained to her that this meant she wanted to push, but that she absolutely could *not* do that because her babies were very tiny and they needed the neonatal intensive care team on hand before she started to deliver. It was an extremely serious situation and Karen knew that if the babies arrived without specialist medical attention and appropriate neonatal life support, their chances of survival were limited. The team had to travel from Hobart and was flying in by helicopter.

By 4.20 a.m. the woman was fully dilated. Karen requested another GP be called in and the other midwife was called back from leave. 'We were going to have premature twins possibly arriving before the retrieval team,' she explains. 'We were going to need at least one doctor to manage the woman and at least one doctor to manage the babies. We needed as many skilled people as possible because, although we did have a humidicrib, we only had one neonatal resuscitation unit.'

Karen remembers the mother was quite calm. 'She kept on saying she wanted to poo and I kept saying, "Don't even think about that. You really don't want to do that." ' Karen talked and talked and talked, reassuring her and encouraging her to ignore her bowels and therefore not push. In consultation with the doctors on the floor, her main concern was having nobody on hand who was qualified to intubate very premature babies.

In Hobart, the retrieval team, including an obstetrician, was about to take off when they registered they only had one humidicrib and had to go back for a second one. While that delayed them, Karen said it was also a blessing because they picked up a neonatologist as well.

By then, every ambulance service in the state knew that the

situation was dire. The Director of Intensive Care for the hospital at Burnie, 170 winding kilometres to the north, and one of their chief paramedics got in a car and drove to Queenstown to see if they could help.

They and the retrieval team arrived all at once at about 8.15 in the morning. Karen was still talking the mother out of pushing, but with the arrival of the neonatologist and obstetrician, who were happy that everything was right to go, they rolled her onto her back and ten minutes later Twin One arrived and was resuscitated. About fifteen minutes later Twin Two arrived and was also resuscitated, and very quickly they were stabilised and flown out to Hobart.

They're now gorgeous and lively twins, but Karen still remembers their difficult delivery and the relief at the good outcome. 'The last thing I'd ever have wanted was premature twins arriving without a doctor qualified to intubate them. We needed the specialists to intubate them,' she says.

The incident illustrates the isolation that faces nurses in remote areas. And on the west coast of Tasmania it can be particularly keenly felt. The road to Queenstown unravels through stark, copper-rich hills, and it's easy to imagine a blanket of thick cloud settling low in the valley, sealing the town off from the rest of the island.

While Tasmania is small and it's a relatively short distance from Hobart to Queenstown, it's a long journey getting there, winding gently through open farming country and then threading through the mighty forests of the Franklin-Gordon Wild Rivers National Park.

Historically, people on the west coast have either been miners, piners (working in the deep forest) or fishermen – although the majority have been employed in mining. The copper, tin, nickel and zinc hills of the region have ensured productivity for around 120 years, and while some of the workers these days are fly-in fly-out

(FIFO), the communities are very resilient and strong, and proud of their heritage.

A century ago, forty-three lives were lost at the Mount Lyell mining and railway company operations outside Queenstown when a pump house more than 200 metres below ground caught on fire. The inferno bellowed out into the maze of tunnels, causing those trapped beyond to perish from fumes and smoke inhalation.

Gas and fumes lingered in the tunnels for months after the tragedy, making the recovery of bodies slow and dangerous work. The last person wasn't recovered and buried until June the following year. The deceased were laid to rest in unmarked graves in the Queenstown cemetery. The impact of the tragedy continues to resonate with the local populace, which still identifies so strongly with mining. No one forgets, and the memories are very personal, even after a hundred years.

Queenstown is near the towns of Rosebery, Zeehan and Strahan. While the effects of the mining disaster were undoubtedly felt throughout the region, until about ten years ago each town stood segregated from the others by more than just the hills between. Historically a blue-collar, union-oriented area, the people were resilient, strong and stoic in the face of adversity, and immensely proud of their origins – not to mention fiercely loyal to their respective football teams. Unsurprisingly, when the Tasmanian government decided in 2003 to merge formerly independent health services along the west coast, they may as well have insisted that local footballers play for rival teams, such was the opposition.

The government consulted local health care providers and all levels of government to review the various services. Among the paper's recommendations were that services be unified, access improved, buildings updated and allied health services expanded.

It was going to take a Herculean effort to implement the recommendations and, just as importantly, get the locals on board with the changes. But if anyone was capable of pulling it off, that person was Karen Schnitzerling. Despite her gentle good looks and sweet smile, Karen is a tactful negotiator with nerves of steel and infinite staying power. She doesn't start anything she can't finish.

The Schnitzerlings originally came out to Australia from Germany in 1890. Several generations later, Karen is a mix of German, English and Irish. Karen and her two brothers and sister grew up mostly at Leyburn on the southern Darling Downs in Queensland. In praise of her German roots, she says that she has always had a strong work ethic. 'All of my family have always been very hard workers. They set such a high standard in work ethic that, when I work, I have to do it the best I can. And, of course, there's always something else to do, another job that needs attending,' she says. Her mother, who is in her early eighties and who is one of the few women in the family who wasn't a nurse, still works for the education department.

While 'pigheaded' as a description seems a little excessive, Karen is certainly determined. She was six months into her nursing training at Toowoomba Base Hospital before she decided she even liked it, but there was no question of her dropping out if she hated it. Her pride wouldn't let her. 'We all lived in the nurses' quarters,' she says, 'and on the first Sunday night we were all in the kitchen and a couple of girls said, "Well, we know that there'll be a large dropout rate so let's work out who's still going to be here in three months, six months, etcetera." They picked me as one of the first ones out. I was so naive I didn't even know what they were talking about. I didn't even know we had to do night duty. I thought you just put the people to bed and then you went home. When we finished three years later, there were only nine out of the original twenty-five of us still in the course, and two years later only a few of us were still nursing.'

By then, Karen was totally hooked. Over the years she's worked her way through a cardiothoracic certificate, midwifery, a Diploma of Applied Science, and her Bachelor and Master of Nursing, all the while working in some of the busiest nursing units in Brisbane. She worked in adult intensive care nursing and then as a charge nurse at the Mater Hospital, where she really began to appreciate some of the finer points of the ethics of her profession. 'The DON [Director of Nursing] and the few nuns who were still there were insistent that the philosophy of the hospital be written into the position descriptions,' she says. 'When we undertook a performance review or when we interviewed staff for new positions, we had to ask the question about how they identified with the philosophy. This wasn't necessarily Catholic principles; it was principles about human rights and how people were treated. I came to realise that it was incredibly powerful. That influence has been profound within my nursing practice.'

While she loved her work in intensive care, Karen had always had a particular interest in the different ways people respond to their circumstances. She grew up in the bush where there weren't any formal health services. There was no community health, not even an ambulance service, but, she says, 'My great-grandmother and grandmother were bush nurses and really resilient and sensible about what you did and how you managed things and I always thought that was such a good thing. I was passionate about critical care, but I kept on thinking how people from the bush would handle some things differently. I wanted to explore that and the health of country people.'

Consequently, in 1995, Karen and her partner, Doug, moved to Wanaaring, a small community about 200 kilometres west of Bourke in north-west New South Wales, where she was the only nurse at the community health centre for three years. Karen and Doug had both been accustomed to testing their endurance – Karen had trekked up Cooper Creek as well as being a skydiver and Doug had represented Australia skydiving and had done a number of base jumps – so being in such an isolated location didn't faze them.

However, in one instance, Karen was starkly reminded how weak links in communication and access can affect medical services. 'On one occasion,' she begins, 'we woke to the phones not working and we had only radio communications. The policeman was out of town so his wife had radioed a message to Dubbo police to advise Telstra that we had no phone connection. Apparently Telstra didn't believe that the whole area west of Bourke could be out so they did nothing about it. Back in Wanaaring, we had no way of knowing that it wasn't being fixed. At the same time, there were high winds, which interfered with the long range radios.'

That night there was a car accident out on the road at about 9 p.m. Three young men were involved and two of them walked 5 kilometres into a station homestead to get help. The station got a short-wave radio message to someone at the post office, who got in touch with Karen at about 11 p.m. She and Doug headed out to the station in the ambulance and found one young man with a chest injury and the other with a back injury. They loaded the patient with the chest injury into the ambulance and proceeded to the accident scene accompanied by a couple of men from the station. They found the third man dead.

Leaving the men from the station to watch over the body so wild pigs didn't get him, Karen got the young man with the chest injury to the clinic and sent Doug and another local to the station to retrieve the man with the back injury.

The policeman's wife had been trying to get some help via radio. At about 2 a.m., she managed to get a radio message through to the Broken Hill police asking them to get the Royal Flying Doctor Service (RFDS) to come with at least one doctor and flight nurse and also to get a message to Bourke police to come asap.

Meanwhile, in the clinic, Karen managed the two casualties. The man with the chest injury appeared to have a pneumothorax (air in the pleural cavity between the lung and the chest wall) and it now appeared that the other patient had both back and head injuries. The RFDS and the Bourke police all arrived around 4 a.m. Karen sent Doug off to meet the plane with instructions for them to bring in appropriate equipment to treat the pneumothorax. The police headed out to the accident site to investigate and organise the retrieval of the body. The RFDS took off with the two injured men at about 6 in the morning.

In the end, the phone system was down for two days and Karen was furious when she found out they had dismissed the report. 'I was so angry with Telstra,' she recalls. 'It's one thing to be isolated; it's quite another to be cut off from the rest of the world because someone didn't believe a report.' The only good thing to come of the incident was that, as a result, a satellite phone was provided for the clinic at Wanaaring.

Karen and Doug moved to Tasmania in 1998 and she worked for the first few years at the St Helens District Hospital as a registered nurse and then as the manager, but in 2003 she was the successful candidate for a job as the acting director of nursing at the West

Coast District Hospital (WCDH) in Queenstown. She'd only been there for a short while and was working on the floor one winter's day when they got a call from Rosebery asking for help. It was snowing steadily and, in those days, the ambulance service operated out of the hospital in Queenstown. Karen was told that two women had turned up at the Rosebery Hospital in labour and they'd heard another woman in labour was also on her way in to Rosebery from Zeehan.

The ambulance at Queenstown was an old 4WD Troop Carrier – aka a troopy – so they loaded it up with all the neonatal gear they could muster and sent it off to Rosebery with two midwives and a driver. The ambo service managed to get hold of the snowplough from Waratah and there was a doctor in Rosebery to assess all the women. Ultimately, with the snowplough clearing the way ahead of them, they managed to get them all out to the much larger hospital at Burnie.

For Karen it illustrated just how remote the west coast could be. 'Contrary to how it might appear, the west coast of Tasmania is *very* remote, and even more so when it's snowing or foggy,' she explains. 'Because of the terrain, the airstrip here at Queenstown is considered quite dangerous. There was a move to close the airport in 2008, but you can't do that in such a remote area because we have to be able to get the RFDS in when we need them. But most pilots wouldn't be prepared to land on it at night.'

With the review of health services on the west coast completed, Karen was appointed as manager and DON. 'When I came on board we started with the first recommendation, which was to bring everything under one umbrella that would be branded Health West,' she recalls. 'Recognising that most people in the community weren't aware of what services were available on the west coast, we held forums around the region and used the media to outline what we were doing.'

A less passionate person might have been daunted by the challenges ahead but, according to her colleague and friend, Maggie Johnson, 'Karen is very capable, extremely courageous and incredibly tenacious. If she has a job to do, she will stick at it until she has achieved her goal. She was always clear with her staff about what she wanted, and that was an efficient and effective rural health service that was sustainable and safe.'

Before the restructuring, there were different services overseen by different bodies in each different town. There was little cohesion, collaboration or cooperation.

Even so, there was a great deal of resistance to the proposed changes, and not only from the community at large. Safe in the traditions of the past, a lot of staff in the different locations and services were threatened by the idea of reform and reacted antagonistically. Luckily, Karen is more inclined to work collaboratively and empower people to make changes, rather than simply dictating what needs to done.

And so it was that Health West began in 2004. Under the state health department the staff are all employed as public servants. The success of Health West is underpinned by an ethos of teamwork. From the beginning Karen established the practice of talking to everyone involved with an issue, inviting their opinions and encouraging their inclusion in the process. Eventually, as staff gained ownership of their transformed services, they took charge of their own futures.

'The changes were really interesting,' Karen says. 'When I became manager I got the management team together and set standing agenda items. When we started, some of those people knew each other but they had no working relationship – they weren't even friends – and sometimes the atmosphere was a bit cold, but I just pressed on. We were going to create an integrated health service for the community's benefit and we were going to make access to it available to all people across the west coast.'

Once that theme was established, Karen suggested to the managers that they could also share staff; when a facility or service was short-staffed they could bring staff across from one of the other communities. It works particularly well with personal care staff, especially in the aged care arena, and isn't just for nursing services. If a cook or cleaner, for instance, is off sick, they can juggle staff across the whole west coast health service. Karen is delighted with the outcome. 'It's broken down the parochialism and it's been lovely to see that these people have become friends.'

As locals became aware of the improved access they had to a broader range of services, most slowly accepted that the changes were positive. The exception was Rosebery, where people totally rejected the proposal that their hospital should be transformed into a health centre. There had been low activity in the hospital and it was deemed that a centre providing primary health care would be more appropriate. However, the community saw the loss of the hospital as a totally negative thing. Rosebery does not have a volunteer ambulance service and many in the town worried about what would happen in an emergency. Initially, in the new centre, the A&E stayed open, but only from 8 a.m. until 6 p.m. That was unpalatable to residents and the staff, who foresaw a loss of access to medical help and a loss of jobs.

Like the Mount Lyell mine outside Queenstown, the Rosebery mine is an important part of the economy and social fabric of Tasmania's north-west coast. It has operated continuously since

1936 and currently has a mine life that extends to 2024. Just like other locals, the miners were by and large strongly against the proposed health care reforms in their community, which presented a further hurdle for Karen and her management team. Karen was even threatened personally and she very nearly pulled the pin – but, in the end, she didn't walk away, because there were other things to do as well as all the community nursing services they were able to initiate there. Eventually the new service opened.

Yvonne Armstrong is the manager of the Rosebery clinic. She has lived in Rosebery for thirty years and her parents originally came from there. Yvonne always knew that the towns in the area were very separate and that no one knew what health services were available in the neighbouring hamlets. 'What's available now has gone far beyond the expectations of people on the west coast,' she says. 'Before the integration there were very few accessible services. People were very sceptical, but Karen was assisted by people with local knowledge. She is a team player and although she had a lot of barriers, because she stayed and stayed, people eventually came around. They were used to people promising things that never happened, whereas Karen delivered. Her strengths are that she knows the direction she wants to go in and can see an achievable result and that she's a meticulous, very structured planner. She had a vision and the knowledge to support it and she's a voice that people respect.'

One of Karen's strengths is her capacity to look at broad issues and broad health needs and devise systems to make them happen. 'I'm a good planner and organiser,' she admits. 'I like to make things happen and I'm good at keeping things on track.' Her friend Maggie agrees, saying, 'She's very good at getting people to do what they need to do to make things happen.'

Clinically, Karen believes in collaborative meetings wherein everyone concerned with a patient – including doctors, allied health workers, hospital staff, local nurses and, in some instances, paramedics – takes a part in deciding their care plan. The idea is to make the care as efficient and relevant as possible. As a consequence, they hold these meetings every week at Queenstown and Rosebery and every fortnight at Zeehan and Strahan. They use video conferencing to link up people and keep travel to a minimum. 'If you have a clear action plan, it is much better for the client,' says Karen. 'They're not mucked around as much.'

She worked from a primary health perspective. 'As health professionals we have a responsibility to identify gaps in health service and access,' she says. 'We do that by keeping really good data.' When she first arrived on the west coast there were no A&E or community nursing registers. Now they document everything and they have a whole pile of information available; for instance, how many chest pains present in a month, how many cases of asthma are treated, how many people in community nursing need palliative care or how many have chronic disease. 'Therefore,' Karen adds, 'we know what needs attention, and how to most efficiently and effectively resource and provide services.'

Karen's strengths rest on the foundations of her childhood growing up in the country. Her family worshipped every second Sunday at St Augustine's, a beautiful little Anglican church at Leyburn, and every other Sunday she went to Sunday school. Her mother played the organ in church and Karen says she developed a sort of missionary zeal until she got into high school and started learning about history. 'By the time I was fourteen I'd become a communist, then a socialist and then an atheist by about the time I was fifteen. I still went to church because one had to, but believing in the resurrection just didn't gel for me, so I've been an atheist ever since,' she says.

Despite that, she does appreciate philosophical teaching. 'Whether that's through the church or some other way, it's important,' she says. 'I do lots of thinking and I do lots of driving, so I like to make that positive thinking time and I don't dwell on unfortunate incidents. If they pop up, then I like to sort out a solution as soon as possible so then I can feel happy about it.'

She is, by nature, a positive person.

When Karen found a lump in March 2009 just below her jaw on the left side of her neck, she assumed that it was connected to a root canal she'd had treated a few months before. As she was taking some long service leave in the following June to go to Vietnam, she had to go to her GP to get her travel immunisations. She mentioned the lump and its suspected cause so he ordered antibiotics for ten days but recommended she return if there was no improvement.

Ten days later he referred her to an ear, nose and throat (ENT) clinic, as, unlike Karen, he was already considering that it might be a tumour. In April an ENT specialist immediately ordered scans, X-rays and a needle biopsy, as he thought it was a secondary tumour and wanted to find the primary. The inconclusive results were back by the end of the month but the biopsy showed up dead tissue in a growth measuring about 6 by 3 centimetres.

Although she never considered it to be anything other than a nuisance, Karen was surprised by the measurement as 'it only felt about 2 by 2 centimetres. At that point I had only told Doug, as well as a close friend at Queenstown and my immediate manager, as I kept thinking that it would all be fine and did not want family and friends to worry,' she says. Doug was in the US on business at the time but due to return in time for the surgical investigation her specialist ordered.

In May, Karen's tonsils were removed and some tissue biopsied at a private hospital in Burnie. She returned to work to hand over to the relief DON who was coming to cover her while she was in Vietnam. At that point she informed her family, friends and staff that she'd had her tonsils removed. Two days later she returned to the ENT specialist who delivered the distressing news that her left tonsil was a squamous cell carcinoma and that the lump was definitely the secondary tumour. He thought no further surgery would be needed but referred her to an oncologist for radiation and chemotherapy.

The oncologist prescribed six weeks of radiation and some chemotherapy, and predicted an eighty per cent chance of survival. Karen cancelled the trip to Vietnam and travelled home to Queensland and then to Adelaide to explain her health issues to her family.

On her return she went to see a dentist for assessment, as radiation is known to have a major impact on teeth. Further investigation by an oral and maxillary surgeon resulted in a recommendation that she have six to seven teeth extracted surgically prior to radiation. Throughout the whole process, that was the most shocking news for Karen. 'I was very upset about this, but Doug convinced me I should do it,' she explains. 'They removed them on our wedding anniversary in June. And then as soon as the suture lines were healed, radiation commenced.'

After radiation she began a course of chemo but didn't finish it as she had a bad reaction and refused the last dose. Although she suffered inflammation and ulceration in the mucous membranes lining her digestive tract and some hair loss, most of the time Karen insisted on driving herself to and fro. The exception was when she reacted badly to the chemo. She had to give in and let Doug drive her to her next appointment. One month after treatment she went back to work and four months later her tastebuds began to kick in again and her ability to swallow was much improved.

Four years on she is still having ENT checks every three to four months and oncology reviews every year. Everyone thinks she's over the hump but she won't be fully cleared until September 2014.

It is a measure of her tenacity that she needed very little help and refused to ever consider anything other than a good outcome. Karen launched herself straight back into a huge workload, including some clinical work. 'Professionally, as the DON, one of the biggest issues has always been recruitment and retention of staff, so I've always maintained my clinical skills,' she says. 'At times I worked on the floor at the Queenstown Hospital and I've covered shifts in Rosebery and Strahan and Zeehan when staff weren't available. I think it's good for staff and people in the community to see I am a real nurse, and I'm happy to do the work. I enjoy nursing and I work from a primary health care perspective, working with the community to improve their options rather than just providing them. I think people need to be responsible for their outcomes.'

There have been consequences to her work commitment and fortitude, though, and in 2010, Doug recognised that her work-life balance was way out of whack and insisted she take notice. She took her postponed long service leave and went home to reconsider her options. While Doug's business keeps him in Launceston and hers in Queenstown, they have always reconnected at home at St Helens. Karen acknowledges that the years of overseeing the transition to a unified health service on the west coast have taken a toll. She is a perfectionist who can't sit down, even on days off.

Ultimately she went back to work, but with a determination to get some proper balance in her life. She discovered a talent for linocuts and took to attending art classes, but before long she was consumed once again by the doings of Health West and had to make a choice about her future. In late 2012 she opted to resign from her role and return to clinical nursing, doing eight-hour shifts, a few days a fortnight.

Maggie Johnson has never had any doubt that Health West would be sustainable and safe even after Karen left. 'We have credibility now, and the initiative will survive because the people of the west coast own it,' she says. 'The community has drawn together in ways that were unimaginable ten years ago. Karen gave us that.'

Since then, Karen has recognised a new frontier to conquer. Having resigned from her job, she put her Queenstown house on the market and orchestrated a move back to St Helens, where she will continue to do some casual clinical work, simply because she loves it. In the meantime, she and Doug have established a new business, Rural and Remote Nursing Solutions, a consultancy service for organisations operating in a health context across outback Australia.

Karen has much to be proud of in her career. Her pivotal role in successfully merging the health services of the west coast of Tasmania is testament to the virtues that underpin her personality: a strong work ethic and an unfailing determination to achieve her goals. Above all this, her ability to listen and empathise with others made her not just a good nurse, but a valued community member as well. It's a combination of attributes that have helped her through her own personal hardships, and will see her through as she follows a new mission in life.

11

FINISHING-UP BUSINESS

Fred Miegel, *Alice Springs, Northern Territory*

On first impressions, Fred Miegel looks like he could be a teacher or an electrical linesman, or maybe even the farmer he would have been if he'd followed his father's footsteps. He certainly doesn't seem like a man who deals with death every day. And yet, when you look into his wise, gentle eyes and see the wealth of compassion and kindness that shines from within, his career choice is not so surprising.

In fact, Fred is the manager of the Central Australian Palliative Care Unit based in Alice Springs, and his days revolve around a theme of supporting people through the process of dying with as much dignity and consideration as possible. The unit supports anyone needing palliative care but most of their clientele is Aboriginal and ninety per cent of their referrals come from the Alice Springs Hospital. Often, for a variety of reasons, it is not possible to return Aboriginal people to their communities to finish up, but sometimes Fred's team does find a way, against the odds, to get someone home to country.

For one such old man, renal failure meant there was no choice but dialysis, since his kidneys could no longer be relied upon. He was wheelchair-bound and suffered an ataxia – a loss of coordination of the muscles – that prohibited movement in his hands. His family came into Alice Springs with him so they could learn how to manage his dialysis at home, instead of him having to live in town where he could access the renal dialysis unit. After a week they said it was too difficult; that they could not and would not do it. So he was further condemned to living in one of the town camps in Alice Springs – where different communities of Aboriginal people live, based on language and kinship groups – hundreds of kilometres from his country.

As the weeks passed, the Tangentyere Council, which provides services for the camps, looked after him. Their palliative care team got involved and they then talked to the Congress Aboriginal medical service. Together they discussed getting him home. The MacDonnell Shire Council said they could organise Home and Community Care funding to pay for someone to care for him at home and the Ngaanyatjarra, Pitjantjatjara and Yankunytjatjara (NPY) Women's Council were on board to help with respite options. Everyone pledged to help if they could just get him back to his community.

However, because of their already heavy workload, the nurses at his home community were reluctant to have him back if his family couldn't help. The nurses' workload was undeniably demanding, but, as Fred Miegel says, 'Sometimes you just have to do what you have to do.' Fred returned from a couple of days off to discover that one of his nurses and his Aboriginal liaison officer were planning to surreptitiously deliver the old man home to his country.

FINISHING-UP BUSINESS

*

Growing up as a farm boy at Temora in the Riverina of New South Wales, Fred went to a little one-teacher school in the district until it was closed at the end of his fifth year. After several years at bigger schools in the town, he finished his final two years at boarding school at Walla Walla, just north of Albury-Wodonga.

Imagining his future as a social worker, he was disappointed not to achieve the required marks, but enrolled in a tertiary course in welfare work. After several months in a classroom with recovering drug and alcohol users, grandmothers, retired teachers and a variety of people with a lot more life skills and knowledge than he, at only nineteen, Fred realised he didn't have the life experience to be a welfare worker.

Unsure of his alternatives, he spent the following year with his sister up in the Pilbara region of Western Australia. He worked as a jackaroo, a wine waiter and a storeman, before moving back to Temora, where he worked as farm labourer.

Before he'd gone to the Pilbara, he'd hedged his bets and applied to train as an enrolled nurse (EN) at the Temora hospital, where his mother was a midwife. She came home one day and told him he had an interview at the hospital if he still wanted to undertake the training. He jumped at it. He reckoned it would be pretty good – twelve months' work with a qualification at the end of it, and he could live in the nurses' home. To his surprise and delight, he found he loved the work.

While Fred was training as an EN, he encountered his first death. 'He was a little old man who'd lived not far from where I lived. We had a lovely nurse educator who talked a couple of us through the process of managing our first experience with death,' he says. After

183

the last rites were administered, they washed the man and shrouded the body. Fred found it was a really lovely event and not at all the traumatic one it might have been. 'When we had finished, we had to walk the body on a trolley down to the morgue. Outside it was a beautiful, balmy spring night with lots of stars in the sky and I found it wasn't scary at all. In fact, it probably set the scene for my future career path.'

As soon as he completed his EN training, Fred applied to do his general nursing training at Royal Adelaide Hospital (RAH). 'New South Wales had gone over to university-based nursing training by then, but RAH still offered hospital training,' he explains. He started in January 1986, met the love of his life, Karen, also a nurse, and graduated early in 1989. Choosing to stay on at RAH for another twelve months, Fred did his graduate year, during which time he and Karen got engaged.

She wanted to go north on her own for a year, so he went to Hobart for the same amount of time, specialising in haematology and oncology. Karen worked in Alice Springs, laying the foundations for their return years later. Fred returned to the oncology unit at RAH and started a six-month course in the field a month before he and Karen were married. After time off for a quick honeymoon, Fred rotated through all the cancer wards: haematology, oncology, radiotherapy and the day procedure centre. At the end of the course he worked in the chemotherapy department. Looking back, he acknowledges he probably always had an underlying passion for palliative care.

In the mid-'90s, there was increasing talk of establishing a palliative care unit in Central Australia. Pivotal in these discussions was a report on the subject by Dr Lyn Sampson – and she, along with Sandra Clyne and a handful of other passionate advocates of palliative support, began the work to make it a reality. It was at this time that the Northern Territory government was working on the Rights of the Terminally Ill Bill – which became an Act in 1995 – and was boosting the palliative care services across the Territory.

Karen and Fred were living in Adelaide at the time but had planned on moving north to Alice Springs. 'We both grew up on farms. Karen comes from the Murray Mallee in South Australia and I grew up in the Riverina. Ultimately, we wanted to get into a regional hospital,' Fred says.

Thanks to Dr Mary Brooksbank, Fred had the opportunity to work as the acting clinical nurse in the palliative care unit at the RAH. During this time, a colleague rang from Darwin and said that they were looking for a palliative care nurse in the Alice and that he should contact Sandra Clyne. Fred wrote her a letter to which she replied positively, telling him to write to Del Hird, who was the manager of Community Health. He wrote to Del and sent her his CV.

Meanwhile, he and Karen moved to Alice Springs. Fred started work in the relief pool at the Alice Springs Hospital, which gave him an opportunity to familiarise himself with the complexities of the clientele. During those first two weeks Del rang and offered him the position with the palliative care unit for three months, adding that they would fly him to Darwin the following week to meet the rest of the team.

Over those first years, Fred says his learning curve was 90 degrees straight up, especially going from being a clinical care nurse in Adelaide to a community-based one in the Alice. 'The euthanasia stuff was a bit all-consuming at the time,' he recalls. Fred had heard about the euthanasia bill being passed while he was still working in Adelaide and realised a lot of people had a range of very different opinions about it. As a practising Christian, he'd never really thought about it himself but, suddenly, in his new job, he had to consider it very carefully. 'It was confronting thinking about dealing with death in that way, about actually killing someone,' he says. When Fred moved to Alice they were still negotiating some of the finer details of the Act.

There were twenty-one steps a person had to go through before they could actually be euthanised and the only doctor prepared to do it was Dr Philip Nitschke. 'Over the period of months before the Act was repealed by the federal government, Dr Nitschke helped four people to be euthanised,' Fred recalls. 'They did it themselves using a computer program that then activated a syringe driver, but he guided them through it. There were lots of steps to the actual process and time to change your mind if you wanted to.'

There were two parts to the legislation that Fred couldn't agree with. One was that the palliative care service had to review the patients, which, he felt, made the care services the rubber stamp for the deaths. 'In the end, we didn't have to deal with it directly down here; the Darwin team copped the brunt of it,' he says. He spent a lot of time talking and listening to his colleagues in Darwin, trying to provide them with as much support as possible.

The second part he didn't agree with was the question, 'Have you talked to your family about this?' that the GP had to ask the patient. It was a yes or no tick box and Fred felt very strongly that, if someone was going to go through with the process, they should have their family on board to do it, rather than just ticking a questionnaire.

Other than that, he says there were lots of checks and balances that were reasonable in the circumstances. His next challenge was deciding how he would deal with somebody asking him to help them through the process. 'In hindsight, I think most people asking about euthanasia are looking for choices rather than thinking of definitely doing it. They're looking for the opportunity to have a conversation about the options, to gather information,' Fred says.

When it came down to it, if it was going to happen in Central Australia, he had to decide as an educator, for the palliative care part of the process, what his role would be. 'I spent a lot of time soul-searching and ultimately decided that I would be comfortable to sit and hold someone's hand, but I wouldn't be comfortable drawing up or administering drugs or doing anything that directly led to someone's demise. I was willing to be a witness but not to play an active part,' he says.

Happily for him, he was never tested. In 1996, the Euthanasia Laws Bill was introduced into federal parliament to overrule the Northern Territory legislation. It was successful in becoming an Act.

In Fred's opinion, a lot of the politics behind the repeal had more to do with the Territory being able to enact their own legislation or not and not so much about the issue of euthanasia itself.

'Either way, the fallout across the Territory was enormous because there was so much misinformation put out by the different interested parties. For a long time, giving injections for palliative care in remote communities became an issue because people were wondering if they were getting a euthanasia injection and the syringe drivers were viewed with great suspicion. The other problem was, every time the media mentioned euthanasia, they linked it to palliative care. So there were lots of mixed messages and it took some years to repair the damage.'

As the dust settled on the new legislation, Fred refocused on establishing the Central Australian Palliative Care Unit in Alice Springs. In March 1996, Dr Lyn Sampson joined Fred for about eight hours a week until her husband, who was the Anglican minister in Alice Springs, was transferred to Kalgoorlie, where he became the Bishop. In 1998, Dr Ofra Fried joined the unit and then, about eighteen months later, a second nurse, Emma Corcoran, joined the team.

Now the staff has grown to include a social worker, a third nurse who is focusing on people in remote areas, a fulltime consultant palliative care specialist, a resident medical officer/GP trainee, a part-time admin officer and an Aboriginal health practitioner position, which he hasn't been able to fill since the last person in the role was offered another job. 'Replacing our Aboriginal health worker is a bit problematic because someone who comes from Central Australia can be caught in the cultural and kinship issues of obligation and the subject of death within their own country,' Fred explains.

'But I've been lucky to have good, passionate staff; they make me look good,' he says. 'I am not a natural manager in the true sense but love working with a good team.'

As manager of the palliative care team, Fred considers them fortunate to have a good staff–client ratio. However, he points out that his area of health work has unique complexities. 'We work with very remote Aboriginal people who are still very strong culturally, and we also work with very urbanised Aborigines. There are a lot of people in between so it's all very complex,' he says.

An Aboriginal translator once told him that you can't talk about death in Aboriginal families unless you talk about it very abstract terms, because, the way they see it, if you're telling someone that they're going to die, you are actually wishing them dead. 'If there's a car crash and someone dies in it, the doctor might say this person died because of a head injury caused by a motor vehicle accident.

The Aboriginal people will say, "But who killed them? Who's responsible?" Long before whitefellas came along, there were sit-down discussions to work out exactly why someone died. It's a very spiritual thing. Very traditional people in the more remote communities would still do this but it is all changing as the culture changes,' he says.

The Palliative Care Unit serves an area of about one million square kilometres down into the Pitjantjatjara lands of South Australia, over into the Yankunytjatjara lands of Western Australia, and up as far as Elliott, 700 kilometres to the north of the Alice. It's a very big area with a population of about 60 000 people. While Fred used to travel out around the communities in the early years promoting the unit, he knows word of mouth is the best advertisement for their services, and he also knows the nurses out in the communities are so busy they don't want to know about anything they don't immediately need. He says supporting them when they do need palliative support is far more valuable than trying to ram information down their throats when they are flat out.

While they will try to return patients home to country to finish up, some of the time, it's not possible. 'People who've been on renal dialysis ten to fifteen years, who've been away from their communities for all that time, when you talk to the community about them coming back to finish up, they say, "They don't belong here anymore" or "That family gone",' he says. 'We've had very important members of the community about whom the community have said, "No, that's too hard for us. We can't manage them dying out here." People generally accept that.' Fred says they prefer for the community to tell patients that decision, which is a hard thing for them to do, but it is their business and hopefully the right person of their kin is there to support them when those decisions are made.

From a practical perspective, it takes at least two people to look after a person who is going to die at home. One can sleep while the other cares and vice versa. Fred says sometimes it's actually a relief for people to be told they can't go home. Some years ago, he looked after a non-Aboriginal woman who had breast cancer. In time she ended up with some brain metastasis and had to go to Adelaide for radiotherapy. Now they go to a new unit in Darwin but the same risks still exist. It's two hours either way by plane and occasionally people don't make it back. 'These are vulnerable and fragile people and sometimes the body can't take the trip,' he says.

This particular lady had told Fred that she wanted to die at home. Before she'd been diagnosed with the brain metastases, she and her husband had made a pact that she could die at home. She went down to Adelaide as planned for radiotherapy and then came back to the hospital in Alice Springs. Her husband was working in a fulltime job and he wanted a timeframe so he could work around the challenges of caring for her. In the meantime, she lost her confidence and began to fear going home, but they had made the pact, so neither of them said anything to each other about their concerns.

Fully aware of their dilemma, Fred advised the specialist of their situation and suggested that he might perhaps tell them that she couldn't go home, that she really needed to stay in. The specialist then spoke with the couple. 'The look of relief on their faces was amazing,' Fred says. 'She spent the next two weeks organising her funeral while he went to work, possibly taking some comfort from the routine. She died in hospital two weeks later, very peacefully. Things do change on the pathway to dying.'

One of the many attractions of his job is the characters he meets, or at least hears about, like some of the single blokes who are out

FINISHING-UP BUSINESS

there running away from someone or something. One fellow, who was pretty itinerant, would travel from place to place, staying until he got into a blue with someone and then had to move on. Fred got a referral from a remote clinic in the Barkly for him one day but then couldn't track him down. About two months later, he turned up at the Alice Springs Hospital and Fred talked him into staying and getting a proper review done as he had been diagnosed with liver cancer. The social worker who was there at the time had known this man and said he had two stories he told consistently. One was that he was a truck driver whose whole family got wiped out by Cyclone Tracy. The second was that he used to fly helicopters in Vietnam. 'It gave credence to why he was so footloose,' Fred comments. They admitted him to hospital, sorted out some pain relief for him and reviewed him. 'One morning the silly beggar went over the road to the servo to get a packet of cigarettes and fell over and broke his hip,' Fred continues. 'Consequently, he had to have a hip replacement and spent a bit of time in hospital.'

A few weeks later, Fred went on holidays and when he came back the man had been transferred to a nursing home in Alice Springs for rehabilitation. Then one day, out of the blue, he was gone. Piecing the story together, Fred heard that the man had been talking to one of the other patients who told him he could leave the nursing home any time he liked. 'He'd been in hospital for a couple of months, so he had a fair few pension cheques saved up. Apparently he caught a bus to town, bought an old car and took off,' Fred says.

Casting a net out across the bush telegraph, they tried to track him down but he'd just disappeared off the radar. About three or four months later, there was much excitement when the patient the man had been speaking with received a postcard from him, sent from a town halfway between Alice Springs and Tennant Creek.

Fred rang the town, only to be told they'd just missed him and that he was heading for Queensland. Still hot on the trail, Fred warned the hospital at a major regional centre in North Queensland and sure enough he eventually turned up there and had to stay put, as his condition had deteriorated.

'He must have rung the publican at the town he had visited in the NT, because next thing, the publican caught a bus to where he was in Queensland and drove him back to stay at his pub,' Fred says. 'He looked after him there and every day they'd set him up on the hotel verandah and he'd keep track of whatever trucks were going by while he drank the odd beer and took his tablets under the publican's watchful eye. They looked after him so well up there.'

Eventually he deteriorated further, but he still didn't want to go back to Alice Springs Hospital. Then, around Easter, the Palliative Care Unit got a phone call from the closest clinic to where he was staying. The nurse there said they needed more sedation and medical supplies to keep him comfortable. The Unit consultant spoke with the nurse and decided that the patient also needed a syringe driver. So, that night, someone from the Unit drove to do a halfway meet with the man's nurse to deliver the driver and other resources. The man died surrounded by a handful of people, who, supported by the Unit, had cared enough to look after him.

Fred's commitment to palliative care goes above and beyond what's simply required. With the help of his colleagues in other services, he stitches together strategies that make it possible for people to finish up their lives as well as they possibly can. A couple of years ago, there was some funding available that enabled Fred to establish a respite house in Alice Springs. It opened in late 2013. The next challenge was to make it work, so Fred took some time off from his management role to be a project officer and to look at how the house was going to function. 'We didn't have the numbers for a fulltime palliative day-respite but I figured, if we shared with other services, we could help some of the chronic disease people who are a bit homeless, who don't have anyone watching over them, who don't have regular meals, don't have regular medications and have nothing to do,' he says. 'If they came through the house a couple of times a week, they'd get a meal, it's safe for them to sit down and watch a bit of TV and we can give them a shower and generally check up on them. We don't want to over-extend ourselves, but that would help keep them out of hospital. We have funding until the end of June 2014. It's helping two other organisations at the same time as it utilises our new facility.'

'And that,' Fred continues, 'is the secret to our success. Out here we work together and support each other in providing these services. There are plenty of people who come into rural and remote areas with big ideas and talk the talk but never walk the walk. They don't stay long; their credibility is shot and they move on. We all work hard at keeping our networks up to date and viable because we're all in this together, and if you can't help each other out you're buggered. We couldn't do half the work we do without the relationships we have with people like the Tangentyere Council, the NPY Women's Council and Carer Respite. Organisations like that are really flexible and ready to look outside the square.'

The Central Australian Palliative Care team is one of the few government teams that deliver services in a hospital, out in the community, in the town camps, in houses and in remote communities. They intentionally have great flexibility and have an extraordinary insight into the whole story of the people they work with. Fred is adamant that 'you can't judge them. You might not like it or them but we still look after them.'

Even the toughest nuts get well looked after. Years ago, there was a man, reputedly a pretty obnoxious fellow, who lived up the road from the pub at a community on the North Stuart Highway. Taciturn and cranky by nature, he was the local clinic nurse's least favourite person because he was so rude. Despite his reputation, the locals rallied to look after him when he became seriously ill, supporting him with meals and lifts. He'd just turn up on the doorstep of the clinic and growl, 'I'm in pain. Get me something now.' He died during the night and they found him early the next morning. Fred was later told that the local council was able to get the grave dug that day and he was buried before sunset with a small gift on his coffin of his favourite vices. About a week later the nurse was talking to Fred and filled him in on the details. Laughing now, Fred reckons she told him she'd 'double-checked to make sure the bastard was really dead. We chucked some cigarettes and a beer in the hole with him to see him on his way!'

Other people are gems. There was a female renal patient who had succumbed to cancer. She had battled through dialysis for ten years, during which time she lost a leg and acquired an artificial one. She came from a little community on the edge of a creek about 100 kilometres south-west of Hermannsburg. Magnificent red cliffs stand over the community and she very much wanted to finish up in sight of those cliffs. The Palliative Care Unit had taken her back to her community in the past for respite, but when her health reached a critical point, they knew it would be the last time. She would not have any more dialysis and they all knew she would not survive for more than two weeks. The doctor and social worker working for Palliative Care at that time drove her back one Friday afternoon.

FINISHING-UP BUSINESS

Her family were overjoyed that she was coming home and thankful to be able to care for her to the end. When the staff returned to Alice Springs, they drove through the smoke of some fires off the side of the road and then, when they got to Hermannsburg, they hit a thunderstorm. The social worker told Fred later that it was like they had been smoked and then washed clean . . .

When Fred returned from his days off to discover that one of his nurses and his Aboriginal liaison officer were planning to surreptitiously deliver the old man in the wheelchair home, he knew he'd have to bear the consequences if it didn't go well. The nurses at the patient's community had baulked at having him back if his family couldn't help.

Their plan was to deliver him home, drop in to the clinic and tell the nurses he was there, and then hightail out before they could do anything about it. Since they were going anyway, they arranged to take another old lady home for a visit as well.

As they headed out of Alice Springs, the old man in the back seat of the vehicle stirred, he straightened his shoulders slightly as his dark eyes brightened in his ravaged, ancient face and he understood that, finally, he was going home.

The trip took them four hours and, as planned, they dropped the old lady off to her family before delivering the old man home to his. They let the clinic nurse know and quickly left.

The next day, the barrage of resulting emails started with, 'Fred, please explain!'

'Well, isn't it great they're out there now?' Fred replied with his usual positive outlook.

It could have ended badly and Fred recalls it took a fair bit of negotiating and schmoozing to make it work. 'The DMO [district medical officer] and all the staff out there were great. They understood what had been done and the nurses at the clinic looked after him beautifully until he eventually died,' Fred says.

Fred reserves his highest praise for the nurses who work in the remote communities. 'They are the ultimate practitioners and we couldn't do what we do without them,' he says. 'Sometimes they have to be gatekeepers, especially if there is only one nurse out there, but in this case there were three nurses in the community and other services helping out. It was enormously satisfying to have enabled him die at home, in his own country.'

After eighteen years in the Palliative Care Unit in Alice Springs, Fred Miegel doesn't envisage doing anything else. He and Karen have established strong roots in the community and their two children are true blue Central Australians. Karen's professional role is clinical nurse manager of the neonatal unit at the Alice Springs Hospital. She brings tiny people into the world and Fred shepherds other people out – an irony that escapes neither of them and provides them with a grounding balance between the opposite ends of health care.

12

WALKING HER MAGIC LINE

Jo Appoo, *Elliott, Northern Territory*

As the on-call registered nurse and manager of the Elliott Health Clinic in the Northern Territory, Alan Thompson grabs the ringing phone as he rolls out of bed, at the same time murmuring to his wife Nell to go back to sleep. It's ooo and there's been a road accident about 100 kilometres down the Stuart Highway. It's another rollover though details are sketchy. As Alan throws on his clothes and heads for his car, he's already dialling the number for Jo Appoo, an Aboriginal health practitioner based at Elliott and Alan's 'right-hand person'.

'When I accepted the position of manager, I asked for Jo to be appointed here,' says Alan. 'I'd met her up near Yuendumu [about 300 kilometres up the Tanami from Alice Springs] about six years ago. She's a great example of how effective a good Aboriginal health practitioner can be. She's got plenty of common sense and we work well together as a team. If she doesn't know how to do something she'll tell you, but once you've shown her, she knows. She can pretty much do anything.'

On this night, Alan meets Jo at the clinic. He calls the second on-call nurse to let her know what's happening, flicking the main switchboard phone through to her number while he's away. Meanwhile, Jo is loading gear in the ambulance, typically a Toyota Troop Carrier (troopy). Realising that time is of the essence, Alan grabs the drugs they might need and, as quickly as possible, they're on the road heading south.

Elliott is situated about two hours north of Tennant Creek, where the nearest hospital is located. The accident is about halfway between. It's nearly 2.30 a.m. by the time they reach the accident site, where the single vehicle appears to have rolled off the highway, landing right side up. The police are already there and report their concern about one of the men. Alan and Jo, mindful of the trucks plying up and down the highway with their spotlights splintering the black night, check the casualties. No one is dead, but two of the men are lying on the ground. The third is sitting in the driver's seat, and all three appear very drunk. There is a pile of empty cans littering the floor of the car and the smell of beer hangs heavy. Alan and Jo breathe sighs of relief that they are all adults.

'Some of these accidents are shocking,' Alan explains, 'and you see some things that no one should have to see, especially if kids are involved. When you get to an accident and see a child's car seat, it's like, *Please, God, no . . .*'

They start checking each of the casualties and sorting out what's what. Alerted by the police, Alan is very concerned about the status of one of the men when he calls Alice Springs Hospital on his satellite phone, to be connected to the district medical officer (DMO). Jo works steadily, taking blood pressures, checking pulses and breath rates, and looking for further injuries. Acknowledging Alan's thoughts about the possibility of the driver having a very serious injury, the DMO requests they load the patients as soon as they are stabilised and shoot them through to Tennant Creek, now only a bit over an hour away.

With help from the police, they load the driver onto a stretcher and into the troopy, then guide the other two into seats and strap them in. Leaving the police to clean up, Jo drives while Alan sits with the injured man in the back, checking his vital signs and generally ensuring he remains stable. Both Alan and Jo are relieved when the lights of Tennant Creek flicker across the horizon. Safely handed over to the staff in the emergency department, they turn around and head for home, arriving with the rising sun.

It's just another day in the life of the Elliott Health Clinic, and while they'll grab some sleep straight away, they'll both be back at work later in the day. Located about halfway between Alice Springs and Darwin, Alan and Jo agree that the accidents are the downside of living in a highway community. 'People get out on these long, straight stretches and just want to get where they want to go,' she says.

Surprisingly, Jo has never actually been to an accident at which someone died, a fact for which she is grateful. 'My goal is to stabilise them and get them out alive; that way I know I did a good job and I can walk away and not worry what happens next,' she attests. It's a measure of her level of detachment in an environment and culture that generally demands immersion. 'I'm probably different from most people in that I leave work at work. If I have to go out, I do my best, and when I go home I leave work at work. I forget about it. If someone's really badly injured, if I walk away knowing

I've safely delivered that person into the hands of someone else and they die later, I can detach myself from that. So far no one's died while I'm there, but if that happens, I'll manage.'

Born beside the Tweed River in northern New South Wales in the 1950s, Jo knew from when she was young that she was Bundjalung from the east coast of Australia. She knew they were a big mob who spoke many different dialects. That was all she really knew about her country until she went to the desert years later and began to learn what culture was and why it and country might be important.

As a child she went to the local school along with her nine brothers and sisters and, until she went to the desert, she never really experienced discrimination. 'Our friends and I would have sleepovers at each other's houses when we were kids and my mother reckoned she never knew whose head was what. There were dark heads and blonde together,' says Jo.

They moved around a lot though, and she later realised her mother was afraid of someone taking her kids away from her as she'd been taken as a child. Jo's mother and her mother's siblings were taken from their parents, though they saw them once a month and always knew who they were. Although it must have been terrible, Jo says her mother always said it benefited her because she got an education, but she acknowledges that not all stories are like that. 'Even though she said it was good for her, Mum always said she was the only one looking after her kids and she was wary of the dangers of the past,' Jo explains. Then there were the traditions of their people; someone once told Jo's mother that the community should be looking after her children, but Jo says, 'She was a very wise lady and she always said, "The only person looking after my ten kids is me!" She was quite determined about that and she didn't go in for this kinship kind of thing.'

Jo worked from a young age, as did all her family. At thirteen she was helping out at the Markwell Fisheries, sorting seafood as it came in off the boats. For six weeks of the year, with the whole family loaded into their old Holden FJ station wagon, her parents drove down to Mildura in Victoria for the fruit-picking season. While it was a transitory lifestyle, Jo remembers a happy childhood and none of the racism she's come to recognise as an adult.

When she turned eighteen, Jo and some of her female cousins packed themselves up and headed south for four months, starting at Mildura and working across to Renmark, South Australia, where they picked oranges. Eventually, back on the Gold Coast, Jo met and married her husband, a white man from Sydney, and moved to live at Kirra, just north of Tweed Heads, near where she'd grown up. She always worked and after her first two daughters were born, she moved her family to Nerang, where her third daughter was born. Because Jo had grown up not knowing much about Aboriginal culture, it never occurred to her to miss it in her life. Still, like her mother before her, she never subscribed to the notion that the community should bring up her daughters; she knew she could raise her children without interference from anyone else.

While they lived in Nerang, Jo worked as an assistant in nursing (AIN) in aged care, but following the pattern of her parents, once their two older daughters had grown up and left home, she and her husband moved around looking for work. In 1997 they were living in a caravan park in Berri in South Australia with their youngest daughter, when someone in Centrelink told Jo that there was a job going in Kaltukatjara, otherwise known as Docker River. She didn't have a clue where it was but she had two important qualifications:

she was Aboriginal and she had experience in aged care. By the time she got back to the caravan park, there was a message waiting for her to say she had the job.

Docker River is located at the north-west end of the Petermann Ranges in the south-west corner of Northern Territory, next to the Western Australian border. By road, it is about 680 kilometres to the west of Alice Springs, much of the latter part of the journey on very rough dirt roads. There was work for both Jo and her husband, so they set off with their daughter on the long trip. Jo herself just wanted any job. 'I always wanted to work and make my own money,' she says. Ultimately it was a turning point for Jo in all sorts of ways she could never have imagined.

Right from the beginning it was an eye-opener and a culture shock, and when she first walked into the nursing home at Docker River, she says she remembers thinking, *Oh shit, what have I done?*

'But,' she adds, 'it was lovely.'

At the Tjilpi Pampaku Ngura aged care service, she found she really liked working with the old people and they seemed to like her being there. One night, not long after she went there, a couple of old ladies came to her and said, 'You have to come with us.' Warily, she asked why, and clearly remembers them saying, 'You need to learn some women's business.' The army was in town at the time and Jo remembers they went and picked up a couple of white army nurses as well. 'They took us out and painted us in real pretty colours and we danced till about three in the morning.' For the first time, dancing under the Central Australian sky with those women, Jo realised why people might want to learn about culture; that for some, culture and country might be significant.

Not long after, she recalls one of the old men asking her if she was Aboriginal and when she acknowledged she was, he suggested she should train as a health worker. She had no idea what that meant but promptly went to the local clinic and asked the registered nurse (RN) about it.

With the RN's support, she took the idea to the local council, which was very keen to have her train up. Jo enrolled at the Batchelor Institute of Indigenous Tertiary Education and from then on, when she wasn't on duty with the aged care service, she volunteered at the clinic.

Because of her isolated location, she did the practical side of her training at Docker and then took leave and went to Alice Springs to complete her Certificate III in Aboriginal Health Work. She completed the course in record time.

They stayed at Docker River for two years. Then, with her qualification safely in hand, Jo applied for and got a job on Bathurst Island, one of the Tiwi Islands off the north coast of the Northern Territory. Once again, she was the new chum. 'I had no idea where I was going or who the Tiwi people were,' she says. 'And I really had no idea what I was doing but I learnt real fast. I was there for five years and set up and managed their first aged care program.'

Jo's first job was to build relationships within the community and help propose a plan for establishing the program. She says the biggest challenges on Bathurst were the same as those everywhere in the communities: drug and alcohol abuse, violence and young people suiciding; that and getting the appropriate bodies to understand that logistics are very different in remote areas. 'The wording had to be changed for the recurrent funding agreements; for instance, because they'd only included "rural" and "urban". We had to get it changed to include "remote". Everything is different when you're remote,' she says.

She identified the resources and infrastructure they would need and worked with architects to plan residential facilities. 'We planned it so the bedrooms and living areas looked out over the water and everything else looked up the street,' she says.

Nothing happens quickly or easily in remote areas and especially not on remote islands. And then there were things like respite. Given that the facility was being established on the island so the old people didn't have to leave their country, Jo told the authorities that the community didn't need respite beds. 'When the old people came in to the residential facility, they'd stay there,' she explains. 'They had regular meals and people to look after them. They weren't going home again.'

Jo is very keen on learning and, in turn, training others. While she was on Bathurst she started teaching young Aboriginal women to become carers in the nursing home, encouraging them to enrol at Batchelor and get a qualification. 'I love learning more about health and I think I learn every day,' she says. 'Someone can always teach you something. I love learning about why we give the treatments we give. I love the training. I loved learning about immunisations, for instance. I'd much rather give the immunisation than treat the illness. So I love teaching others to love learning too.'

After five years on Bathurst, Jo recognised that she needed a break and moved back to Central Australia. She ended up working as clinic manager for Central Australian Aboriginal Congress. At some point she had parted ways with her husband, deciding to rely entirely on her own abilities and resources to journey through life. Her youngest daughter had grown up and moved back to the coast, so, following the nomadic tendencies of her youth, Jo wandered around working where she was needed until 2010, when she decided to retire. She moved back to the Gold Coast but soon realised she had unfinished business in the Territory. 'The thing is, I do feel for the people of the Northern Territory. So I went back and based myself in Alice Springs and went once more wherever I was needed,' she says.

Then came the day, in 2012, when Alan Thompson decided he needed Jo at Elliott. She initially agreed to a casual appointment because she's never wanted be tied to one place, but Alan and Nell, who have both become her firm friends, apparently won her over, and she has since accepted a permanent role.

Now employed as a clinical health practitioner, and based on her personal experience as well as seventeen years working in Central Australia, Jo Appoo has very clear views about certain things.

Despite understanding other people's need to embrace culture and country, Jo doesn't feel the need herself. 'I'm not into the culture thing. We grew up with no culture. We were just a mob of kids growing up in the Tweed. We didn't know about racism. I think white people can belong to the land. Some of them have been there for generations, so it's also their country. Sometimes someone will say they come from the Gold Coast and I might say, "That's my country", but it's also their country. I'm not that precious about it.'

On occasion, Jo has heard people say that they can't see any Aboriginals at the Gold Coast. She says they're not looking. 'They're there but they're in offices and shops and businesses working just like everyone else. They're not sitting on the riverbank getting on the grog. Most of them are doing what they need to do to make a quid to survive,' she says.

Jo gets frustrated with a multitude of things that she says are complicating the main issues. 'All this being politically correct and polite stuff is starting to annoy me,' she says. She recalls going to a meeting at the Gold Coast with one of her daughters a few years ago. She was sitting up the back listening to young Aboriginal teachers talking about culture and language and finally the facilitator asked if anyone had any questions. She says it got too much for her and she had to have her say. 'I said, "I have a question for the whole group here. How can you tell anyone about your culture? I've been around a long time and my parents and grandparents were born and died here and we weren't brought up with a culture and we weren't brought up with language." They said, "We're speaking the language," and I said, "Bundjalung has many, many dialects. What part of Bundjalung are you talking about and who're you going to talk to? Please tell me because I'd love to know who you're going to talk to." They just looked at me.' The facilitator asked who she was and Jo told him she was from one of the biggest Bundjalung families on the Gold Coast.

Reflecting on that incident, she says, 'They don't have culture back there. They don't have their own dances. They don't have language. They don't have stories because it was all lost. They are copying what they see other people do. I walked away when they started dancing. They were dancing other people's stories.'

Despite her personal views on culture and country, she loves working among Aboriginal people. 'I love doing what I do. When they see a black face here in the Elliott Clinic, they know I'm here to help them. That's all they want; someone to help them. Mostly I like Aboriginal health being in the hands of Aboriginal people,' she says.

As an Aboriginal health practitioner, Jo can provide initial consultation and basic physical examination to patients, as well as advise on the treatment and management of health problems. She can manage follow-up sessions and schedule activities such as Pap smears, blood tests, ECGs (electrocardiogram tests) and routine chronic disease checks. She can prescribe and dispense pharmaceuticals, treat injuries and general malaises – consulting, as required, with either the RN or doctor on call.

Elliott is, by anyone's definition, a tough gig. Apart from the added exposure to highway accidents because of its location, some nights in the town are tougher than others as alcohol and drugs wreak havoc on people.

On the other hand, according to Jo, there are advantages to being there. She actually thrives on the challenge of emergency work. 'There's more emergency work here than at the communities that aren't near a highway,' she says. Because of their location, they also have good communications. 'I carry a mobile phone at all times and know my girls can ring me any time they need me. In some communities, I'd have to give them the clinic number and rely on messages. This is much better.' Being permanent, she also has her own house.

Jo and her girls are pretty tight and she has a handful of friends around the country that she spends time with. She does not make close friends in the communities; not even at Elliott where she is permanent staff. She says there is a magic line you never cross if you don't want to get sucked into the whole business of family and the associated responsibility.

Jo doesn't believe it's a good thing for anyone. 'Some white people have told me they've been invited to join a family and offered a traditional name [bestowed to enable non-Aboriginal people to fit into an Aboriginal family structure], but I tell them to really think about it because, if they accept, they're a part of that family and they're looking after that family. A lot of the nurses think they need to keep in contact with those families, and some of them have two or three skin names. That's a lot of responsibility!' While the people

NURSES OF THE OUTBACK

at Elliott know Jo is there for them at the clinic, she says they also accept her as she is, and don't expect anything else.

While she's clear about her magic line, Jo does love to communicate with other Aboriginal people and especially the old people. She likes helping them fix things and helping them to help themselves. 'I tell them, "You are the only ones who can make this better. You have to want to help yourselves." Fifty years ago these people used to work on the stations. They earned their keep and got a bit of money so they had pride in what they did.'

Though Jo was only taught English as a child, she understands people's need to learn their traditional language. 'I've worked with Greeks and Italians and they learnt English at school and their own language at home. I don't see anything wrong with our people doing that too; it's the same thing. But they must learn English at school,' she says. Jo doesn't believe that people in the communities don't speak English. 'They all speak some English or at least pidgin English, but pretending not to allows them to put up a wall and shut white people out.'

She loves the old people but, even with them, doesn't ever step over her magic line. 'People here see my black face and see me as one of them, but I still keep a distance. I love helping them with their health issues and I get a lot of satisfaction out of the work here,' she says.

Jo pays attention to people and she's always keen to apply the learning she undertakes along the way. A few years ago, she was at another community and spent some of her time reading the CARPA Manual (Central Australian Rural Practitioners Association manual), which is used widely throughout the Territory.

About a week after she'd read it, she had two children come in with swollen ankles, aching on the balls of their feet, sore joints, sore throats and high temperatures. She recognised the signs and symptoms of rheumatic fever – having read about them in the manual – and alerted the DMO who later rang her to congratulate her on her work. It gave her great satisfaction and endorsed her love of learning.

The nursing staff at Elliott are generally transitory and RNs come sometimes for a few days, sometimes for a few weeks. Often the first couple of days are taken up with orientation, especially if they've never been 'remote' before. If Alan had his way, RNs would come for block periods on a rotational basis so that they had some continuity, but that's extremely unlikely to happen. 'Retention is much cheaper in the end than recruitment,' he says, 'but things happen slowly in the Territory and money has tightened up.'

Jo, on the other hand, stays. Alan relies on her, knowing that she's aware of the routines and that they work well together. In fact, he leaves her in charge when he goes on leave for a few accumulated days every few weeks. 'Jo's got a wealth of common sense, bucket loads of it, and she doesn't rattle easily. It would be an insult to make an agency nurse in charge when Jo's the one who's consistently here. I have every confidence in her abilities. As the manager, it's my job to organise these things so, when I'm going away, I just send an email up the line saying Jo is "acting up" in my role while I'm away,' he says.

Alan says there are more Jo's out there in remote health care – not many, but some, both men and women. Apart from the obvious clinical tasks, their job is to liaise with the community. According to Alan, a good Aboriginal health worker makes all the difference to the outcomes of any clinic. Jo believes it's because most people don't trust the white faces at the clinic and they won't declare the real reason why they have come. 'A good health worker will quickly assess what the real reason is and guide the way to appropriate treatment,' she explains.

If Aboriginal health workers are employed in their own community, sometimes they don't turn up regularly because they must abide by the rules of being a member of the community before the rules of being a health worker. They have family commitments that affect them, so it's an advantage that Jo does not belong to that country.

When she's in charge, she expects the Aboriginal health workers to toe the line. She knows if they're asked they will go but, finding a balance, she tells them, 'If someone comes and asks you to drive them somewhere, you have ten minutes. It's not your car, it's the clinic's, and you can't take it away for an hour or more.'

Jess Pascoe was the administration officer at the clinic until she decided in 2013 to train as an Aboriginal health worker. She's already well known in the community and readily accepted in her new role. Following her transition, Jo's daughter, Trish, relocated to Elliott to take on Jess's former role. As a result, Alan and Jo agree that they're establishing a good team in Elliott and they're both confident about the future of health care in the community.

'You need great people skills to work in the remote clinics,' Alan says. 'That's the thing about Jo particularly. She's an excellent clinician as well as a good people person.'

While she wasn't so sure in the beginning, Jo now loves nursing. 'I love getting out of bed and coming to work. I love the everyday stuff. In general, I just love my job. I never wanted to become a nurse, I never planned that, but now I'll work until I'm sixty-six and then I'll see. Maybe I'll work a little bit longer . . .'

13

FINDING HOME

June Andrew, OAM, *Marree, South Australia*

Located at the junction of the Birdsville and Oodnadatta tracks, on a hot summer's day, the town of Marree shimmers like a mirage on the desolate gibber plains at the southern edge of the Lake Eyre Basin. A dusty 700 kilometres north of Adelaide, in South Australia, Marree nurtures a cluster of historic relics, serving as ghostly monuments to the history of the outback. The remnants of a replica mosque created from mud bricks and a bower roof preserve the forgotten voices of sixty Afghan cameleers and their families, who ferried freight on long camel trains throughout the Red Centre in the late 1800s and early 1900s. Timeworn, battle-scarred locomotives stand like sentinels beside the railway tracks that used to carry the Old Ghan, the train that eventually replaced the camel trains in 1929. When a new track was built and opened in 1980 to standardise the rail width, it was relocated well west of Marree and, consequently, the last train whistle echoed out of town.

Opened in 1883, the Marree Hotel still does a busy trade through tourist season, especially when Lake Eyre is full. Marree is a launch pad for several charter flight companies who fly circuit after circuit, day after day, allowing tourists to see the magic of Australia's largest salt lake. For the rest of the year, the pub gets through the summer the same way that everyone left in Marree does: one day at a time.

The Marree Health Clinic, built circa 1916, reflects the same aged facade of the other monuments but, like the pub, it continues, as it has done for nearly 100 years, to serve the needs of the community and that of anyone who passes through.

Despite the turning of a new century, nothing much has changed in Marree since the last train left. Even the Stateliner Bus Service stopped running to the town in 1988. The bitumen airstrip is relatively new and electric lights guide incoming aircraft at night, but they run off a generator, as does most of the town. The Marree Roadhouse – which acts as a café, general store, bakery, fuel station and post office – office has embraced solar power because they use more than most, but everyone else relies on the town generator and pays through the nose for it. The population has decreased, with about a hundred people living in the town and about another seventy in the district. The sheep and cattle stations don't have the staff they used to and, apart from government institutions, there's not much work around most of the time, although the tourist season has spiked in recent years thanks to four seasons of water in Lake Eyre.

All in all, Marree sounds a bit of a dim prospect and yet, when registered nurse (RN) and midwife June Andrew roared into town in her Ford Laser in the summer of 1982 to take over running the local clinic, she zapped the community alight. Jollying everyone along with her endless enthusiasm and irrepressible giggles, thirty-plus years later, there's not much happening in Marree that June doesn't have a hand in or an opinion about, and the people of the community love it.

Although June is firmly settled in Marree now, she wasn't always so sure about where she belonged. However, as she shared the joys and tragedies of the people in this small community, she built connections that have bound her firmly to the district. With her quick thinking and innate common sense she has overcome many of the challenges peculiar to remote area nursing.

Born in 1953, in a little village in Devon, England, June migrated to Australia with her parents and three brothers when she was just three. They settled in Gawler, north of Adelaide, where June went to school until she was twelve and made the decision that would set her on her pathway to Marree.

A bright, somewhat precocious child, she always thought she'd like to be a kindergarten teacher. That changed when she went to hospital for the first time after breaking her arm. She'd never been before and had no experience of nurses. She was affronted when one of the nurses didn't believe she was feeling sick and, consequently, didn't provide her with a vomit bowl. June promptly threw up all over the bed. In the aftermath of the clean-up, she thought to herself, *I could do so much better than that!*

So it was that she enrolled at the Technical High School in Elizabeth where she could do the science and maths subjects she needed to enter nursing. She started her training at the Hutchinson Hospital in Gawler at the end of her fourth year of high school and was working on the wards by Christmas. 'The lecturer was going away so they started our group early,' June recalls.

There was only a handful in the intake and although the nurses were assigned to specific areas for their shifts, they did get to move around the small hospital pretty readily. 'It was an excellent introduction because, in that smaller country environment, we had lots more opportunity to directly assist the doctors and so we got a broader exposure to a wider range of conditions and treatments,' she says. 'We did lots of tonsillectomies and tooth extractions, so there was always lots of blood involved.'

Just before the second Christmas of her training, there was a very serious road crash in Gawler and a number of young people were killed. It was her first encounter with a really bad accident and she found it confronting, but discovered that she felt almost detached from the emotion of it all and was easily able to respond in the calm, collected manner that underpins the persona of a good emergency nurse. The ability to stay composed and focused in sometimes horrific circumstances is integral to successful outcomes.

At that time, the nurses who started in Gawler routinely transferred to the Royal Adelaide Hospital (RAH) to complete their training. While June felt a little nervous about going into Adelaide, when she transferred to RAH, she found she slotted comfortably into her new medical environment, thanks to her solid grounding at the Hutchinson.

By nature a studious girl, June recognised that 'there were a lot more rules and regulations at Royal Adelaide and more hierarchy, but I wasn't too worried'. Learning her way around and coping with an assorted crowd of young women in very large nurses' quarters presented much more of a challenge. While most of the young nurses were shortening their skirts, partying and dreaming about the Rolling Stones' impending tour, June was working hard, even though she wasn't sure what she wanted her future to be like. 'There was much more freedom at the nurses' quarters in Adelaide. We weren't locked up like in Gawler. You could stay out very late, but I mostly just studied.'

After graduating and still being unsure about what to do with her career, June stayed on at the RAH to undertake a twelve-month certificate in ward administration. Unfortunately, when she finished, she couldn't find a job; not even a cleaning job. She didn't know about nursing agency work then and was looking for something casual to fill in her time until she started her midwifery. June moved home to Gawler and, thanks to one of her brothers, found employment packing wine bottles at a winery in the Barossa Valley for several months.

In 1976, beginning to think that she'd prefer to work in a country setting, June moved to Mount Gambier Hospital to do her midwifery training then stayed on for eighteen months working as a midwife. She loved delivering the babies and has always thought she'd have liked her own, but has never met the right man to make it happen. Looking back now, from the isolation of outback South Australia, she does concede she may not have been looking in the right place!

Back then, still unsure of her future, but building the foundations of a nursing career, June undertook her Maternal and Child Health certificate in Hobart and then stayed on in Tasmania working as a relief nurse doing home visits to babies under five years old and their mothers. She'd had to learn to drive to get the job and bought her first car, a Mini. As her driving confidence grew, June developed a secret fondness for getting around the back roads of Tasmania quickly. However, while she loved her work, she didn't think she wanted to stay there forever.

In 1980, June took her parents home to England for six months so that she could meet some relatives and see where she came from, and so that her parents could reminisce. 'When we got sick of each other, I would park them somewhere with family and go driving around on my own for a while.' Once again, she really liked it but didn't for one minute think that she'd start a life there.

Returning to Australia, she joined the Medstaff agency based in Adelaide. While she knew by then that she didn't want to work in the city, she hadn't found a place that really felt like home. Starting at Peterborough, June worked her way around several country hospitals; through eleven months of night duty at Wallaroo delivering the babies on night shift on her own; and then through several weeks of night duty in Cowell. She worked for one night back in Adelaide, but that just confirmed she definitely didn't want to be there. Then she moved to Keith for five months, by which time she was heartily sick of moving and not having a place to call home.

June was reading through the job pages one day when she found an advertisement for a well-qualified nurse to go to a town called Marree on behalf of the Royal District Nursing Service (RDNS). She thought it sounded different and quite interesting, though she had absolutely no idea where it was. When she found it on the map, her first wide-eyed thought was, *Wow, I haven't been up there!* She went for an interview with the RDNS in Adelaide and, when they rang a couple of days later asking if she was still interested, she committed herself to at least five years in the new role. 'I was looking forward to unpacking and settling in one place,' June says.

With her car already packed and ready to go, she finished her last shift at Keith at 8 p.m. on a Saturday night, then excitedly zipped 200 odd kilometres to her parents' home at Gawler, where she spent Sunday unpacking and repacking.

Very early one Monday in December 1982, she took off, heading north on her new adventure. Later in the day, still driving along a seemingly endless dirt road, June admits she wondered if she was ever going to get to Marree. She finally arrived in a cloud of dust in the late afternoon, just in time to see the Royal Flying Doctor Service (RFDS) plane take off for the very last time from the old Marree airstrip. The next plane landed on the new strip. Noting that it wasn't that long since the Old Ghan had stopped running, June giggles and says, 'I arrived in town just as everyone was leaving!'

Because it was the end of the year, the teachers were wrapping up and a number of people were leaving town, so there were farewell parties most nights at which the remaining residents welcomed June and the parting ones wished her luck. Meeting most of them in the dark, she found it difficult to recognise them in daylight during her first days in the clinic, which caused her a little confusion and lots of giggles.

She had a week's handover with the departing nurse. Then, as now, on any mid-summer day, when the temperature regularly tops out in the very high 40s, Marree almost hovers on the hot air waves of the simmering desert gibbers. In June's first week, towards the end of more than six years of drought, she shovelled foot-high dunes of dust off the verandahs of the clinic at the end of almost every day. 'There was just no way of keeping it out. Depending on which way the wind blew, the dust storms just rolled straight in through the gauze screening. And the wind seemed to blow nearly all the time.' She confesses to thinking, *O-kaay. What have I got myself into?*

The dust wasn't her only challenge. She had to learn how to check the dirt airstrip and light the flares for night landings and departures by the RFDS. Part of the job was checking there were no kangaroos on the strip. 'It was always interesting and you have to drive really fast to check the surface for the planes.' She admits to secretly enjoying the excuse to whizz up and down the airstrip very quickly.

The other difficulty she faced in those early days was mastering the HF radios. Although the town got an automatic telephone service and television not long before June arrived, the pastoral stations didn't have phones back then and they still used HF radios for communications. June well remembers the twice-daily radio sessions were one of the trickiest things to learn. 'There were two sessions a day and I would call in to either session and talk to a doctor about any problems. The hardest thing was learning to tell the doctor what the problem was without saying much. Everyone with a HF radio could hear both sides of any communication so you had to be careful what you said because half the outback would hear it if they happened to be listening in. The stations could call in throughout the day if there was an emergency so I kept the radio on all the time, just in case,' she says.

As it happened, the alert for June's first major emergency didn't come over the radio. Not long after she began working in Marree, a man walked in and said he'd come across a road accident about 30 kilometres south of town. He had brought in the two boys involved; one was dead and the other barely injured.

June remembers the adrenaline kicking in as she saw the dead boy in the car. They ferried the injured lad into the clinic before she called the RFDS, which dispatched an aircraft to come and retrieve him. Meanwhile, they relocated the other boy's body to the morgue to await the police plane, which eventually came from Adelaide to take him for autopsy prior to a coronial inquiry. 'They were local lads and it was pretty terrible because the injured boy was the driver and things got pretty awful between the families for a while. Everyone knew them both and it was the focus of much speculation in the community. People took sides a bit,' she says.

It's not the worst thing she's had to deal with, although she's inclined to block out the memories of those incidents that are too awful to think about, including a couple of shootings and a murder. 'I can't talk about them and I don't think about them,' she says. Very clear about what she believes and what she's prepared to do, June admits that one of the things she most hated was going out to fights, 'especially when there was alcohol involved. They could get very nasty and that was a bit scary. People don't seem to drink quite so much nowadays. There was a time back in those early years when I would judge the mood of the town by the music I could hear at the pub. I wasn't a great fan of Slim Dusty before I came up here, but I soon became one. If I could hear Slim, I breathed a sigh of relief knowing I could relax.'

June herself has never voluntarily drunk alcohol, although she says when she first went there a couple of the local yahoos used to say they'd get her into it eventually. 'They spiked my drink a couple of times, so I gave up orange juice and now I only ever drink water. I wasn't happy about it, I can tell you, and I let them know it. Ever since then, I keep my water bottle in my pocket with the lid firmly screwed on.'

For the first few years June was there, Lyn Litchfield worked with her for two days a week, particularly on doctor's days when they were often very busy. Lyn and another local registered nurse, Anne Morphett, still relieve June all these years later. Resident relief staff is a luxury most remote nurses don't have. Lyn worked at the Marree Clinic before her marriage and relocation to Wilpoorina Station, 60 kilometres south of Marree, and Anne and her husband moved into the area not long after June when they bought Callanna Station, 30 kilometres west of Marree. Working alternate weeks,

Lyn and Anne relieve June during her annual leave and when she takes patients who have no private transport to Port Augusta or Adelaide for medical appointments. Since the Stateliner Bus Service closed in 1988, there has been no public transport service in or out of Marree.

'We understand that it helps the community having nurses on hand to relieve June but it's also given us the chance to keep up to date with our clinical skills,' says Anne. 'We're lucky to have kept June here for so long and she really is an important part of the community. I've enjoyed being able to work occasionally and the RFDS is very supportive of all of us.'

Lyn agrees wholeheartedly and, having known June the longest, says she hasn't really changed much in the thirty-plus years she's been here. 'She's always been very stable and sure of herself. She enjoys the same simple pleasures she's always enjoyed and isn't given to flights of fancy,' she says.

Assisting June works well for Lyn and Anne because they're happy to do things the way that she does them. 'June's pretty set in her ways, but then, her way generally works. She's got faith in her ability,' Lyn says.

As clear as June is about the way she does things, she is clever at utilising whatever is at hand and likes problem solving. It's a trait that has served her well during emergencies. A few years ago, a lady out on one of the stations was prescribed diabetic medication by a city doctor who also told her to change her diet. June thinks they didn't understand exactly where she lived, and that she probably should have changed her diet first and then introduced the medication later. The patient did both at the same time and June was called out one day when she appeared to be having a seizure and was struggling to breathe. She had drastically changed her diet as

220

FINDING HOME

well as taking the medication, which caused her sugar levels to drop suddenly, resulting in a hypoglycaemic attack,' she explains.

June talked to one of her family on the radio and had to work out how to get oxygen to her quickly. Once she knew they had a cylinder of oxygen in the shed for welding and braising, she got them to fashion a mask out of a plastic cup and deliver some of that oxygen until she could get there with the ambulance. After alerting the RFDS and requesting assistance, she jumped into the ambulance and took off. 'I've been on that road a fair bit and I knew where the bumps and things were. It usually takes about forty-five minutes, but I did it in twenty-five,' she says. When the RFDS arrived, they took the lady to Port Augusta to stabilise her.

June's ability to think on her feet and the extensive knowledge she's built up of the Marree region and its inhabitants over the years have enhanced her capacity to respond in an emergency. While these would be invaluable assets in many professions, in a nurse, they're potentially lifesaving.

For June, nursing and awareness of the welfare of the community go hand in hand. While she's so involved in what's happening in the community, she can keep an eye on exactly what's going on with everyone who lives there. It was Lyn Litchfield who instigated June's first foray into helping out in Marree back in 1983. When Lyn's children were small, she was unable to join the kindergarten committee because she lived out of town. So she asked if June could go in her place.

June happily signed up and started to feel just a little bit of belonging. By the time she'd been in Marree for five years, she'd become entrenched in the fabric of the community and opted to stay another five years. The more involved she became, the more at home she felt. So it was that she kept adding 'just another five years' to her contract.

According to Lyn, 'June gees everyone up with her enthusiasm. At the gymkhana, held every October to raise money for the Progress Association, they hold a Calcutta where anyone can bid on the horses competing in the events next day and then, if that horse wins, the bidder "wins" the event. June loves bidding on the horses and, if "her horse" wins, she loves to go up and get the prize and the ribbons and be a part of the celebrations. She gets pleasure out of winning and is actually very competitive. She belongs to the tennis club and plays to win. She manages the pool for the school and challenges herself every day to swim further.'

Another old friend, Sue Dadleh, has worked at the local school for even longer than June's been at the clinic. The way she tells it, June gets just as much pleasure out of directly helping people as she does out of winning. 'She'll run people down to Port Augusta for appointments and come back in the same day. She does love the drive and while she's down there, she'll shop for other people and run errands. She'll go to KFC and have a meal then collect her passengers and head home. She doesn't stop for anything once she gets going.' The trip there and back is 800 kilometres and some weeks she does it more than once if someone suddenly gets a long-awaited appointment or needs to go for an X-ray or special test. Testament to June's generosity, she will transport anyone who doesn't have their own means of travel.

When she's not helping, she's managing things. June organises the darts competition that rules the pub on Friday nights. She's the local Avon lady, selling cosmetics, skin care and hair care products to the ladies of the community and anyone passing through who might be interested. She is also the captain of the local Country Fire Service and loves the thrill of driving the fire truck. She's the treasurer of the Race Club and helps out at the annual gymkhana once she's sorted her Calcutta entry. Naturally, for both events, she's also the ambulance presence, juggling her various hats with all the confidence of someone who knows if she needs it, someone will always pitch in and help.

While Marree may seem like it's slumbering away on a hot horizon, the social life is surprisingly hectic, and June Andrew is right in the thick of it.

The one organisation she's not involved with is the Marree Youth Group and even then she commandeers their building on Saturday nights in winter and Friday nights in summer (before the darts competition) to run movies in June Andrew's Cinema. The cinema was part of a gift presented to June in 2009 when she was officially recognised by Scott Cam on Channel Nine's *Random Acts of Kindness* program. While the gesture was instigated by someone within the community, it was soundly supported by the RFDS, which helped orchestrate the surprise. The cinema has four rows of authentic seating, an overhead projector with surround sound and a popcorn machine, and is a source of entertainment for anyone who's into movies. The cinema was accompanied by a wedge of other gifts, all of which June appreciated and enjoyed, but the pièce de résistance was a large trophy cup, which takes pride of place in her flat.

The RFDS took over responsibility for the Marree Health Service in 2006. Cheryl Boles is an RFDS Community Health Nurse based at Port Augusta, who regularly visits Marree with an RFDS doctor as part of the fortnightly GP clinic run to the town and to stations up the Birdsville Track. She says June is as much a part of the landscape as the old clinic itself and pretty much runs the clinic just the way she likes it. 'She has strong points of view and she's very experienced. She can treat a lot of things herself, so we know if she rings us then her patient is very ill or badly injured. She has the confidence to make decisions and doesn't doubt herself. We all respect her for who she is and, if she sometimes chooses to do things her way, that's okay. I'm the visitor there in her clinic, which is really a part of her home.'

Every Christmas, June endears herself to the RFDS GP team by organising a party for them. 'She makes all the food and gives everyone a gift,' says Cheryl. She takes great pleasure from the simple things in life and spends a lot of her time helping fundraise for Daffodil Day and Biggest Morning Tea, as well as for the RFDS. She makes lucky dips up and then sells them at race meetings and other town functions to raise money.'

Despite the huge part June plays in the social complexities of Marree, her predominant role is as the RN at the clinic. That takes priority over all else. She is open for business from 8 a.m. to 5 p.m. on weekdays. She organises and coordinates the doctor's clinics at Marree every second Wednesday. She doesn't make appointments as such; rather, she suggests an approximate time and then calls people to tell them to come. In summer, if they don't have transport, she'll go and collect them and return them later because it's so hot outside.

Most of the time she's the only staff at the clinic, so she does all the jobs, including cleaning, filing and ordering stock; whatever needs doing. There's a lot she likes about it, especially the interesting people who sometimes unexpectedly cross her path. Occasionally that's been challenging, like the time a busload of tourists turned up with gastroenteritis. The clinic didn't have enough medication for that large a group so she triaged them, putting IV lines into the worst cases and providing electrolyte drinks for the rest. One man had a heart complication and needed to be collected by the RFDS. For June, it's all in an interesting, varied day's work.

Like many outback nurses, June soon became the unofficial town vet as well. She sutured her first horse out in a paddock years ago. While she didn't sign on for this role in the beginning, she accepts it as a normal part of her role as the resident nurse. Over the years she's injected and sutured nearly as many animals as people. She's also been on hand to put local pets down when they're struggling to live. In fact, it's that readiness to do whatever it takes to look after anyone or anything that has endeared her to the community.

June is not concerned about having the best and newest resources and loves the old clinic. However, she's aware that a new clinic is a possibility and looks forward to it. 'It will make things a bit easier, as there would be a bit more room, especially now all these allied health people are coming,' she says.

Somewhere along the way, June Andrew realised she'd found home. The people of Marree have become her family and she enjoys the special place she holds in the community. If anyone needs anything, they know they can rely on June to help.

She's the nurse and as such, priceless. The acknowledgment from *Random Acts of Kindness* is not her only recognition. She was one of the first community nurses nominated by a school for an award in Children's Week and she was a finalist in the Nurse of the Year in 1999. But the icing on the cake was the Order of Australia Medal (OAM), which she was awarded in the Queen's Birthday Honour's List in 2009. It was a richly deserved honour, acknowledging the huge impact June has had in the region, as a nurse, charity fundraiser, volunteer, ambulance driver, impromptu vet and beloved local. She's grateful for the recognition this remote community has bestowed upon her and they have truly become her extended family.

All going well, according to her plan, June's not going anywhere, any time soon. Cheryl Boles reckons it's one of the best remote jobs going and actually offered to swap places with June for a fortnight so June could fly around and visit the other clinics. But June wasn't having any part of that. She knows she's onto a good thing and, for as long as she's able, she's going to keep doing her thing in the community that became the home she was looking for.

Giggling she says, 'Just for another five years . . .'

Photo courtesy of Kimberley Visions Photography

14

CALLING AUSTRALIA HOME

Shamiso Muchando, *Derby, Western Australia*

When Shamiso Muchando arrived in Broome in late 2008, on her way to Derby on the northern coast of Western Australia, she was truly startled to see Aboriginals. As a black Zimbabwean, it wasn't that she was shocked by their skin colour. 'We didn't do European history at school, but I expected Australia to be an English country,' she explains. 'I was just expecting to see white people.'

It was the very first step on the roller-coaster of social, cultural, economic, environmental and professional changes that faced Shamiso when she first arrived. Some she expected, some she hoped for, but others she never even imagined, and they tested every bit of her willpower and inestimable patience as she tackled the initial challenges of relocating halfway around the world from her homeland to a small coastal town in remote north-west Australia.

Shamiso trained as a nurse at the major central hospital in Harare, Zimbabwe. Before the nation reached independence, the hospital was only for white patients. When Shamiso trained, she did a general nursing degree and ultimately became a registered general nurse.

Her training was demanding in the beginning, because she didn't really want to be a nurse. 'When you leave school you have these ideas of a fancy job,' she explains. 'I wanted to be a marketing executive or a lawyer or something. Nurses and teachers were looked down upon, so I wanted to do something else. However, my mother said, "While you are waiting for a place at university, why don't you do nursing if an opportunity presents itself?" I wasn't really keen. My mother was like, "You can take a job nursing while you're waiting, and if an opportunity comes up to join marketing you can leave nursing or you can finish your nursing and become a pharmaceutical sales representative because you'll have a medical background." It was a way of a mother talking to a child who is full of fantastic ideas but is not ready to receive reality. So I started doing the nursing training and it was challenging.'

Shamiso was more surprised than anyone to discover that once she got into her studies, the subject became fascinating. 'It was different to school. You've got incidents to relate to, like, "This is what was happening to my uncle when he was suffering from this" and "That was what was happening to me when I was suffering from that". I got interested and I diverted my mind from the marketing thing,' she says.

She was the top student during her first round of training, and felt she had to retain that position. 'It was not always the case!' she says with a laugh. 'But I worked very hard and I got very interested in what I was doing. We had everything on site and I liked it to bits.'

When she was a student, she found the most stimulating place to work was in the emergency department (ED). 'We were always on our toes and learning something new every day. It was very busy and there was never a time when you could sit and watch the clock tick,' she says. The other thing that attracted Shamiso to ED was that, being in a major central hospital, anything significant was brought to that department.

Consequently, when she graduated, Shamiso wanted to stay working in ED and, happily, got a place. She was appointed to the resuscitation team and loved it, explaining, 'We were always on our toes. I felt good about it because, although we were all nurses in the hospital, in ED I felt we were special nurses. When a problem arose in the wards they would call in an ED nurse. For instance, in the ward, nurses never used to insert cannulas and they never did vena punctures, so when they couldn't locate a doctor to do those procedures, they called one of us in to do them. I felt good about it,' she says.

In 2012, Shamiso was appointed as the Director of Nursing at the Numbala Nunga Nursing Home in Derby, in the Western Kimberley region of Western Australia, and, today, both she and her husband, Owen, are Australian citizens. Their lives began in Harare but, nowadays, they call Western Australia home, and their daughter, Aimee, is Australian born. So how did that nurse so in love with emergency nursing end up working at a predominantly Aboriginal nursing home in outback Australia?

Growing up in Harare, Shamiso's family was quite well off and lived well in a low-density area. While she came from a stable home, with her father working as a doctor and her stepmother a nurse, the future looked very uncertain for Shamiso in the early 2000s. Economically, things in Zimbabwe were getting tougher. While she never felt frightened when she was growing up, as a nurse working for the government she was not getting paid much, and she began to feel anxious about her ability to look after herself.

According to Shamiso, it is not true that Zimbabwe is a bad place to live, but economically it is hard. 'Before dollarisation, when they introduced the US dollar as our currency, our money didn't have value; you could not do much with our money, which is what was frustrating me,' she says. 'Now things are more affordable, but you can't compare it to Australia. We were professionals and yet we knew that we could not make ends meet. We could not think about building a house. All our money went on basic food and shelter.'

She had friends in the United Kingdom, but they also said the cost of living was very high and that many people were doing two jobs just to make ends meet. 'My friends in Australia were not complaining,' she recalls. 'They said they were doing fine.'

Shamiso decided she wanted to come to Australia. When she met and married her husband, Owen, he was also keen to immigrate, so they initiated the process of applying for skilled-work visas, officially known as '457 visas'.

In Zimbabwe, if you train in a government hospital, you have to commit to a three-year bond when you finish your training. Consequently, Shamiso had to wait to complete her bond before applying for a visa. 'The 457 visa process itself is very long and costly. When I finished my bond in 2005, I applied to get my academic transcript – you can't start any process without it. I started applying directly to the South Australian (SA) Nurses Board but it took a year to complete the process of verification from the Zimbabwean Nurses Board. When they finally got my transcript and verification and some other references, I was registered in SA, so then I was able to start looking for a job.'

Shamiso and Owen had started saving towards their airfares long before she got a job because the flights are very expensive and they were only able to save a little at a time. She got her SA registration in 2006 and then suddenly, in 2008, she got the longed-for email. 'It said that if I was still interested there was a job application I had to sign and send back. I could not believe it! In those days we didn't have internet at home and we used to have to go to the internet café to check our emails. Because I was getting a bit frustrated and thinking it would never happen, I did not check my emails frequently. In fact, they had sent two that I had not seen. That was in July 2008 and I had to send all the papers they needed. I had to send lots of documents, including reference letters, and I had to get medicals done and so forth,' she says.

Finally it was all organised. Shamiso was employed by All Recruiting Services Agency, which told her that another nurse named Memory was going to Australia at the same time. Shamiso and Memory got in touch with each other and booked the same flights with adjoining seats. 'We met for the first time at the airport,' Shamiso says. 'We were chatting and anticipating the journey. Everything was overwhelming. It was my first time to be in a plane and I did not know how to move the seat or anything,' she recalls with peals of laughter.

Shamiso was twenty-eight at the time. Her 457 visa was valid for four years from December 2008. The two nurses assumed they were going to work in hospitals and that, because they were agency nurses, they would be moving from one hospital to another. Because they flew to Sydney, they assumed that's where they would be working. Their liaison in Australia was named Bronwyn. It was not a name they were familiar with and because they had only communicated by email, they had no idea whether Bronwyn was male or female. Bronwyn emailed Shamiso, saying, 'I'm a redhead, short and of a medium build, and I wear glasses.' Shamiso recalls wanting to ask if Bronwyn was a lady but, 'I thought it might be offensive. I didn't know how best to ask. The problem is, when you are coming from another country, you don't know what offends and what doesn't. You don't know how best to put something without offending or crossing the boundaries.' It was one of many conundrums to face the Zimbabwean nurses in the months ahead.

Bronwyn had reassured them that she would be coming to meet them and not to worry because she would find them in the crowd. She told them about border checking and that they might be asked questions. 'One of the emails said, "Don't worry, you are LEGAL," ' Shamiso recalls. 'Bronwyn told us to have our work permits at hand in case they asked for it and she gave us the appropriate contact names in case they asked us questions, but they never did.

'When we heard "Hello girls", we said, "Okay, yes, she's a lady." She was very nice to us, checking if we were tired, but we weren't because we were so very excited. She had phones ready for us so within fifteen minutes of landing we had mobiles. That was so exciting for us because in Harare you have to apply for one and you have to wait and wait and wait for them. I rang my husband and he said, "Whose phone are you using?" I said it was mine. "Really?" he asked. "So this is your number?" I kept saying "Yes, yes, yes". As soon as I said goodbye, he phoned straight back just to verify it really was my number,' she says, through more laughter.

They spent the first five days getting oriented, setting up bank accounts, tax file numbers and so on. During the orientation, Shamiso asked Bronwyn which hospitals they were going to work

CALLING AUSTRALIA HOME

in. She said that an opportunity had come up in Western Australia where they would be working long hours and their accommodation would be provided. 'We were comforted by the fact that, for the first three months, our accommodation was provided and that we would not have to look for transport,' she says.

Shamiso and Memory were shown on a map where Derby was and realised that it was quite a long journey. They were also told that it would be quite hot.

When the pair arrived at the airport to depart for Perth, they were bamboozled by the large crowds and somewhat confusing check-in process. 'It was overwhelming, but I just said to Memory, "Within a month we will be doing these things without thinking,"' says Shamiso. And so it was they flew first to Perth.

Perth airport was easier than Sydney as there were fewer people, and they continued north the next day. The plane touched down in Broome at about 11 a.m. but the bus didn't leave until that evening, so they waited at the depot, sleeping on top of their bags. 'I didn't have any idea of the distance between Broome and Derby,' says Shamiso. 'This was going to be our final destination and I was very anxious. Along the way there was cattle and I was thinking, *Is this the right area? Maybe there are just farms.* We didn't have any idea, and when we got there it was late at night. There was this guy who met us and brought us here to Numbala Nunga. It was dark and what frustrated us was, when we drove in the gate, we saw a sign that said 'nursing home'. We said to the man, "We were not supposed to go to a nursing home."'

Shamiso had never even visited anyone in a nursing home. 'Back home we had nursing homes, yes, but only for rich white people who are too busy to take care of their parents. With us, we take turns; everybody looks after their parents. So, I had no idea of what

233

a nursing home looked like or how they functioned,' she says.

'So there we were, late at night, nearly 10 000 kilometres from home, at a nursing home in Derby. The accommodation was not what I had expected. On the inside they looked good but on the outside they were not like the Australia I had in my mind. None of it was like the Australia I was expecting. But I did not worry because I thought I would just do the three months and then they would send me back to Sydney!'

They went over on the first morning to meet the Director of Nursing (DON), expecting to get an orientation into the procedures and protocols of Numbala Nunga, but none was forthcoming. 'It was a bit of a culture shock,' Shamiso recalls. 'We had an orientation for the whole of Australia in Sydney, but now that we were here in Derby we expected that we would have one for Numbala Nunga. We expected she would say, "Can you come back tomorrow morning so that we can go through some things?" But she just said, "We are waiting for your registrations; when they come through you can start work."'

They had their South Australian registrations, but they had not had time to process the Western Australian registrations, so they had to wait for them to go through.

However, later in the morning, the DON sent for them, telling them to come to work straight away as carers. Shamiso and Memory found everything completely different. Shamiso explains, 'This was a nursing home and the clients were different. I had worked in hospitals and I had bathed patients before but they were critical – accident victims or CVAs [cardiovascular accidents], for instance. I had never really bathed someone who was just old. To us, in a hospital set-up, everyone who is bedridden is a bed bath, but here they differentiate between a shower and a bed bath or a bath; it was a bit tricky.

Someone said, "Use the hoist," and I said, "How do I use it?" I didn't know how it was supposed to be used.

'I went to the office and said to the nurse there, "I am having difficulties. Can I have a bit of orientation?" She said, "I thought you were an RN [registered nurse]? RNs are supposed to know what to do." I said, "Yes, I am an RN, and when it comes to the medication trolley and the resident or when it comes to me nursing the patient's medical condition I will know what to do, but right now I do not know what I am supposed to be doing."

'I began to regret going there because now she made me feel I was not competent,' Shamiso adds. 'So then I was scared to ask anyone, in case it made me seem even less competent. I was in a nursing home, not a hospital, and I just needed to be told what was expected so I could get on and do my job. Then when our registrations finally come through we went back to the DON and asked her if we could have orientation now and we were given a folder. I didn't understand it. It made me feel even worse.'

Then the DON went on leave and the clinical nurse manager (CNM), who was supposed to come on duty in the afternoon, disappeared. Shamiso had worked the morning shift and didn't have anyone to hand over to. Because Shamiso and Memory were the only registered nurses there, they had to devise a way to cover the shifts. For a week, they worked twelve-hour shifts and because they'd had no orientation, they asked everyone everything. 'Everyone used to give us instructions!' Shamiso recalls.

One day a lady turned up who said she was from accreditation. Shamiso asked her, 'Why are you here?' She said she was there to help and to ensure that quality in the nursing home was maintained. Shamiso said, 'Thank you! You are the very person I need here.' She poured all her problems out, saying, 'We have come straight from Africa, from Zimbabwe, and my problem is orientation. Any problems I am having here are simply because we did not have any orientation. The CNM has not turned up for work and we are covering the shifts.'

Simultaneously, Frontier Services was called in to take over running the nursing home and hostel. The next day, more people arrived. They wanted to know where the keys were and Shamiso and Memory had to tell them they didn't know, so a locksmith was brought in. 'We did not even know the passwords for the computers. Within twenty-four hours the DON was back.'

Shamiso and Memory had been taking temperatures three times a day and blood pressures twice a day because they were doing what they would have done in a hospital. 'But it was not what was supposed to be done in a nursing home,' she says. 'Even with dressings, we did what we would have done back at home, but we were doing it wrong.'

Numbala Nunga was hit with sanctions and training became more rigorous, which Shamiso was very pleased about because she and Memory learnt a lot during that time.'We had someone there every day until the sanctions were lifted. I am very grateful because it was a blessing in disguise. I learnt how to do things from scratch and I learnt to do it the way they wanted. In between, we would have audits to tell us whether we were worsening the situation or actually getting somewhere.'

They were difficult days but people from Frontier Services were there, including DONs from other Frontier Services centres, teaching them what they needed to know. 'They were assessing us there and then. It taught me a lot, especially about accreditation – how they want things done and how they want them presented and how they look for those things. It was a good learning curve,' Shamiso says. The sanctions were in place for six months. The existing residents were able to stay there but no more could be admitted, and the facility did not get any further funding from the government until the sanctions were lifted.

Despite Shamiso's belief that she would be returned to Sydney after three months, she missed Owen and wanted him to come out as soon as possible. While she never really questioned her decision to relocate to Australia, the challenges at Numbala Nunga did take the edge off the excitement she felt transitioning to this new life she'd been seeking. To ensure Owen's speedy arrival, she had to secure accommodation in one place for twelve months, and so, in those first couple of months, she decided to stay in Derby and was happy to sign a lease on a house for a year. 'I wanted my husband to come over and I didn't mind that it was Derby. I wasn't used to working one place to another. That's not me; I like a sense of belonging,' she says.

Owen arrived about three months after Shamiso. He had worked in marketing in Harare but when he came out to Derby he decided to do his Certificate III in Aged Care, although he was certain he didn't want to work at the same place as Shamiso. While he was studying, he got a job packing shelves at Woolworths and then later out at the airport as a ground handler.

Finally, after six months the sanctions at Numbala Nunga were lifted. By then they had a new permanent DON, a fulltime CNM and more staff from the agency. Shamiso decided she was happy to be there and by then felt like she belonged. They had pitched in when things were messy and felt they had achieved something for their efforts.

Shamiso continued working for the agency and then after a year she started applying for permanent residency. Frontier Services offered her a permanent job as an RN but she didn't accept because under the terms of her visa they would have had to pay the agency around $5000 to transfer the visa, and she didn't want them to do that. She wanted to become an independent permanent resident first.

When Shamiso and Owen married they had wanted to have a baby, but they knew that if Shamiso became pregnant, the agency in Australia would not process the papers she required to work. So they waited until their permanent residency papers were at an advanced stage before trying for a child. 'With immigration, you submit everything they want and then you hear nothing for months. It was very frustrating because they kept asking for more things without telling us what's happening with our application,' she explains. 'During that period I had a phone call one day and I thought *What now*? 'The person who processed my 457 was the same person who processed this application, so when she called, I said, "What have I forgotten now?" And she said, "You have your permanent residency." I couldn't believe it! I was heavily pregnant but I ran looking for my husband. He wasn't at home so I had to run shouting. Everyone thought something must be wrong.'

Because they were applying independently, without a sponsor, they had to leave the country and come back in, so they flew to Malaysia and went to the Australian Embassy to get their paperwork stamped. They got their permanent residency in July 2010 and Aimee was born in August 2010. 'You cannot rush immigration, so we were lucky we got our permanent residency status before the baby was born,' Shamiso says, laughing happily.

'It is not easy to get in here,' she continues. 'There are so many forms and hoops to jump through. It is also very expensive. Sometimes it seemed too hard, but we could not give up. Sometimes we would think they had everything they wanted and they would want something new. We had to have police checks in Zimbabwe and fingerprints over here. It was very stressful and takes a long time, but it was definitely worth it.'

After getting permanent residency, Shamiso accepted a job at Numbala Nunga as a clinical nurse manager with Frontier Services, although she was initially reluctant because she was also having the baby. She says she was very lucky though. 'I had a very, very supportive DON, Meredith Barrett. She helped me go through the pregnancy and she helped me through the first stages of being a mother. She already had one baby and was pregnant with her second, so she helped me learn to juggle things. Back home, in Zimbabwe, your parents come over to help but we did not have that privilege here, and when you are a nurse everyone thinks you will know how to nurse your child, but motherhood and nursing are two different things, and Meredith helped me through it.'

Apart from taking two months off to have Aimee, Shamiso worked as a CNM for eighteen months. Then, in June 2012, she was offered the position of Director of Nursing. She knew it would be difficult work, but she was well prepared for the challenge. 'This time I was excited, though a bit scared because when I was a clinical nurse manager, I had back-up from Meredith; I always had someone to run to on site. But now I thought, *Who will I have to ask?*' In fact, Shamiso found there are always people at the other end of the phone, so while it was a challenge, it was one she enjoyed.

Numbala Nunga has twenty-five permanent high-care patients, one respite bed in the nursing home, and sixteen permanent and one respite bed in the hostel section next door. Most of the residents in both are Aboriginal. In her experience, Frontier Services always tried to employ people with a Cert III in Aged Care, but sometimes interested people didn't have the qualification. In that instance, at Numbala Nunga, if they had the experience, they could do their course through TAFE while they worked. There are Aboriginal health workers on staff, which is advantageous. 'There are so many languages and dialects,' says Shamiso, 'so the health workers interpret. One of the Aboriginal girls knows quite a lot of languages, which is particularly helpful. Often, instead of families coming to visit, we'd take the patient home to the community. Sometimes they just wanted to go home to country.'

There have been other African staff working there, who Frontier Services recruited directly from Zimbabwe. Thanks to Shamiso, they were very well oriented when they arrived at Numbala Nunga. She understands that it is the simple things that other people take for granted that can be difficult to comprehend for new staff.

Although Shamiso knows that sometimes people look at her and doubt her competence, she has not felt direct racism. 'Sometimes when I have been the RN on the floor, people have run past me and gone to the [white] enrolled nurse and asked whatever they want to know, and then the EN has directed them back to me. They know very well you are the RN on the floor, but their first impression is to doubt your competence. I don't mind; they're led to believe by the media that we have not been educated properly. With my clients, because I'm not sure what their experience is, I identify myself when I'm with them so they know who I am. It is about building personal relationships. With some of the white patients I have had to prove my competence. Sometimes they will check I know what medications I am giving them. You have to prove above and beyond doubt that they can trust you. It does make me feel uncomfortable, but I think over time I gained their confidence.'

While Shamiso loved ED nursing, she has come full circle and now loves aged care work. 'With ED nursing you take patients where they need to go and then they go home,' she says. 'There is no time for relationships. In a nursing home you establish a relationship with the client, you get to know them and give them better care because you know them. It is a home, so it feels like a family. True, it doesn't have the bustle and hustle that you have in emergency, but although I was at work there, at times I did not feel like I was. It is now a part of me, part of my life. I think of ED but I don't think I want to go back there. I liked being here.'

With Shamiso's cultural and nursing background, having patients die was confronting for her, although she has learnt to embrace palliative care. 'Back in Zimbabwe, we never talked about death because then we could pretend it was not coming. Back there, we do not express it. We do not plan for it. Working in ED, you fight for life. I was not a good nurse with palliative care in the beginning. I would find excuses not to give morphine because, while it relieves pain, it also suppresses respiration. Letting go was always hard for me but after palliative training it was better. They asked, "Would you rather see them die in pain?" No, we cannot do that, so we promote peaceful death.'

Shamiso acknowledges that, in those first five years, Frontier Services was a very supportive employer. 'They understood and accepted us the way we were and I was very happy working for them. Those visiting DONs who helped during the sanctions, they must have been very patient. I was very raw but they never asked why I did not know things. They just taught me what I needed to know.'

By her own admission, Shamiso doesn't give up easily and if she thinks of doing something, she will follow through to the end. She says she has a short fuse but has learned to manage it, discovering in her leadership role that she doesn't have to say everything she thinks or show every emotion. Mostly, she just loved her job.

Owen completed his enrolled nurse training in 2012 and was offered a job in the ED at Derby Hospital early in 2013. He plans ultimately to train as an RN and Shamiso has recently completed a second-stage diploma in mental health. They have juggled study, work and looking after Aimee between them. While Derby is relatively small, very remote and a world away from Zimbabwe, they have both been happy working and living there.

However, at the end of 2013, Shamiso's services at Numbala Nunga were terminated unexpectedly during a time of complete overhaul of Frontier Services programs across the country. After five years at Numbala Nunga, she is looking in a new direction and she and Owen have their eyes on a future in Perth. They will miss Derby. 'We saved money faster here!' she says with a laugh. Looking on the bright side, she says, 'We knew we might have to think about moving when our daughter has to go to school, so now we will already be established in Perth when that happens.'

Under Shamiso's leadership, Numbala Numga was a cheerful place and her infectious, happy laughter was often to be heard around the hallways accompanied by the joyful murmurs and laughter of her colleagues and the residents. She's come a long way from Harare and it wasn't an easy transition, and this latest development in her career has been challenging, but, while she sometimes misses her family and friends back in Zimbabwe, she feels very much at home in Western Australia. 'It's not like we're just surviving here,' she says. 'We go back to Harare to visit but we're very happy to be here. Now we are Australians and we are just fine.'

15

WEST-COAST NIRVANA

Sue Stewart, *Bidyadanga, Western Australia*

A couple of years ago, Dylan Ford spent some weeks staying with his grandparents, Sue and Barry, up at Bidyadanga in the north-west of Western Australia. During his stay, the local Aboriginal men took him fishing and the women took him hunting and taught him the right way to kill a snake. He went to school and made friends with the other kids in the community. He loved everything about it.

It's not unusual for children around the area to spend time with their relatives in another place, and the whole community welcomed Dylan. He'd not been in that country before, so everyone kept an eye out for him, even after they'd taught him about the local dangers, including snakes and saltwater crocodiles on the beach.

When Dylan returned to Victoria, he went to a new school and had to make friends all over again. He was pleased to see quite a few Aboriginal kids in the class.

One day the teacher asked them, 'Who's going to the Indigenous cricket day?'

Several hands shot up, including Dylan's.

'Put your hand down, Dylan,' she said. 'You can't go. You're not Indigenous.'

'I am so,' he said.

'No, you're not!' she replied with just a little exasperation.

'Yes, I am. I belong to the Jadai and Mandijalu families.'

And, indeed, this white kid does – as do his grandparents, Sue and Barry Stewart. 'The Jadais and Mandijalus are two different families, but they tell us we belong to them,' Sue explains. 'They smoked our new granddaughter when she was brought up to visit us. They gave her a bush name and they have said she'll have to come back. But,' Sue adds with a chuckle, 'she won't have to share her things or her money with them. They don't expect that.'

Bidyadanga is located in La Grange Bay, 200 kilometres south of Broome on the West Australian coast, and Sue and Barry have been working there for several years. Sue, a registered nurse (RN), is the manager of the Bidyadanga Clinic and Barry, a retired truck owner and operator, drives the clinic bus to Broome every day to ferry residents to and from medical appointments. He also drives the ambulance and maintains the buildings and vehicles associated with the clinic. For them, Bidyadanga is where their hearts are, and for now, it's definitely their home.

Sue grew up in Traralgon in the Gippsland area of Victoria. She always wanted to be a nurse and trained at the Central Gippsland Hospital. She worked at various country hospitals, ending up in

Tahmoor in New South Wales, where she moved when she married Barry.

Eventually they moved back to Victoria and Barry established a transport company plying freight up and down the east coast of Australia. After the youngest of their four babies was born, Sue was offered an opportunity to do some renal dialysis training. Dialysis is a process for removing waste and excess water from the blood, and is primarily used as an artificial replacement for lost kidney function in people with renal failure. She then set up a dialysis unit in Bairnsdale, before setting up another at the Omeo and Orbost hospitals.

Sue retired from the dialysis unit in 2004, and the following year she and Barry packed up and went travelling around Australia. She had always wanted to work remotely and, having worked with Aboriginal people in the dialysis unit, she wanted to work with them again, plus the autonomy associated with a remote community appealed to her. She used the trip as an opportunity to check out the possibilities. In the end, where they settled came down to pure chance. Heading along the Great Northern Highway in the north-west of Western Australia, they pulled up at the turn-off to Port Smith – a caravan park on the beach about 20 kilometres north of Bidyadanga – to talk to a bloke who was turning onto the highway. They asked him what it was like there and he assured them it was worth a look. Had they not decided to try it for a night, their lives might have turned out quite differently.

They booked in for one night and stayed nine. On Thursday afternoons, during the tourist season, everyone staying at Port Smith is sent out fishing and then, in the evening, the caravan park staff cook up the catch and provide accompanying chips at a total cost of $5 a head. All funds raised are donated to the Royal Flying

Doctor Service (RFDS). The Family Shoveller Band drives across from Bidyadanga to provide entertainment for the evening. So it was that Sue Stewart met Christine Farrer, one of the Shoveller family, who was the receptionist at the Bidyadanga Clinic.

Encouraged by Christine, the next day Sue and Barry went and visited the Bidyadanga community. Something about it resonated with Sue as they continued on their journey for another three months. She rang the Kimberley Aboriginal Medical Service Council (KAMSC), which employs the staff at Bidyadanga, and asked if they had any job vacancies. They did and she went back to the community to relieve as an RN at the clinic for three months while Barry returned to Victoria and the trucking business. By the time Sue finished her contract, she was entranced by the people and their friendly, relaxed attitude to life, the colours and vastness of the landscape – especially the beaches – and the variety and range of the work. 'Every day is different and you never know who or what problem will walk in the door next,' she explains.

Already committed to an eight-month contract with a Gippsland aged care service, Sue went home to Victoria, quietly determined to return.

Meanwhile, Barry was back in his truck, plying up and down the east coast. Things were changing rapidly, however, in the trucking industry and, like everyone in the business, Barry was struggling with rising fuel and registration costs and increasing red tape and legislative rigmarole and was fed up with long hauls, idiot drivers and bad roads. He was an easy mark when Sue arrived home and said she really wanted to go remote.

They sold their business, locked up their house and headed back to Bidyadanga for six months. Sue worked as an RN and did relief work elsewhere in the Kimberley, as required. They both really liked the community and the western Kimberley and when the incumbent manager retired from the Bidyadanga Clinic, Sue stepped in as the acting manager and then, ultimately, as the manager.

Bidyadanga has about 960 permanent residents, who visit the clinic at least four times a year, and another 300 transient inhabitants. It is the biggest Aboriginal community in remote Western Australia.

In 1931 the Western Australian government set aside approximately 180 hectares of land near a traditional meeting ground for a reserve and ration depot for Aboriginal people. This was later taken over, in 1955, by the Society of the Catholic Apostolate to be run as a mission.

The traditional owners of the area were the Karajarri people, but when the Australian and British governments decided to begin missile testing at Maralinga in the Woomera region of north-west South Australia, many of the Mangala, Yulparija, Juwaliny and Nyangumarta people from the western desert and the Pilbara were moved into La Grange Mission. Thus Bidyadanga is home to five different language groups. Wilson Mandijalu, otherwise known as Ahmet, is one of the Aboriginal health workers (AHWs) at Bidyadanga and can remember, as a four-year-old, walking in from the desert with his mother about fifty years ago.

While the Karajarri own the land, the Bidyadanga Community Council is made up of two elders from each of the five language groups. They meet regularly and consider any matters relating to the broader community. Personal issues, however, are referred to the elders of the appropriate language group. 'For instance,' Sue says, 'petrol sniffing was never a problem in the community until the Department of Child Protection moved a young person into the community from another place. Within three weeks of his arrival, six other Bidyadanga kids were petrol sniffing.'

Because it was an issue that threatened the welfare of all young people, the council met as a collective to deal with the matter. They asked to have the child removed and the local kids involved in the sniffing were publicly shamed by the elders, which stopped the problem. Once punished, the matter was over. 'The elders in the community jump on any misbehaviour very quickly,' Sue adds. If the matter is specific to one skin group, though, it will be referred to the elders of that group. Elders never interfere in the business of another group.

Sue goes to the Community Council meeting once a month to report on any concerns within the clinic. Recently there has been a notable incidence of sexually transmitted infections among some of the younger people. They have education programs, but, she says, 'There seems to be a group that just keeps pushing the boundaries.' By reporting to the clinic, Sue can rely on the elders to support the programs and encourage the young people to participate and take notice.

Change looms, though. Barbara White is Karajarri and has worked at the clinic for twenty-eight years. She is currently the community liaison officer (CLO) for the clinic. Sue says she never goes out into the community professionally without her trusted CLO. Barb worries that the young people don't take as much notice of their elders as previous generations. 'Blackfella way is very different to whitefella way. Sometimes young ones want to go with the wrong person; someone of wrong skin. It upsets the elders but the young ones don't always listen,' she says.

Barb has lived her whole life at Bidyadanga. She has two sisters and a brother in the community and she cares for several of the young ones in her extended family. She remembers when she was a child, living in a dormitory at the mission school during the week and going home to her parents on weekends. 'We used to do cleaning up after school,' she says. 'We learnt how to clean the missionaries' houses and how to set all the tables, how to put the plates and knives and forks together. We had to walk to the bakery and bake bread and stuff like that. We used to have a big farm and we used to be weeding and doing everything. We were kids and we did all the work. We had the hospital here near the office. There was a laundry and we used to have big coppers of boiling water and we put all the sheets in there. On the weekends we had to go to see our families. I was really happy to go and visit them.'

Barb became a health worker, in the first instance, to help her people. 'All these white nurses used to come in and the people used to be scared,' she explains. Even now, the remote area nurses (RANs) never go out into the community without a liaison to ensure familiarity and connection. Usually it will be Barb, if she's available and it's not to visit someone in her own family. Sometimes new RANs don't understand the need for a liaison and they often don't understand when one of the Aboriginal staff suddenly disappears – which is where Barb comes in handy. Sue does have some specific rules of her own to impart during clinic orientations, but Barb educates and guides the new RANs so that they quickly learn the customs of the people. She will explain the intricacies of family, language and skin groups and make sure the nurses understand that the Aboriginal workers will disappear when one of their own family comes in, as it is taboo for some members of the family even to be in the same room. 'KAMSC trained the Aboriginal health workers in the first place so we could work together to help our own people,' Barb says.'

As CLO, Barb keeps a weather eye on everyone in the community. She coordinates all the recalls, chats to old people and keeps gentle tabs on the young people. She accompanies people for tests and X-rays and she rounds up patients who have appointments with visiting health professionals. But her most important role is connecting the nurses of the clinic with the people. Sue relies on Barb to guide her when she needs it. 'If I have any doubts or concerns about how to manage something or what is the correct way to do something, I will ask Barb,' she says. 'She is wonderful at her job and, as a health worker, she can do most things. The only thing she can't really do is give medications as she is not endorsed for that.'

There's clearly mutual admiration between the two women. 'Sue is a good boss,' Barb says. 'She's very good to work with.' With a moment's thought, she adds, 'All the RANs are good to work with. We work well as a team. Sometimes stuff happens – someone gets cross, but we say we're sorry and everything's all right again.'

Recently Barb was given an award at the NAIDOC (National Aboriginal and Islander Day Observance Committee) ceremony for her contribution to Aboriginal health care over the previous twenty-seven years.

KAMSC is a training school for Aboriginal health workers and they have three trainees at Bidyadanga. The clinic has three fulltime AHWs, as well as the trainee students – two boys and a girl, who go to Broome for their classes. 'They do their prac work here,' explains Sue, 'and undertake their required competencies, which any of the RANs can sign off on to confirm their proficiency. We can always use more health workers, especially for when we get the new clinic.'

Much has changed in the community over the years. Back when the mission was functioning, most people had work either there or on the surrounding cattle stations. Sue says many of the elders talk about the old days as better, and not just because there was no alcohol. Rather, they say that the young people listened to their elders and everyone knew and understood the law. 'They say that, before the station owners were forced to pay full wages to their workers, they all lived in station camps where they were all provided with food, clothes and tobacco. The men had good jobs as stockmen and the women worked in the house. They had self-respect,' she says.

There's not so much work around Bidyadanga now and, unless the young ones move away, there is not much prospect of a career for anyone who does not want to be a trainee health worker or a liaison officer at the school. The Bidyadanga school caters from pre-school to the end of high school and a couple of the teachers are Aboriginal, including Frankie who is Karajarri. The retention rate at the school is one of the best in the state but most families don't want their young people to leave when they finish school, so they stay. And even the ones who do go usually come back, anchored by the responsibility that accompanies obligation to family. While building programs are happening in the community, some of the young people can be employed as labour, but there is no opportunity to learn a trade because when the building projects end, so to does the opportunity to learn.

Housing is another issue that Sue says causes some grief. While the Karajarri own the land, Homes West owns the houses and members of the community rent them. Sue feels very strongly that, ultimately, Aboriginal residents should be able to buy the houses. 'The houses are generally well looked after and the community employs people to clean up and maintain the surrounds,' she says. 'But people would feel a lot better if they could own their own homes. We all want to own our own homes, so why shouldn't they be able to?' It's one of many inconsistencies that irks Sue Stewart.

Unemployment and lack of ownership are just part of the conundrum that underpins a lot of unrest in some communities, but Sue

NURSES OF THE OUTBACK

says Bidyadanga remains a great place to live and work. 'When I first came here, a man came into the clinic one day and called me a "f***ing white c***". I was a bit stunned and said to him, "How would you feel if I called you a f***ing black c***?" He said angrily, "You can't call me that. That's racist." I told him that it was a two-way street and asked him to leave the clinic. Two days later, he came back and apologised. Another time a lady physically threatened me and the next day she was gone. The Community Council told her to leave because they value the nurses and won't abide bad behaviour. The elders do keep on top of things pretty well,' she says.

Theoretically, Bidyadanga is a dry community. Some people have signs on their houses saying 'No grog. No gunja', and people respect that, but Sue says that there is always plenty of both going around the community at large.

Prior to Christmas in 2012, the wet season was running late and everyone was getting a little edgy. By Christmas Day, trouble was brewing. Sue and one other RAN were on call and they spent two days treating one injury after another – all alcohol-related, which, Sue says, 'is a great pity because it was all avoidable'. She and Barry eventually ate their Christmas dinner at 9 p.m. on Boxing Day. With some people fired up by grog, there were several violent incidents out in the community, culminating in two evacuations. It definitely tested Sue's metal and she did think about pulling the pin, but, she says, 'I know I'd really miss it. Usually this is a really lovely place to live.'

Barry and Sue enjoy the community lifestyle and paint an idyllic picture of their leisure time. Barry spends a fair bit of time with the men in the community when he's not at work. 'We go fishing quite often, although I'm not much of a fisherman. There can be twenty blokes standing along the river and I can be right in the middle and they'll all catch fish and I won't even get a bite. They get a great laugh out of it,' he says. Fishing at Bidyadanga is not just a recreational pastime. 'They're catching their next meal,' he adds.

He and Sue both say it's a relaxed environment to live in. 'We go out camping on one of the beaches sometimes, eat fish cooked over the campfire . . . Time is not so busy up here,' Barry attests.

Like most remote area nurses, once back in the clinic, Sue enjoys the autonomy that goes with working in a far-flung location. Even though there is a doctor based in the community, and they have visiting GPs two days a week, Sue has special standing orders for when a doctor is not available for consultation, such as to give antibiotics and pain relief. 'It's part of being a RAN and one of the many things that make this a great place to work.'

It's an opinion substantiated by the good staff retention at Bidyadanga. The four RANs based there are on twelve-month contracts and Sue is hoping that KAMSC will engage two particular RANs as permanent relief staff, giving them even better continuity of service. 'We all work well together as part of the overall team and the work conditions are pretty good for nursing staff,' she says. 'They work 8 a.m. to 4.30 p.m. and are on call for one week in four. Sometimes they might be called out night after night and sometimes they mightn't be called much at all. I'm always on call as well, of course. If I want to go away for a weekend, then someone else will always back up. If something major is happening everyone pitches in. It's that kind of team.'

Located, as they are, just off the Great Northern Highway, the staff at Bidyadanga are often called out to road accidents. Technically, they aren't required to go anywhere, so Barry, who drives, and any of the RANs, actually volunteer their services. They cover an area 70 kilometres in each direction, but in reality they go where they're needed. It's a fine line deciding how to respond in any given situation and Sue says she is mindful always that, if they go out in the ambulance, they are leaving the community without an emergency response vehicle and without some of their staff, although one of the RANs always stays in the community on call. 'At a really bad road accident we can be gone for four or five hours, plus the travel time. A lot can happen back in the community in that time.'

Consequently, she walks the same fine line when deciding about evacuations. As a rule their policy is *If in doubt, ship it out*. There is no question, for instance, with snakebite. They do three to four evacuations for snakebites every year, even if it's only a suspected snakebite. A child died from a bite years ago so they take no chances.

Her most challenging day took place in 2010 when they had all hands on deck in the clinic with an eighteen-year-old pregnant girl having a seizure and another man having a cardiac event. Sue was doing an electrocardiograph (ECG) on the man when she spun around, caught her foot in a cord and went down on her hip, breaking it. In the scheme of things, she had the least urgent problem there, so the RFDS flew the girl and the man out before returning for Sue – everything is prioritised.

Whatever happens, if it's serious enough, she calls the RFDS base at Derby. If they can't come within five hours – the community's turnaround time by road to Broome – then she'll call St John's Ambulance in Broome to do a halfway meet. If they can't come, Barry and one of the RANs will take the ambulance right through to Broome themselves. However, road evacuation is sometimes hampered by flooding on Roebuck Plains, a wide-open plain that sits only about 8 metres above sea level and runs from the coast out across the Great Western Highway. 'Some people wonder why we're considered remote when we're only two hours from Broome but, apart from the fact that we're *all* more than 2000 kilometres from Perth, during the wet season we can be cut off from Broome for days, or even weeks.'

In absolute emergencies, when the RFDS couldn't come straight away, Barry has driven the ambulance through water up over the running boards of the Troop Carrier. But it's a situation they consider carefully with all the appropriate authorities.

As with most of the Aboriginal population in Australia, diabetes and renal failure are among the most pressing issues in the community. 'In fact, Bidyadanga has the highest per capita incidence of renal failure in Australia,' Sue says. Anyone with renal failure has to move in to Broome to be near dialysis but they come home sometimes for the weekend or for 'sorry time'.

The statistics on renal failure and diabetes in Bidyadanga seem almost a contradiction given that people in the community eat a bush diet; the men hunt for kangaroo and bush turkey and eat a lot of fish, turtle and crabs caught out on the beach. The local shop has run the healthy diet program using a traffic light system to designate good food and bad food. However, one of the favourite foods is damper, made with refined white flour, baked over coals and loaded up with plenty of golden syrup. And many people consume a lot of soft drink and chips.

On the other hand, there is a lot of physical activity. There is an AFL team, the Bidyadanga Emus, that plays against Broome, Looma, Eagle Bay and Derby. The football oval at Bidyadanga has perished somewhat but, when they get a grant, there are plans afoot for the oval to be resurfaced so they can have home games. There is also a new basketball complex and a 25-metre swimming pool that is well maintained, well organised and well patronised. In addition, everyone goes to the beach regularly, though lately they've seen crocs, so nobody's swimming there.

According to Sue, it's one of the challenges of working in health in any forum. 'We can teach people what is correct but, in the end, they must make their own decisions about exercise and about what they put in their mouths.'

Visiting KAMSC services work closely with the clinic to support the old people in the community. They have community care packages (CCPs) and extended aged care at home (EACH) packages in place, and although nobody is employed for personal care, someone in the family will undertake that role. Sometimes the clinic will bring people in for a shower when it becomes too hard to manage them at home. When, finally, the community can't maintain people at home, they go in to the Bran Nue Dae nursing home in Broome.

All of this ultimately leads to palliative care and death in the community. Palliative care is provided by the clinic staff and Barb checks on every case at home every week and will call in the RANs if needed. When a death occurs, everyone concerned retreats to another house for sorry business.

One of Sue's few rules is that the new nurses are not to go to sorry business (the Aboriginal term for the funeral and social arrangements after a death), unless they are specifically invited. 'In the beginning I didn't ever go but after a couple of years I started to go if I was invited. Sorry camps can last for several weeks until the funeral can be organised, so, obviously, I don't stay there but I will go and pay my respects to the family and then leave.'

It raises the question of crossing boundaries. Sue has been in the community for long enough to feel some genuine connection with the people and the place. She says she tries to maintain some level of detachment but it's getting harder the longer she is there. She had been there two and a half years before she was given a skin name. 'The ladies were coming in and hanging around for a couple of weeks saying they were finding the skin name for me. I wasn't at all sure it was a good idea.'

Barb explains they called her Whyntamurra. 'It's a beautiful tree. It grows in the western desert with a yellow flower. We don't want her to leave,' she says.

Sue's name is a mark of respect, and Barb says they hope she'll stay indefinitely. However, a nurse once asked for a skin name just after she got there to work and they called her Winja. She didn't like it and another of Sue's rules for the nurses is, 'Don't ask for a skin name.' Her own name, Whyntamurra, means she's part of the whole community, so she doesn't feel the responsibility that goes with belonging to one family. There's no humbugging (demanding or begging members of the family, especially older people, to hand over cash) for her. Barry doesn't have a specific name but she says a lot of people, especially the kids, call him Namu, which means 'old man'.

What pleases Sue most is her belief that she's broken down some barriers and people have realised they can live together, side by side, black and white. She'd been told when she first went there that racism was alive and well, but she always thought that was a two-way street. She thinks, on some level, she's contributed to decreasing the incidence of racism and that these days everyone in the community is much more respectful of each other. 'I don't always tell people what they want to hear, especially about health, but they do listen and they know I'll listen back,' she says.

Sue says she's learnt at least as much as she has taught. She doesn't worry about material things anymore, having learnt that 'it's all just stuff. Having nicer, bigger, better things used to seem important but not anymore. People are much more important. One of the things I've got out of this is to realise that we're all just people. You know, I think Aboriginal people are treated quite differently in society to how white people are and I think everyone just needs to realise that we are all the same. Just because they have a different culture doesn't make them any different as people.'

Late in 2013, Sue regretfully submitted her resignation and she and Barry left the community early in 2014. They say the elders asked them not to, which made them realise they were valued as friends as well as professionals.

The Stewarts did consider the possibility of staying in Bidyadanga for the rest of their lives and, every now and then, Barry used to tell the elders that he was going to claim land rights – a joke they reciprocated by telling him they might consider it one day.

However, in the end, family commitments have forced their hand. Sue says she can't imagine life without nursing as it's all she ever wanted to do so she will be available to return to the Kimberley as a relief nurse. 'I've always thought I was so lucky because I've always had to work but I've always had a job I really love doing,' she says.

They'd both like to come back to visit Bidyadanga and they know that Dylan is breaking his neck to go back. Then there's their baby granddaughter who has been smoked; chances are, one day, she'll be curious to see where and to whom she 'belongs'. Sue and Barry have had the most wonderful few years living and working at Bidyadanga and say they will carry the memories, influences and lessons learnt with them for the rest of their lives.

Acknowledgements

My heartfelt thanks to publisher Andrea McNamara, who knew that nurses working in the outback would be fascinating when she offered me the opportunity to write about them. More of the same thanks to editor Adrian Potts, who not only finessed my words into much better shape, but also gracefully and tactfully managed my assertions, 'But that's what it's called out here . . .' As the old blokes down at the tree of knowledge would say, 'Ya blood's worth bottling, Adrian!'

Thanks also to text designer Samantha Jayaweera, proofreader Brooke Clark and cover designer Alex Ross. Gratitude also to freelance photographer Louise Cooper, who cheerfully ventured up into the Queensland Gulf Country to photograph Catherine Jurd on her home territory for the front cover. And special thanks to Catherine herself for devoting a precious day off from her nursing roster to accommodate this vital modelling assignment!

Getting around Australia to interview everyone was great fun in the company of my old friends Margie Greenway and Judy Treloar, especially since they did most of the driving. More thanks to Judy for also reading the stories and interpreting modern nurses' speak, and to Helen Miller, who has read nearly everything I've ever written, including job applications, and bravely given me an honest critique. Thanks to my mother, Patricia Ford, who taught me to love written words long before I knew I could write them, and to my sister-in-law, Julie Ford, who proofread for me when I could only read what I thought I wrote.

Heart and hugs to Ian, who always encourages and supports me, and to our family and extended family, who unashamedly applaud from the sidelines.

I am grateful to Marie Williams and Maree Green for cheerfully stepping in to my part-time job whenever I've been away, and also to Cordial Stephson and Rabbit Warren, who, at different times, minded the fort.

Last, but never least, thanks to the nurses in this book who entrusted me with their stories. My respect for you all is exceeded only by my admiration for you and the extraordinary contribution you have all made to remote Australia. I salute you!

BUSH NURSES

Edited by
ANNABELLE BRAYLEY

It takes something special to be a bush nurse working in rural and remote Australia. These remarkable women patch people up and keep them alive while waiting for the doctor to arrive. They drive the ambulances, operate the clinics and deliver the babies. They are on call around the clock and there are no days off. They often make do with whatever is at hand while working in some of the most isolated places on the planet.

Be they devastating family tragedies, close scrapes with bushfires or encounters with true larrikins of the outback, some stories will make your hair stand on end, others will make you laugh and some will make your cry. With tales from Birdsville to Bedourie, Oodnadatta to Uluru, you'll be amazed at the courage and resourcefulness of these nurses who have been the backbone of medical practice in remote Australia for more than a hundred years.

'Full of battle tales, with all their comedy, farce and sadness.'
WEEKEND AUSTRALIAN